Hedayat's *Blind Owl* as a Western Novel

Hedayat's *Blind Owl* as a Western Novel

Michael Beard

PRINCETON UNIVERSITY PRESS

PRINCETON, NEW JERSEY

Library of Congress Cataloging-in-Publication Data
Beard, Michael, 1944–
Hedayat's Blind owl as a Western novel / Michael Beard.
p.   cm.
Includes bibliographical references.
1. Hedāyat, Ṣādeq, 1903–1951. Būf-e kur. 2. Hedāyat,
Ṣādeq, 1903–1951—Knowledge—Literature. I. Title.
PK6561.H43B8334   1990   891'.5533—dc20   90-33738

ISBN 0-691-03137-1 (alk. paper)

Publication of this book has been aided by a grant from the
Persian Heritage Foundation

This book has been composed in Linotron Sabon

Princeton University Press books are printed on acid-free paper,
and meet the guidelines for permanence and durability of the
Committee on Production Guidelines for Book Longevity of the
Council on Library Resources

Printed in the United States of America by Princeton University Press,
Princeton, New Jersey

1   3   5   7   9   10   8   6   4   2

In memoriam
Alessandro Bausani (1921–1988)

_____

CONTENTS

PREFACE

THIS BOOK has very little in common with *The Blind Owl*. For one thing, it is longer. It does share with its subject, however, the peculiarity that its writer is not sure whom he is talking to. Specialist readers will know in advance that *The Blind Owl* is a major work; others will find me in the role of advocate, attempting to introduce new readers to an insufficiently known masterpiece of world literature.

The issue is the creation of new audiences for a book whose relation with its audiences has always been equivocal. We should acknowledge for *The Blind Owl* at least four separate groups of readers. First, there is the rather small audience Hedayat reached during his life, a readership of intellectuals, many of them acquaintances. Second, we can cite the larger audience among whom Hedayat became a kind of cult object after his 1951 suicide, and third, the international readership who has access to him in translation. This third category is the group my study is meant to enlarge. But there is a fourth audience we might describe with reference to Walter Ong's famous essay "The Writer's Audience Is Always a Fiction" (*PMLA* 90.1 [Jan. 1975]: 9–21), the audience Hedayat's speaker posits for us.

On the face of things Hedayat's speaker does not care whether anyone reads him or not. He writes, as many readers have observed, "for his shadow"—whatever that means. But his protestations of solitude are after all fictional. They constitute, in fact, a literary reference: recurring, often insistent references to other texts suggest tacitly, indirectly, that familiarity with a specific set of forebears will orient us in the fiction. Some of those references are common knowledge to an Iranian reader (the folkloric references, commentaries on Iranian popular culture, and the linguistic innovations that make *The Blind Owl* difficult to translate); others require a different, perhaps surprising kind of grounding in a Western literary tra-

dition to which Iranian readers had no access. This shadowy
background invisible to its original readers may in fact have
added to the effect of mystery and uncanniness that so struck
its early readers, but this does not mean that we are better off
not knowing his sources.

There is a critical commonplace that suggests that the meaning of a work cannot fully exist at a particular moment in
time; it has to evolve through the reactions of future readers.
In the case of *The Blind Owl* we find a phenomenon that takes
that notion farther still: *The Blind Owl* seems to have been
designed quite systematically to be unreadable within its own
culture at its own moment in history. It becomes itself, so to
speak, only as it goes forth, masked, in its translated forms. It
requires its shadows. This is why readers like myself, from
outside, claim our usefulness. We locate the work in a territory
where there are no native speakers.

This leads me to inquire who my intended reader may be.
Novels from outside our tradition are often taught as representatives of their cultures, ambassadors for a presumed national character, meant to give access to the glories of a national mode of being. This is a disciplinary habit that I hope I
have avoided, but I felt it pressing me as I wrote, urging me to
restrict my audience to Middle East specialists and to students
of Persian. Indeed a reader could perhaps make it through
Chapter Three of this study on the assumption that it is tar-
geted at specialists. The first chapter is meant to fill in the
background a Western reader is likely to need, and in the process it stakes out the usual disciplinary turf. In the second
chapter I sketch a wide category of comparison, the genre of
romance, through the stylized pattern of Dante's *Vita nuova*;
here I would be grateful for a reader who sees that *The Blind
Owl* does not inhabit that pattern passively, that it interro-
gates the pattern and transforms it. The third chapter may be
read as an interpretive gesture, but it is my purpose to make
the interpretation emerge from the patterns of imagery that
contain the work and its generic neighbors. When I deal with
more specific Western narrative traditions, such as the Gothic
romance in Chapters Four and Five or the story within a story

in Chapter Six, the nature of the relationship between Hedayat and his tradition leads to a discourse that abandons Hedayat for pages at a stretch.

I insist on the seriousness of Hedayat's participation in an
esthetic system that is international, which makes *The Blind
Owl* a commentary on our own tradition, a mirror in which
Western culture sees itself transformed. Among the many elements that make *The Blind Owl* an extraordinary work of art
is a design that puts into question the very notion of national
literature.

A Note on the Transcription

To approximate the pronunciation of Persian more closely
than the standard transcription, I use the following equivalents for long and short vowels: â and a, u and o, i and e
(rather than the Arabic î and i). The usual problems of transcribing proper names consistently remain unsolved.

ACKNOWLEDGMENTS

PORTIONS of this book appeared in different form as articles: "The Hierarchy of the Arts in *Buf-e kur*," *Iranian Studies* 15.1–4 (1982): 53–67, and "Character and Psychology in Hedayat's *Buf-e kur*," *Edebiyât* 1.2 (Dec. 1976): 207–18.

Summer grants from the American University in Cairo and the University of North Dakota intervened at crucial moments in the framing of this project. A year I spent as a Mellon Fellow, doing other research at the University of Pennsylvania, allowed me to discover parallel lines of inquiry that turned out to intersect with this.

As for the individuals whose help made this book possible, thanks extend to Robin Magowan, who directed me to Iran in the first place; to Fazlollah Zahra'i for long-distance friendship, wisdom, and a lot of books; to Emile Snyder, Breon Mitchell, and Salih Altoma, who guided this project through its early stages; and to an always surprising number of patient readers willing to go over various later stages of the manuscript: William Hanaway, Lee Sterrenburg, Jane Lilienfeld, Ahmad Karimi-Hakkak, Walter Andrews, Barbara Harlow, Ralph Flores, Hasan Javadi, Michael Hillmann, Jerry Clinton, and Fedwa Malti-Douglas. Their opinions remade this book, though they may find my subsequent revisions puzzling.

There are others, so many that if I named them all, the acknowledgments would threaten to grow longer than the book. Criticism is a joint project and the intellectual debts I have accumulated require a good intellectual accountant. Fortunately I have one.

ABBREVIATIONS

THE PERSIAN TEXT is *Buf-e kur*, 14th ed. (Tehran: Amir Kabir, 1973). References in English are to *The Blind Owl*, trans. D. P. Costello (New York: Grove Press, 1957). Page references to *Buf-e kur* will cite first Costello's English translation and then the Persian text.

AA 'Aqâyad va afkâr darbâre-ye Sâdeq-e Hedâyat pas az marg (Opinions and thoughts about Sadeq Hedayat since his death). N.p.: Bahr-e Khazar, 1967.

ANTH Ehsan Yarshater, ed. *Sadeq Hedayat: An Anthology.* Modern Persian Literature Series, no. 2. Boulder: Westview Press, 1979.

ASH M. F. Farzaneh. *Ashnâ'i bâ Sâdeq-e Hedâyat, qesmat-e avval: Anche Sâdeq-e Hedâyat be man goft/Rencontres avec Sadegh Hedayat, première partie: Souvenirs d'un disciple.* Paris: H. Samuelian, 1988.

CWP *Collected Works of Edgar Allan Poe.* Edited by Thomas Olive Mabbot. Cambridge: Harvard University Press, Belknap Press, 1978.

FYA Michael Hillmann, ed. *Hedayat's* Blind Owl *Forty Years After.* Austin: Center for Middle East Studies, 1978.

NP Sadeq Hedayat. *Majmu'e-ye neveshte-hâ-ye parâkande* (Collection of scattered writings). 2d ed., ed. Hasan Qa'emyan. Tehran: Amir Kabir, 1963–1964.

SQKh Hedayat. *Se qatre khun* (Three drops of blood). 1932. Reprint. Tehran: Parastu, 1965.

SR Hedayat. *Sâye rowshan* (Chiaroscuro, or Contrasts). [1933], 5th ed. Tehran: Amir Kabir, 1963.

ZG Hedayat. *Zende be gur* (Buried alive). [1930], 7th ed. Tehran: Parastu, 1965.

Hedayat's *Blind Owl* as a Western Novel

Chapter One

NATIONALIST POETICS AND ITS SHADOWS

I

BY AUTHORSHIP, language, and setting Sadeq Hedayat's short narrative called *Buf-e kur* (*The Blind Owl*, 1936) is a Persian novel. But it is a novel so profoundly informed by Western narrative conventions that it defies the reader to lodge it securely in an accepted category of Western or non-Western writing. And it is informed by more than one Western convention: Roger Lescot's French translation, *La chouette aveugle* (Paris: José Corti, 1952), is reprinted in a series with Gothic romances and *contes fantastiques*; D. P. Costello's English version, *The Blind Owl* (1958), flourishes in the company of *nouveaux romans* and the theater of the absurd. Western readers have evidently found it meaningful, since both translations are still in print. Criticism meanwhile has treated it as a *lusus naturae*. It exists somehow on the margins between vague cultural entities called East and West, like the imaginary dwelling portrayed in its opening pages, away from the inhabited world in a landscape of ruins.

The purpose of this study is to classify a single text, taking classification to be a relational process: it requires us to focus on the tradition that holds the work in place, its predecessors and its influences, and on the fields of force that make intertextual pressures sensitive issues, for the writer and also for the critical reader. My purpose is not to demonstrate how *The Blind Owl* imports Western techniques and utilizes them to deal with a new set of cultural and social problems. Nor is it my purpose to follow the other polemic line of arguing that the importation never took place. My focus is on the process of "dealing with" cultural and social problems. How does any novel deal with (that is, process, alter, continue, swallow, digest, define, evade) the narrative traditions and social issues it finds in its way? The importation has undoubtedly taken place, but the means of transport are no less mysterious across cultural boundaries than they are between writers in a single tradition. There are two distinct processes—the process of influence and the process of communication between cultures— and the additional variable complicates the analysis.

I propose to simplify the object of study by limiting it to the forces at work between *The Blind Owl* and the Western narrative traditions. The result may be to help determine what the non-Western properties of the text might be, though this is not my primary concern. It is my contention that *The Blind Owl* is a masterpiece of world literature (even in translation, despite the fact that many of its virtues in Persian are totally unavailable to the translation process), but it is not my primary concern to belabor that point. This study is not "about" *The Blind Owl* in the sense that previous explications have been about it.[1] I propose to let critical attention flow in the other direction, to examine *The Blind Owl* as a commentary on its Western predecessors, to use it as a lens through which to see, as if from outside, aspects of our own narrative tradition. The difference is one of point of view: the texts cited, the endnotes, the "substance" of the book would be largely the same in either case. The advantage is to help the Western reader avoid what might be called the doppelgänger effect: to recognize, that is, when the alien under our scrutiny is in fact ourselves.

Ironically, the book through which I have chosen to inspect Western literary conventions professes in its title to be blind. It is a first premise of the argument that the speaker of *The Blind Owl* is an unreliable, in fact an insane, narrator. This results in two specific kinds of blindness: the blindness of the narrator, who sees only what his obsession allows him to see, and the blindness incurred by the reader, who has access to the narrated world—to the extent that it can be said to have an independent existence—only through the mechanisms of the speaker's distortions. Through most of this study we will leave aside the blindness of the writer, who, under the perhaps false security of the madman's disguise, may speak more personally than he intended.

Both instances of blindness are relative. The narrator's ability to perceive his outside world varies. The reader, once aware that the narration does not mesh with a consistent narrated outside world, reverses the process of misperception and extrapolates a reality concealed behind the narrated surface. We might speak of two narrative motions proceeding at different rates: the narration of the narrator, consistent in its repeated obsession but undependable in its interpretations of them, moving inexorably toward the revelation of the murder scene that is the climax; and a complementary pattern, the reader's gradual realization that the speaker is mad. Two acts of narration at right angles to each other. The blindness of the text forces a slower reading or, more likely, multiple readings—whose ultimate effect, inevitably, is to make the reader aware of the importance of artifice and conscious conventionality, which are characteristics of modernity.

The purpose of this introductory chapter is to indicate, from a distance, a series of legitimate fields of inquiry that are not part of this book. Although my aim in giving priority to formal elements of *The Blind Owl* is not to keep it indefinitely out of the hands of social scientists and literary historians, there is an element of protection in my attitude toward the perception of total form, which is easily broken. (Inevitably broken, we might add, and always a tentative project.) No book suffers more from summary or injudicious quotation: it is a narrative made to order for New Critical analysis, and yet in the course of that analysis the critic feels certain directions mapping themselves out on the other side of the *explication du texte*. Outside the boundaries of this inquiry I perceive two specific issues that seem relevant, two boundaries: that of national identity and that of biography.

II

The first issue we will look at is that of national identity. Latent in the project of examining *The Blind Owl* as a Western novel is an unstated question: what are the properties of an Eastern text that are being left out of consideration? The question is usually understood to break down into two parts: what does an Iranian text reveal about an Iranian national character and, second, what modes of presentation characterize contemporary Persian writing? The two of course intertwine: presumably the kinds of behavior we designate with the term "Iranian national character" will be the content presented through the characteristic Persian modes of writing; presumably the Iranian national character will be one of the factors determining what modes of writing will be congenial to the Iranian writer. Even if we isolate such cases as Gobineau's *Nouvelles asiatiques* or Galway Kinnell's *Black Light*, where a Western writer portrays Iranian behavior, and Ali Hejazi's *Sereshk* (Tears), where an Iranian describes life in the United States, we have probably still not separated the two questions.

It is not my purpose to consider the validity of the concept of an Iranian national character,[2] nor to deny what is sometimes said informally, that *The Blind Owl* is in the final analysis a profound statement about that concept. Its imagery of walls and barriers, its insistence on the privacy of significant experience, its juxtaposition of highly romantic and intensely physical depiction of the erotic, its brilliantly concrete treatment of feeling—all could be taken as analogues for modes of behavior and expression Americans commonly think of as distinctly Iranian. As L. P. Elwell-Sutton has pointed out, *The Blind Owl* is "a veritable mine of folkloric and mythical motifs" from Iranian popular tradition.[3]

But seeing *The Blind Owl* in this way does not account for the complex effects the text achieves, nor does it help us distinguish it from ephemeral literature and expressions of popular culture that might express the same content more directly and efficiently. The possibility that *The Blind Owl* may embody characteristic Iranian styles of writing is a question of greater complexity, which by and large has been answered by fiat. "Despite its French influences," writes William K. Archer in a frequently quoted article in the *Saturday Review*, " 'The Blind Owl' is, above all, deeply Iranian." We can see what this means as a sentence in a book review—that *The Blind Owl* expresses anxieties of concern to Iranian intellectuals (Archer cites "the terrible Persian awareness of time, of the past, of the direct burden of a great and antique culture"),[4] and that (by suggestion) it is a "deep" book (since "deeply Iranian") rather than a superficial one—but what would it mean as literary criticism? What model of the text permits us to say that one book is more Iranian than another? (Had it been a superficial book could it have been deeply Iranian?) Can national identity be quantified? If we look hard enough for national identity, we can find it everywhere.

Christophe Balaÿ and Michel Kuypers's *Aux sources de la nouvelle persane* (1983), a sensitive and meticulously documented study of the prehistory of the novel in Iran, perhaps demonstrates the limits of that search. It insists on the coherence between the novel and indigenous narrative forms, and in the course of the argument presents the clearest and most detailed account we have of their evolution in Iran.[5] Its virtues, however, are independent of the central premise. The reader can assent to individual steps in the argument without being convinced of the essential oneness of the tradition: the examples could be run the other way to emphasize the differences and to confront the two traditions with their mutual strangeness. In earlier criticism Iranian national identity is often asserted by a visible force of will. Peter Avery, in a 1955 article, speaking of the popularity of the short story in Iran, depicts a continuity of narrative tradition that makes foreign influence inconsequential:

> The short story is very old and dear to Iran. Modern authors have been influenced by Western writers in this genre and the names of de Maupassant and Edgar Allan Poe are often mentioned in this connection. But in using this form, writers of this present day are simply returning to the traditional *Hekiyah* [*sic*, apparently a misprint for *hekâyah* or *hekâye*] or anecdote, though this has been given a new kind of plot and subject matter.[6]

Here again we are not so much in the realm of literary criticism as that of compliment. It is a significant compliment: the Iranians had no need of an imported short story because there was an indigenous tradition of short narrative already. It is still a compliment rather than a neutral commentary.

It is not demeaning to the *hekâye* tradition or to Persian classical culture to point out that the two traditions of *hekâye* and short story are profoundly different. The distinctive set of narrative conventions we designate by the ambiguous term "short story"—which developed over the course of the nineteenth century, primarily in France, but which today seems a genre most practiced outside of Europe—appealed to Iranian writers as a revolutionary vehicle for commenting on a changing society. With its specificity of setting, its awareness of social detail, and above all the interaction of character and environment, the short story made incidental the anecdotal qualities (marvel, adventure, stratagem) that were central to classical Middle Eastern narrative styles. There has been occasional interaction between the *hekâye* and the Western short story. An example from the Arab world is a collection of anecdotes by the Egyptian writer Zaki Najib Mahmoud, *Qasâsât al-zujâj* (Pieces of broken glass, 1974).[7] There narrative situations dissolve and reconstitute in interplay with an expository narratorial voice; the result is hard for a Western reader to classify—popular philosophy that keeps solidifying into *exempla*, narratives that never quite get started because they drift off into commentary. It is clearly a crossbreeding of Eastern and Western traditions, but such exchanges are more frequently the result of conscious experiment than the crying out of the writer's Middle Eastern blood.

We enter the same obscure area in a moving short story by Samad Behrangi titled "Mâhi-ye kuchelu-ye siyâh" (The little black fish), where the accoutrements of the beast fable (an Aesopian genre popular in the Islamic world at least since Ibn al-Muqaffa' 's *Kalila wa Dimna*) are used in the service of a modern political statement about the necessity of questioning established beliefs. In a review of the English translation, Ahmad Karimi-Hakkak has argued for the importance of its Eastern origins: "All discussions of whether this short story . . . is to be viewed in the genre of children's literature or not stem from irrelevant superimpositions of Western categories

alien to the Persian tradition of story telling, itself largely
rooted in the ancient idea of instruction through animal fables."[8]

He is right that Behrangi's story cannot be written off as
children's entertainment, but Behrangi is no more immune to
the Western categories than anyone else in our century, and
"The Little Black Fish" is hardly any closer generically to Persian classical literature than the oriental tales in the *Tatler* and
the *Spectator*. The strangeness to Western (and Eastern) eyes
of much contemporary Iranian narrative traces back more
often to the absence of relevant tradition than to a surfeit.
Wishing the Iranians a strong cultural identity is a strangely
ambiguous gesture. On the one hand it portrays them as self-
sufficient, as possessors of an indigenous narrative tradition
that obviates importations; on the other hand it puts a wedge
between our world and theirs, which prevents the possibility
of comparison on equal terms, and in a sense forestalls taking
them with complete seriousness.

If criticism in the West tends to emphasize the alien properties of Middle Eastern writing, it is not the result of an im-
perialist conspiracy to make all non-Westerners seem to be
gibbering aborigines. The area-studies orientation in Middle
East studies, like the philological orientation of a previous
generation, naturally draws the attention of Western students
to differences, with the result that the coherence of Middle
Eastern cultures is exaggerated. Consequently, the profound
break that separates classical and modern styles in every Middle Eastern literary tradition is insufficiently acknowledged.
The novel, like the short story, is a borrowed Western innovation. There is no indigenous tradition for it to graft on to,
and to some extent its early practitioners have no choice but
to speak in a borrowed voice, even in an alien voice. Edward
Said, in a passage on the Arabic novel (a distinct but not unrelated development), suggests particular philosophical limits
to the success of the transplantation:

> Modern Arabic literature includes novels, but they are almost
> entirely of this century. There is no tradition out of which these

modern works developed; basically at some point writers in Arabic became aware of European novels and began to write works like them. Obviously it is not that simple; nevertheless, it is significant that the desire to create an alternative world through the act of writing (which is one motive underlying the novelistic tradition in the West) is inimical to the Islamic worldview; thus the word *heresy* in Arabic [*bid'a*] is synonymous with the verb "to innovate" or "to begin." Islam views the world as a plenum, capable of neither diminishment nor amplification.[9]

It may be in the final analysis an oversimplification to suggest that either readers or writers in any culture make esthetic decisions according to such visible, coherent philosophical concepts. And if we hold that they do, I should think that the desire to create an alternative world is equally inimical to the Christian world view prior to the intellectual ruptures of the seventeenth century—the transition from, in the phrase Koyré uses for the title of his book on that period, finite world to infinite universe. But the point is well taken that this is a case of literary borrowing beyond the sporadic interchange of texts we are used to in borrowing among European cultures—it is a massive importation that makes available a new mode of seeing. Literary criticism has only begun examining to what extent the novel is a neutral tool that can be applied to social structures outside the Western cultural sphere, to what extent it is bound by peculiarly Western problems. But even if the traditional concerns of the novel are Western ones, we export our peculiarly Western problems as rapidly as we export our modes of perceiving them. As Middle Eastern societies are increasingly exposed to Western technology, Western artifacts and patterns of life, the non-Western culture is also increasingly alien to itself; we might even formulate a Westernized Iranian literature that succeeds in being "deeply Iranian" not in Avery's or Archer's terms but because it questions the coherence of personal and cultural identity. Similarly *The Blind Owl* may be "deeply Persian" in exactly those qualities that Hedayat borrows from the West.

The Iranian writer Jalal Al-e Ahmad, in a sensitive study of

The Blind Owl written shortly after Hedayat's suicide, describes an important feature of the book, the curious middle style that was so utterly new to Persian writing. *The Blind Owl* is, he says, "an example for the proof of the fact that Persian, simple Persian, is capable of describing the most novel sensual states [*bayân-e badi'tarin hâlât-e nafsâni*] of a writer and can be employed for introspection."[10] The meditative, silent feeling of the unpeopled scenes with which *The Blind Owl* opens derives largely from the fact that the narrator paints a familiar, desolate village scene without any of the anticipated Islamic formulas and proverbial sayings, the village dialect, that had become familiar literary topoi in the wake of Mohammad Ali Jamalzade's famous short story collection, *Yeki bud o yeki na-bud* (Once upon a time, 1921). The opening scenes of *The Blind Owl* conjure up a village setting without the anticipated villager's voice, but also without the ornamented impersonal style of the traditional detached narrator. This unprecedented level of discourse, which fills the gap between high and low styles and taps new resources in the spoken language, is derived from an analogous style Hedayat encountered in European writing. Jamalzade, who was more open about indicating foreign models, cited Villon and a local colorist named Jean Richepin (1894–1926) in his introduction to *Yeki bud o yeki na-bud* as models for his experiments in a Persian low style.[11] What do we call this, a Persian or a Western innovation? The two amount to much the same thing.

The seeming paradox of an imported form that is more expressive than indigenous forms of what readers feel to be their national identity occurs regularly in literary history.[12] It suggests that the two components of national identity that we isolated above—the kind of behavior perceived as characteristic of the culture and the forms available to express it—may frequently be at odds. There is no natural principle that outfits each culture with precisely the literary forms that most directly express its peculiar concerns—no guaranteed relation between content and form. The particular case of the novel in Iran, or in the non-Western world generally, presents the problem in exaggerated form, first because the growth of the novel in industrializing Europe, over a series of innovations so gradual that they seem to justify the biological metaphors of growth that suggest themselves so regularly to literary historians, has given it a central position in the West's awareness of itself; second because the rupture in Iranian literary history that begins with the adoption of Western narrative conventions is not just a break in development. It is a break after which the idea of development becomes problematic. A clear-cut literary evolution of the Balzac-Stendhal-Flaubert-Zola-Proust kind is a luxury of the European nineteenth century. If a non-Western culture could be inoculated with translations of Scott and Balzac, isolated for a hundred years, and then flooded with specialists, we might be able to produce a literary history of the proper Western sort. But the environment is confusingly and unpredictably permeable. All Third World writers are comparatists: either they know foreign languages directly or they read translations, and the result is a tradition that refers inevitably outward.

The project of literary history progresses most smoothly when a chronological listing of works can be reconciled with historical cause and effect, when a chain of literary influence is visible and traceable in a close literary family. The relative cultural self-sufficiency of the European community is such a situation: a family that fathers its own texts. (Perhaps the real subject of Harold Bloom's analyses of the affective components of literary influence in *The Anxiety of Influence* is the peculiar hothouse, city-tenement closeness of the Western literary family.) But in Persian—or in Arabic, or for that matter in modern Greek—exogamic unions are common, and the apparently indiscriminate textual coupling that results often leaves mongrel offspring with no one to claim it.

The modern literary history of any non-Western culture will suffer from such discontinuities, but Iran is perhaps unique in having one of the most opaque and cryptic narratives of the twentieth century left summarily on its doorstep at a time when a narrative tradition resembling the Western novel was perhaps forty years old, the short story only twelve. I date the first from Hajj Zayn al-'Abedin of Maragheh's turn of the century *Siyâhat-nâme-ye Ibrâhim Beg* (The travelogue of Ibrahim Beg, ca. 1900), the second from *Yeki bud o yeki na-bud*. The *Blind Owl* stands as a barrier to the formulation of any symmetrical conception of modern Persian writing, and even a sensitive literary history like Hassan Kamshad's *Modern Persian Prose Literature* (1966) feels its decentering effect. Kamshad devotes a separate section to Hedayat, a third of the book in length, this in itself separating Hedayat from the chronological stream.[13] Hedayat's short stories can be made to fit into a pattern of developing indigenous realism, but in a chapter devoted to *The Blind Owl* titled "Hysterical Self-analysis," he is clearly uncomfortable with its central position in Hedayat's works. Read as part of a national tradition of social commentary (which Hedayat did write, indeed created in his short stories) *The Blind Owl* becomes inept naturalism, the product of a bad mood:

> now and then came moments of intensity when a glimpse of purpose, sympathy, or anger made him focus his attention on his own immediate environment. These observations produced two conflicting results. On the one hand they left for us an immense wealth of realistic writings, mainly in the form of short stories. . . . But on the other hand, as the morbid realities of life unravelled before him, a sense of *Weltschmerz*, a sort of nausea at anything real, earthly and alive grew in him little by little. He mistook effects for causes: instead of attacking the political system, the social and economic conditions that had made simple people so blind and unfortunate, he condemned the people— condemned his own self. That is where his "sardonic grins" began to appear [the term Kamshad uses to characterize the satirical works of the early 1930s], leading him gradually to the black pessimism of *Buf-i Kur*.   (Kamshad, 166)

The suggestion that Hedayat's pessimism developed gradually runs counter to Kamshad's own account of it earlier (140–41), but it is called for by the constraints of the literary historical project, where visible cause and effect is the rule.

Although his own premises put *The Blind Owl* into a negative light, Kamshad is a good enough critic to see that it is an important book, and the result is ambiguous: he quotes favorable reviews of the French and English translations of *The Blind Owl*, apparently with approval, and dutifully recounts the events of the narrative, but he lists them with a curious suppression of commentary. At the conclusion of his synopsis he acknowledges that the opening episode is a hallucination (176), a fact that is presumably important information, but he stops short of using it to construct an interpretation. The black pessimism that characterizes the book in his introductory comments quoted above gives way to a suggestion that the story is a Buddhist parable, and the murder with which it ends an act of affirmation (172–74).[14] If there has been an unwillingness to make *The Blind Owl* a coherent text, perhaps this is because to do so would be to lessen its social and personal referentiality.

There is also the possibility that it might do the opposite. It might expand them. The effort of making it a coherent statement would certainly postpone an understanding of its personal and social contexts, but that postponement is a methodological necessity. If we were to make *The Blind Owl* Kamshad describes a fundamental text of modern Persian literature, we would have a tradition without a center. A more accurate view would have to deal with the notion of a displaced center, a national tradition interpenetrated by world literature. But once we have begun to acknowledge the intrusion of Western literary forms into Persian writing, inherently affective properties of literary criticism begin to interfere with our objectivity as observers. Even if we are familiar with the argument to reinstate nonnovelistic forms of narration in such studies as Scholes and Kellogg's *Nature of Narrative*, the critical language is more or less loaded. How do we say that the novel happened to develop in the West without suggesting a theory of cultural development whereby the novel is seen as a natural step in literary evolution that we "reached" first? Do we call the Middle Eastern novelistic traditions "derivative"? Do we judge them by the extent to which they conform to Western tastes or do we expect them to create something peculiarly Middle Eastern? In either case we impose value judgments that have nothing to do with the project of literary criticism. Relative open-mindedness is probably easier to achieve in dealing with classical Islamic literature.

The Western critic's cultural anxieties are most likely to come into the foreground when, prepared to be tolerant toward an alien style, we encounter something familiar instead. The orientalist G. M. Wickens, discussing Western influences in Arabic and Persian contemporary writing in a 1959 article, articulates the Western anxiety with exceptional clarity:

> in the long run the effect on the development of many writers was not wholly for the good. Both movements were, and to some extent still are, rent by a conflict of Ancients *versus* Moderns: the "Ancients" are loyal to the classics of their respective linguistic traditions, the "Moderns" enthusiastic for a thoroughgoing imitation of a heterogeneous, and often somewhat *démodé*, range of European models. These models have been found primarily in French and Russian literature, less—with certain conspicuous exceptions—in their English and German counterparts. In the extreme cases, Dostoievsky will rub shoulders with Conan Doyle, while Dumas assorts uneasily with Nietzsche![15]

I do not want to suggest that in Wickens we have the orientalist in full colonial dress, but the patronizing tone of the passage, especially when considered in the light of Edward Said's *Orientalism* (1979), is unmistakable. The reader is not likely to expect that fifteen pages later in the same essay Wickens would conclude, "It is for such as the Persians themselves to work out the ultimate terms of the synthesis now demanded" (132). Because the influence of Hedayat is largely responsible for the extreme cases Wickens refers to (the article is in part an attack on Hedayat), it is worth asking whether the issue is Iranians' insensitivity as writers (and readers) or whether it is their failure to accept the hierarchies and categories in which we Westerners, according to fashion, pigeonhole them. (The word *démodé* perhaps answers the question.) If Hedayat has been influenced by Poe, and Poe is out of favor with the English and American critics in 1959, it does not follow that Hedayat has failed to comprehend Western culture. Still less does it make it our role to instruct the Iranians in what models to use. The vision of a fragmented Western tradition, of texts unglued from history, with which the above quotation concludes invokes our anxieties about our own history: the student's fear of failing to observe our received distinctions between naive and sophisticated texts, the fear that naive or uninformed reactions to a text are necessarily wrong. No doubt strangers to Western traditions often misread the relationships between Western texts, but then literary history regularly rewrites the relationships between texts anyway. It is one of the favorite devices of genius to elevate *démodé* writers, as when Borges, in the introduction to *Dr. Brodie's Report*, puts Kipling's late short stories above those of Kafka and Henry James. There is a possibility that the Iranian writer who puts Conan Doyle's shoulder against Dostoevsky's sees something we have missed.

As a statement of critical anxieties Wickens's position is remarkably clear. As an argument it has missing steps; he supplies no explicit reason that we should regard uninformed borrowing as an offense to tradition because we are expected to have the same sense of tradition. The Italian orientalist Gianroberto Scarcia, in his 1958 article " 'Hâǧi Aqâ' e 'Buf-e Kur', i cosidetti due aspetti dell'opera dello scrittore contemporaneo persiano Sâdeq Hedâyat" ("Hâjji Aqâ" and "The Blind Owl": The so-called two aspects of the work of the contemporary Iranian writer Sadeq Hedayat), bases an explicit argument on much the same evidence. Noting "the simultaneous influence of various currents of European thought that, in Europe, have followed one another historically, but that in Iran end up coexisting one beside the other: illuminism, positivism, 'decadentism,' " he sketches an apparent polarity between two styles of contemporary Persian writing, represented by the hermeticism of *The Blind Owl* and the committed social satire of Hedayat's 1945 novel *Hâjji Aqâ*. He argues that the distinction between the two is illusory on the grounds that Persian socialist writing looks at Iranian society with the taste for the exotic that Iranians have learned from the West, and the result is a derivative artificiality in which moral questions are reduced to black and white—a kind of neo-Manicheism that puts it into the same category of escapism and evasion of social realities with the fantasies of *The Blind Owl*. He finds a radical oversimplification of Iranian social problems in the central premise of *Hâjji Aqâ*, a protagonist who functions as a personification of Iranian social evils: Hâjji Aqâ is a kind of Père Grandet figure whose vices are so gratuitous and unmotivated as to obviate the necessity for a social explanation. Similarly, Scarcia sees the speaker of *The Blind Owl* fitting into a common pattern whereby a superior individual is constrained to live among an ignoble crowd. His criticism of *The Blind Owl* emphasizes European borrowings and is the occasion for his harshest words:

> It is simply not permissible to transform the southern districts of Tehran in that way, with their filth, their incredible poverty, with their simple problems, into a cubist backdrop that uses the ancient, solemn name of Rey, in conjunction with imported Parisian fashion, in order to give a color at once "Persian" and "modern" to the theater of one individual's literary despair (literary even if the despair is authentic). There are limits one should not cross. . . . And if it is possible to discuss whether this contempt [*dispregio*] might be justified in Paris . . . where it could be tolerated in its time (not now) as an experiment [*un sofferto esperimento*], it is not possible to discuss it today in Iran.[16]

I disagree with Scarcia's conclusion, but his is by far the most intelligent attack on *The Blind Owl*. The key point for him, as for me, is the profound gap between classical Middle Eastern narrative conventions and their Western post-Romantic counterparts. He does not invoke an exotic presence, an indigenous voice with which the Iranian ought to address us; but latent in his argument he does convey the assumption, not illogical on the face of things, that in realism we have a universal form, unbound by cultural determinants and uniquely licensed to bridge the gap.

Contempt (*dispregio*) is an interesting word to characterize the discontinuity between the realistic setting of *The Blind Owl* (or settings, since they shift) and the antirealistic elements of the story, implying that narrative distortion is an act of aggression against its subject matter. Today criticism has become more aware of the inevitable distortions of realism as a style (the inherent selectivity of narration, the question how to define reality in the first place); it would be easy to defend *The Blind Owl* on these terms if it were necessary. It is more important to point out that Scarcia's essay raises observant questions about the text. The artificial, stagelike quality he describes with the word *cubist* is really there, and the contempt he finds is in fact a central functioning element in the narrative. Scarcia misperceives the focus and scope of this contempt—understandably, because it is a complex phenomenon. I discuss in Chapter Five to what extent this contempt is focused on the "subject matter" of the story, to what extent finely diffused among the narrative's levels of representation. What limits such arguments is in part an unfamiliarity with the variety of possible narrative forms; it is also akin to that which limits Wickens's vision in the passage above, the Western reader's anxiety about the coherence of our own tradition, their common embarrassment over the fact that their subject has seen fit to admire in Western literature movements and writers that we ourselves have been uncomfortable with, or have tried to disown.

The non-Western novel, with its occasional deviation from patterns Western readers anticipate, its hesitation to stray from the thematically obvious, an occasionally audible creakiness in its mechanism, a sense of absence somewhere in the discursive structure, often strikes Western readers as unworthy of their attention—irrelevant to our indigenous novelistic tradition. It is, however, a class of texts of great potential interest to students of the novel who might wish to account for the feelings of presence, fullness, and plenitude that we are taught to experience in our own novelistic tradition. The heavy reliance on conscious artifice that Scarcia finds characteristic of modern Persian writing, and that (as he notes) is certainly evident in *The Blind Owl*, may be its most meaningful link with the esthetics of classical Persian literature; but that quality can also be read as a link with another tradition. Scarcia recalls a comment often heard from Iranian intellectuals at that time: "We are more modern than you Europeans" (112)—spoken, no doubt, in connection with the Western unwillingness to acknowledge the artificial, arbitrary elements of artistic representation (a blindness that allowed the West to develop the novel into a tool of social awareness, but that delayed our comprehension of nonnovelistic narrative). For Scarcia it is a sad irony that our decadent arts should be what appeal most to a developing country, but perhaps twenty years later it is easier to see that they had as much right to the decadent arts as we did. After all, the cultural and social analogues for the sensibility of alienation that became so eminently central to modern writing are nowhere more visible elements of cultural and economic life than in the Westernizing Middle East.

The distrust of mimesis that Edward Said, in the passage cited above, notes as a quality of the Islamic cultures can be a sign of naiveté about narrative, but it can also be a mark of modernity,[17] the suspicion of Nathalie Sarraute's *Age of Suspicion*. It is not the purpose of this study to single out what works fall into the one rather than the other category, but we can be fairly certain about *The Blind Owl*. First, it is not altogether representative of non-Western writing. Though its language, that innovative simplicity with which it bridges the Persian separation of styles, has been extremely influential, its formal complexity did not have a direct impact on subsequent writers. (Hedayat's short stories have been a much more fruitful source of imitation.) Second, *The Blind Owl* is profoundly representative of themes and conventions central to European literature. What sets it apart from Persian writing is, beyond its formal complexity, the uncanny authority with which it adapts a Western heritage to its ends. The most extreme statement of alienation in Persian writing is paradoxically the one most at home in its borrowed style. It is as if the sense of absence Westerners perceive in Middle Eastern writing generally had been absorbed into the work itself and made a functioning component of the narrative.

III

If national identity seems an amorphous resource to use for textual explication, the details of a writer's life seem a more explicit and substantive context. It is easy enough to draw links between Hedayat's writing and his biography—the usual reading of his life explains his reclusion and eccentricity through the violent and frequently pessimistic quality of his writing. This gives us the happy illusion of confirming through his literary expression what we have determined separately through the details of his biography, triangulating on the artist's deepest self. In the perfunctory sketch that follows I attempt to avoid the temptation of filling in the gaps of the biography with the writer's fictions. Relegating the sources to a single long endnote,[18] I shall try to emphasize the details that show why *The Blind Owl* belongs at the center of his works.

There is a photograph in E. G. Browne's *Literary History of Persia*[19] showing Sadeq Hedayat's great-grandfather, the poet and historian Reza-Qoli Khan (1800–1871/72), standing next to his pupil Mozaffar al-Din, later Shah Mozaffar al-Din (reigned 1896–1907). The child Mozaffar is seated with a sword in his hand—the same hand that was to sign the oil concession of 1901 and later, in the last year of the Shah's life, the Iranian constitution. The tutor, his face slightly out of focus and framed by a long straight beard and a tall fez pulled low over his forehead in such a way as to suggest a scowl, leans inward with a hint of a protective gesture. To a contemporary Western eye no one's clothes seem to fit: sleeves look too long, hats too big. The photograph is overexposed and badly focused, but it provokes speculations about the proverbial changes wrought by history and the changing relations of culture and power. Reza-Qoli Khan, as poet and anthologizer, writer of polite conventional poetry,[20] is a representative of Persian tradition at the center of power, such as it is. In his great-grandson's time the crown prince (of a new and even shorter-lived line) was sent to Switzerland for his education, the number of self-respecting writers who would go near the seat of power was limited, and the writer's perception of his function had changed beyond recognition.

Hedayat the great-grandson was born on 17 February 1903, in the sixth year of Mozaffar al-Din's reign, two years before the Russo-Japanese War was to alter the self-image of non-Western countries, three years before Mozaffar signed the Iranian constitution. This makes Hedayat somewhat younger than his most prominent colleagues in Iranian letters: eight years younger than Iran's first experimental poet, Nima Yushij (1895–1960), and eleven years younger than Mohammad Ali Jamalzade (b. 1892). It makes him two years older than Jean-Paul Sartre and A. J. Arberry, three years older than Samuel Beckett, one year younger than Ayatollah Khomeini.

The Hedayat family were landholders in the province of Mazandaran, which figures occasionally as the setting of Sadeq Hedayat's short stories. The unrest that followed the constitutional period would have been the central political fact of his childhood, and the landmarks of that period occur not infrequently in his writing. Shah 'Abd al-'Azim, the cemetery and shrine in the town of Rey, south of Tehran, which figures prominently in *The Blind Owl* and two short stories ("Gerdâb" [Whirlpool] and "Changâl" [The claw] in *Se qatre khun* [Three drops of blood]) was a retreat and place of political sanctuary (*bast*) during that period. The Pearl Cannon (*Tup-e morvâri*) in Maydan-e Arg in Tehran, a landmark used for the same purpose, is the subject of his scurrilous satire *Tup-e morvâri*. The famous Dâr ol-Fonun school, which Reza-Qoli Khan directed long before, and which Hedayat in his turn attended as a secondary student, is the alma mater of the melancholy scholar Mirza Hosein'ali in "Mardi-ke nafs-ash-râ kosht" (The man who killed his "self," *SQKh* 191–218)[21] and of the insane narrator of the title story of that collection.

When we speak of Hedayat as a stranger coming to Western literature from abroad, a writer who views our traditions with the eye of an outsider, this does not imply that he was unfamiliar with them or experienced them only through the mediation of translation or an uncomprehending alien sensibility (a "Middle Eastern mind"). There may have been misreadings, but not the sort that can be explained away by cultural ignorance. Hedayat took his secondary degree from a French high school, Lycée St. Louis in Tehran, where he would have studied, in French, the traditional classical French curriculum of the time. For our purposes we may consider him virtually bicultural.[22] He was a secondary student during the eventful *anni mirabili* of 1921 and 1922, the years of Reza Shah's rise to power, when the two landmarks of modern Persian were published: Nima Yushij's poem "Afsâne" (Fable) and Jamalzade's *Once Upon a Time*. In 1926, the year Reza Shah founded his so-called Pahlavi dynasty, Hedayat left Iran to study dentistry on a scholarship in Ghent, though to judge from the account of his studies in Djannati-Atai's biography, he may not have taken them very seriously from the first. He never took a degree, but spent the following years living in Paris and Besançon. (Besançon is the setting of "Asir-e Farânsavi" [The French prisoner of war, *ZG* 67–72].) He took up painting in Europe, and a number of sketches remain, but to judge from the array of stories he published immediately after his return to Iran in 1930, he must have worked nearly full time at his writing.

It is sometimes said of non-Western students abroad that they become aware of the greatness of their native cultures only after leaving them. Gandhi, for example, became a strict vegetarian and discovered the Bhagavad Gita only after his arrival in London. But as much as we would like to be able to trace visible development in his ideas, Hedayat seems to have formed the opinions he is famous for early in his life. Not only his fascination with ancient Iran, but his vegetarianism, his opposition to Islam, his fascination with death, can all be dated from before his departure for Europe. If Hedayat's ideas were unorthodox, they were indigenous, and his experiences abroad seem not to have changed them.

It is difficult to know to what extent the eccentric direction his life takes at this point is scandalous, but it certainly breaks with anticipated patterns of the student educated abroad. After his return to Tehran in 1930, instead of benefiting from family connections to rise in official circles (the option he would be expected to follow), he took work as a minor functionary in the National Bank, continuing to write in his spare time. The early thirties are for him an extraordinarily prolific period. The sales of his first publications are said to have been negligible—vanity-press level by contemporary standards—but there was a coterie of intellectuals who recognized his talent and among whom he found reinforcement for his unorthodox ideas. This is the group referred to as the Rab'a, or "four."[23]

This is the period during which Hedayat's youthful interest in Omar Khayyam crystallized, an interest that became the occasion for defending the directness of *carpe diem* poetry against the pretension and circumlocution of the *qaside* and against the polite classical tradition in general. The Czech orientalist Jan Rypka has written a memoir of a visit to Tehran in 1934, the year Hedayat expanded the introduction to his edition of Khayyam's quatrains. He recalls that "Hedayat considered Omar Khayyam to be a confirmed atheist, and for that reason he simply rejected as spurious any verse that did not express antireligious ideas or that seemed insufficiently pessimistic."[24] In Hedayat's cultural vision Iran was an occupied country, Islam an alien religion imposed by an alien race, and the true national spirit of Iran was that of its imperial past in Achaemenid and Sassanian times. It is a vision that suggests in miniature an analogy to the revival of classical learning in the Renaissance—a return to patterns of nearly a millennium and a half before—but with the difficulty that there were no specific pre-Islamic literary traditions to return to. There was a history of conquests, monuments, heroes in Herodotus and the *Shâhnâme* of Ferdowsi, and an artistic legacy of pottery and metal artifacts, but nothing like the complex literary, moral, and mythological tradition recorded by classical Greece. It is not a tradition that could generate a sustained exuberance. The absence of models may help explain why when Reza Shah's son co-opted the same view of history in the 1960s and 1970s, it sounded so shrill and hollow.

It is not hard to show the limitations of the pre-Islamic golden age as a concrete ideal or a project of social reform. The pitfalls range from sentimentality to racism. Hedayat's historical plays, in which Sassanian heroes struggle vainly against the Arab conquest, *Parvin dokhtar-e Sâsân* (Parvin the daughter of Sasan, 1930) and *Mâzyâr* (coauthored with Mojteba Minovi, 1933), are probably the weakest of his works. In a short story from his first collection called "Atash-parast" (The fire worshipper, *ZG* 95–102), the voice that validates the pre-Islamic esthetic and thus perceives the real Iran is, with a familiar irony, that of an outsider. In it the (historical) French nineteenth-century traveler and engraver Eugène Flandin recounts to a friend one of the experiences described in his book *Voyage en Perse*, a scene at sunset near Persepolis when he is so impressed by the sight of two Zoroastrians praying at the ancient tomb that he joins them from a distance.[25] Hedayat's portrait of the Iraqi city of Kerbala in a 1932 story, "Talab-e âmorzash" (Seeking absolution, *SQKh* 105–26), can justly be termed racist: the Arabs with which the stage is set have "stupid faces" and communicate in a guttural language "spoken from the depth of the throat and entrails." Images of poverty and filth accumulate gratuitously ("A mother had forced half of her black breast into the mouth of a dirty baby in her arms. . . . In front of the coffee-house an Arab was picking his nose and rubbing the dirt out from between his toes"),[26] and finally they cease to function as social realism; they become allegorical portraits of moral evil. Thus the attempt to separate Iranian from alien elements of his culture leads to a moral dead end, but the project of embedding that cultural polemic in fiction—of adjusting an oversimplified historical vision to the resistance of a narrative medium—is a major source of innovation in his writing.

One of Hedayat's most successful short stories, "Sâye-he moghul" (The Mongol's shadow),[27] conspicuously exemplifies this dialectic. The setting is the Mongol invasions of the thirteenth century. Shahrokh, a wounded Iranian fighter, withdraws into the forests of Mazandaran to die. The nightmarish sketch of an oriental face that Hedayat drew to accompany that story betrays more than the racial anxieties of "Seeking Absolution": it shows the historical thesis turning into something more general and schematic. The racial caricature takes its ominous nature from our fear of the alien, but also from its positioning in the sketch—from the zooming motion of its nonhuman claw (with its incongruous thorned wrist) across the scene. For the Western reader it might be useful to imagine the effect of a mirror image reaching from right to left, contrary to the direction our eyes track across a page of type, against the grain, so that the Mongol reaches not from a place of origin but from a terminus.

But at this point a characteristic ambiguity intrudes: does the sketch illustrate an attitude toward the Mongol or toward death? The skull in the background is more than a representation of what the Mongol brings, death, which is the Mongol's gift to his victim; it is also what the victim becomes—it is a premonition of the victim's fate. But since the Mongol (with his shaved head, flat nose, and seemingly disembodied, neckless head) resembles it, the sign of the skull also occupies the third position of victimizer. Efficiency of representation thus works to undermine the overt message, in a process not unlike that of the story, where a sexual parable is superimposed on the historical one: the Mongols have violated the Iranian community but have also transgressed sexually by raping and killing the hero's fiancée. The juxtaposition of personal and patriotic motive in Shahrokh's quest confuses the historical issue; indeed the theme of innocence exposed to unmotivated demonic intervention and the emphasis on the natural world as a benign setting give the narrative a sense not just of romance but of ritual. We see Shahrokh, in a flashback, take his revenge on the Mongol victimizer and then retire, dying, into the dark forest, where he wedges himself into a hollow tree as if to become one with the landscape he has been defending. (The thorned wrist of the caricatured Mongol suggests a parallel evolution.) In death his skull takes on the appearance of a Mongol (which we understand immediately, having seen the sketch) and two passersby who find him the following spring refer to him in fear as the Mongol's "shadow." The passersby are not Mongols, so there is no question of the epilogue functioning as a warning to future invaders. The pattern of doubling, whereby the solitary hero comes to resemble a demonic enemy, is in small the pattern of *The Blind Owl*.

The best-known works written between Hedayat's return from France and his trip to India in 1936 (primarily his short story collections *Zende be gur* [Buried alive, 1930], *Se qatre khun* [Three drops of blood, 1932], and *Sâye rowshan* [Chiaroscuro, 1933]) are famous for their dominant mood of darkness and melancholy: they focus on tragedies of alienation and loss of identity, again in terms located ambiguously between personal and national (or social) contexts. Even a story with a relatively visible social setting such as "Abji Khânom" (*ZG* 105–19),[28] in which a plain older sister in a middle-class household drowns herself in the cistern on the night of her younger sister's wedding, carries with it a sense of heaviness and foreboding that far outweighs its social commentary. Abji Khânom's homeliness in a superficial society becomes the cause of moral ugliness (her religious fanaticism) and makes her both an embodiment of social evil and the victim of it. But the sexual imagery with which her death is charged (her hair is twisted around her neck like a snake, her dress clings to her body, and the occasion of her death is after all a marriage night) slightly exceeds the requirements of the social theme and, like "Sâye-he moghul," foreshadows the twinned themes of death and sexuality in *The Blind Owl*.

A few stories conclude with Chekhovian understatement ("Hâjji Morâd" [*ZG* 53–63],[29] notably, and the stories set in France), but more commonly we are safe in assuming that a Hedayat protagonist will not get out of the story alive, from the suicidal student in "Buried Alive"[30] to Mirza Hosayn'ali (the Dar ol-Fonun graduate) in "The Man Who Killed His 'Self' "—a kind of Iranian Mr. Duffy who, after becoming aware that he has cut himself off from life's feast, commits suicide—to Khodadad in "Lâle" (*SQKh* 129–44), a solitary old man who is deserted by an adopted daughter and simply fades away. We might argue that the pessimistic Hedayat of traditional biographical criticism can be glimpsed through the text, that the violent Hedayat ending is a response to the dual constraints of his personal vision and his sense of literature as a social force—an attempt to find channels for pessimism that are both socially engaged and communicable as literature. The succession of outsiders and victims Hedayat chooses for his protagonists would be a way of meeting both requirements, with the sort of problematical success we saw in "Sâye-he moghul" and "Abji Khânom." There is, however, a third constraint.

Beside the biographical context of Hedayat's pessimism or the social context that would explain the nature of his stories as a project to shock the complacent reader into recognition of brutal social truths, there is the vastly more visible context, woven from its own complex personal and social referentiality, of the European tradition that Hedayat draws on, which was itself famously morbid.[31] In Chapter Four we will see in detail that Hedayat's Western reading centered on texts with morbid subject matter, but there is no indication that his reading was unrepresentative. In them two modes of isolation, the isolation of the European artist within European culture and the additional isolation of the Westernized artist (none of the available words expresses the complex nature of the relationship) outside the West. Hedayat adds to the stories of *Zende be gur* (Buried alive) the date and city of composition (four in Paris, four in Tehran), as if to chronicle his homecoming and emphasize the idea that he is looking at his country from the outside. After Hedayat a genre was to develop in which returned students see their country in a new light, such as Mohammad Mas'ud's *Gol-hâ'i ke dar jahannam mi-ruyad* (The flowers that grow in hell, 1942) or Jamalzade's *Râh-âb nâme* (Kamshad's English title is "The drainage controversy," 1948). Hedayat's heroes are seldom themselves returned students, but he undoubtedly contributed to the esthetic of disillusionment, which is central to the returned-student convention in *Zende be gur* and in the even deeper sense of isolation to be found in the stories of *Se qatre khun* (Three drops of blood) two years later.

The esthetic of estrangement rehearsed over and over in the short stories was consummated in *The Blind Owl*. The short stories are an extraordinary achievement: new generations of readers have found increasing significance in them (and they are, as we have said, the source of Hedayat's primary influence on later Iranian writer's). But it is in *The Blind Owl* that Hedayat most unmistakably transcends specific national issues and takes a prominent place in world literature. It is hard to focus on an absence: to define the gap Hedayat crosses between his previous writing and *The Blind Owl* would be to contemplate creativity directly, to perceive the difference between innovative, skillful writing and a masterpiece. One way to approximate that impossible project is to begin with the continuities between them—the sense that the stories and *The Blind Owl* are solving congruent technical problems. An additional reason to begin with the links between *The Blind Owl* and the short stories is a tendency in Hedayat scholarship to see the novel as an outright break with the past: for Manoutchehr Mohandessi it is a departure in style from his other work and its first-person narration (quoting Kamshad) "an unusual style for Hedayat."[32]

The first person is in fact, however, rather common in the short stories: five of the nineteen stories in Hedayat's first two collections are narrated in the first person, and two of the most prominent of them, the title stories "Buried Alive" and "Three Drops of Blood," read today as if they were studies made in preparation for the discontinuous narrative style of *The Blind Owl*. The speaker of "Buried Alive" is a young Iranian in Paris afflicted with acute depression, and the story takes the form of a journal found after his suicide. The causes of his depression are not an issue, but it is clear that he is buried alive in the sense that he is trapped in his own tortured consciousness. In "Three Drops of Blood,"[33] we are even further from the possibility of perceiving causes for the narrator's state of mind. Its wandering, discontinuous narration is even more conspicuously like the style of *The Blind Owl*. The speaker describes his life in an insane asylum with a breathless stream of uncoordinated observations and non sequiturs that gradually demonstrate the extent of his isolation from the recognizable world. The three drops of blood in the title are a leitmotif that recurs as an obsessive memory, shed by a cat the speaker believes he has seen killed, and at the conclusion of the story the speaker is discovered to have been the agent of the violence. At the moment of anagnorisis he also merges with a character (or perhaps two) who we had thought previously to be a separate entity, very much in the fashion of similar projections of character that will concern us in *The Blind Owl*.

A strategy that pervades both the short stories and *The Blind Owl* is that of concretion, materialization of the abstract. It echoes everywhere—both on the level of style and theme: in short stories where a sublimated or figurative concept is punctured by exposure to its repressed or literary counterpart (the man who kills his "self" in the story of that title does it not in the mystical sense but by committing suicide) or the plot of "Changâl" (Claw, *SQKh* 169–87), which parodies the events of a well-known children's folktale in sinister ironic terms, even in Hedayat's theory of Omar Khayyam's materialism, which supposedly reinterprets ethereal love conventions into sensual ones. The most thorough such relation is between the two parts of *The Blind Owl*, a relation summed up by the term *mojassam* (embodiment, incarnation), which is a key term in the book. It is visible not just on the level of individual stories but between them as well.

In both collections, *Zende be gur* (Buried alive) and *Se qatre khun* (Three drops of blood), the absence of social context in the title stories, both of which open the collections, is compensated by a concluding story that echoes it imagistically and anchors it in a realistic context. "Buried Alive" is balanced by the concluding story in the collection, "Mordekhowr-hâ" (Eaters of the dead), in which Mashdi, a middle-aged Iranian villager, is literally buried alive after a stroke. The story presents the women of the household—relatives and rival wives—pretending to mourn the deceased but in fact bickering over the inheritance. The conclusion, in which Mashdi enters the scene in his shroud and the women confess to having stolen his possessions already, down to his false teeth, is unmistakably social satire and not metaphysics. In "Gojaste Dezh" (Kamshad's English title is "The cursed castle"), the concluding story of *Se qatre khun*, the blood image from the title story occurs as the essential ingredient (three drops of blood from a virgin) in the alchemical formula the protagonist Khashtun employs to make gold, but the virgin he procures turns out to be his own daughter. The parable is clear: Bozorg Alavi calls it "an allusion to the capitalist exploitation of man by man,"[34] or more in terms of the story, that avarice can make people forget their natural social ties.

It is logical that the device of concretion or *mojassam* should focus on social and realist contexts, but there are times when the emphasis seems to fall on the process rather than the social signification of that device. In such stories as "Sâye-he moghul" and "Abji Khânom" something in the narrative coheres in such a way as to resist, even to countermand, what we perceive as the obvious thematic message—the historical polemic or social comment. Perhaps specific thematic links with *The Blind Owl* are most evident in the stories where the presence of a thematic argument is minimal. In "Suratak-hâ" (Masks, *SQKh* 147–65), social commentary is so nearly absent that we may hardly notice the realistic context. The conflict of ideal versus reality, or illusion versus concretion, is likewise reduced to its simplest form in the central character's romantic illusions. Manuchehr, a wealthy, idle Westernized Iranian, is discovered trying to decide whether or not to attend the masked ball at the Iran Club. He is jealous over his girl friend Khojasteh because he has seen a photograph of her with another man. In a dialogue at the masked ball Manuchehr expounds for Khojasteh his new philosophy (apparently devised since the opening scene, when he was a simple romantic dupe), that desires are masks—that every desire masks a desire for something else; Khojasteh tells Manuchehr that she has to leave town for the sake of her reputation. They leave that night together for his property in Mazandaran (it is unclear how this will help her reputation) and are killed in an accident on the road. The final authorial comment is the description of the wreckage, beside it a pair of carnival masks.

Kamshad provides as a social context for this story, among others, a comment on the Westernized classes. The abnormalities of Hedayat's middle-class characters are "the deformities produced by a deformed society, and it is therefore not surprising that Hedayat should make them all either die violently, by committing suicide perhaps, or end up in a lunatic asylum" (Kamshad, 158). This would be a more satisfying explanation with "Suratak-hâ" if we felt that Manuchehr's shallowness and superficiality were responsible for his end. Indeed, there are details throughout the story that suggest Manuchehr's weakness and decision to be typical of his class, and the central image of the masks, as well as the masked ball, which represents the society by synecdoche, can be taken as an image of a superficial system in which appearances outweigh realities. The problem is that the philosophy Manuchehr outlines to Khojasteh at the ball, which is in the final analysis the only element that holds the story together, is so much like what Hedayat has written elsewhere (most conspicuously in his study of Omar Khayyam) that we lose sight of Manuchehr as a distinct character, representative of a social class with a restricted point of view.

As he enters the ball he is reminded of a former girl friend, and by the time his conversation with Khojasteh is under way that memory has apparently crystallized with his thoughts of the preceding afternoon and produced a full-fledged philosophy of belatedness:

> "You were just a manifestation of someone else for me. You know, there's no truth [haqiqat] beyond our own personal experience. You can see it best in love because anyone who falls in love does it through the force of the imagination. The pleasure he gets from it is from the force of his own imagination, not from the woman who's there in front of him, and still he thinks he loves her. That woman is just a concealed image, an illusion, something far removed from reality."
>
> "I don't understand."

"What I'm trying to say is that you are just the illusion of
another illusion for me; I mean, you look like someone who was
my first illusion."   (*SQKh* 160)

It is not clear from the fragment of Manuchehr's philosophy
that he works out in his conversation with Khojasteh how far
he is willing to extend his theory. Potentially this chain of illusory objects of desire stretches back into infancy. We do not
expect Manuchehr to work out the theory of psychoanalysis
in one evening at a dance, but even in its unformed state Manuchehr's philosophy is like a drop of universal solvent eating
away at the narrative's dynamic shape. (Traditionally, it is the
desire of a central character that sets a narrative in motion;
what happens when the process of desire is questioned not as
René Girard questions it in Flaubert, but questioned by the
central character?)

Some readers will suggest that Hedayat the philosopher has
shown himself here and that such stories as this are philosophical. It may be more profitable to see "Suratak-hâ" in a transitional position, as an attempt to reconcile narrative elements
that resist integration until *The Blind Owl*. The theory of illusory objects of desire, or masks, is expressed in *The Blind
Owl* through the device of shifting identities. The narrative
emphasis on tableaux (the photograph of Khojasteh and the
other man, and later Manuchehr's memory of a painted curtain in his grandfather's house) reappears, much expanded, in
the series of painted scenes and related tableaux in *The Blind
Owl*. The ambiguous, vacillating attitude toward the narrator
is again a feature of *The Blind Owl*, but projected outward
and expanded into a colossal ambiguity, an untrustworthy
protagonist whom we see only from inside. The violent ending
of "Suratak-hâ"—as with other Hedayat stories seemingly unmotivated, even unnecessary—betrays a radical need for narrative closure. It would not have been necessary for Hedayat
to write *The Blind Owl* for us to see in the dynamics of super-
latives and sudden shocks that pattern the short stories a
thinly disguised erotic coloring, but the unmistakable juxtaposition of sexual union and violence at the conclusion of *The*

Blind Owl functions almost as a critical commentary on that esthetic system.

There are other works of the period less concerned with esthetic closure: '*Alviye Khânom* (Madame Alviye, 1933),[35] an amorphous narrative depicting the life of a group of indigent travelers on a pilgrimage to Mashad, and *Vagh vagh sâhâb* (the title contains a comic misspelling, but Kamshad's version, "Mr. Bow Wow," catches the essentials; 1933), a series of ephemeral satires parodying various pretentious styles (they are called *qaziye*, or "cases," in the manner of a detective story)—some of which are still amusing—written in collaboration with Mas'ud Farzad under the pen names Gog and Magog (Ya'juj and Ma'juj). The satires are silly and clownish, but often marvelously inventive. (Among the cases is the story of a diarrhea microbe: "One of the germs was more important than all the rest because we're singling him out for this story.")[36] They are perhaps not worth studying as contributions to the short story, in the sense that the more ambitious creations are, but their artlessness makes them a useful compendium of Hedayat themes, no less useful because in *Vagh vagh Sâhâb* the themes are tied to passing topics of local concern in the thirties rather than the verities of serious social commentary. We will refer to the *qazâyâ* occasionally for this reason: with the short stories they make up a private encyclopedia of recurrent themes that allow us to see the unified set of patterns that take their clearest form in *The Blind Owl*. The same quality that is often held against *The Blind Owl*, its lack of social context, is also the source of its intense coherence and power. What readers may see as a self-indulgent foregrounding of Hedayat's personal obsessions may also be seen as a direct confrontation with patterns of discourse and sunken conventions that had previously been unacknowledged informing powers in his writing. We often refer to such shaping forces as private obsessions, though this is a curious term for themes that are major leitmotifs of post-Romantic writing. The themes that are developed hesitantly in the short stories—doubling, repetition, the metaphor of sexuality and death, the esthetic of horror beneath the innocent surfaces of things—

become narrative commonplaces in the nineteenth century because (among other reasons) the private obsessions of writers
are found to resemble one another. But whether we call them
private or public, something that is bound in the short stories
is set free in *The Blind Owl*, and after *The Blind Owl* Hedayat
was not to achieve such an act of liberation again.

The Blind Owl made its first appearance unpretentiously, in
1937, in the form of a mimeographed handwritten text, apparently for circulation among friends, affixed with a stamp
noting "not for sale in Iran." Hedayat spent the year 1936–37
in Bombay, where he had come at the invitation of his friend
the writer Shin-e Partow, a member of the consular staff there
(*AA* 93). He spent the year studying Pahlavi, the pre-Islamic
language of Iran, with the Parsi scholar Behramgore Ankle-
saria. Available biographical information does not give a consistent picture of his mood at this period in his life. On the one
hand we have the evidence of his enthusiasm for his studies. A
letter to Jan Rypka announces with a sense of excitement balanced by his self-deprecating irony that he intends to devote
himself to the study of pre-Islamic texts: "I've been busy
studying Pahlavi, though I doubt if it will be of any use in this
world or the next. Everyone finds some talent for making his
livelihood; one person, for instance, makes the circle in the
letter *nun* well, another memorizes ancient poetry, another
writes articles full of flattery and gets his bread that way the
rest of his life."[37]

An apocryphal story that, if true, reveals a side of Hedayat's
life remarkably like his fictions has it that during this period
he fell in love with two beautiful sisters in an Iranian family in
Bombay, but was unable to choose between them (*AA* 93–94).
It was in India that he became a confirmed vegetarian. On the
other hand, we have Mostafa Farzaneh's testimony that studying Pahlavi was only an excuse, that Hedayat went to India
to publish *The Blind Owl* (*ASH* 151–52). There is also evidence that he was in bad health: an acquaintance recalls that
he passed out once at the Iranian consulate in Bombay and
adds (attributing it to his vegetarianism) that he would have
died if a doctor had not been on the scene (*AA* 94).

The trip to India makes a convenient pivotal point in his career for a biographer to underline. After it the impulse that created the glorification of ancient Iran and its vestiges in contemporary folklore generates a series of specific projects—translations of Pahlavi texts and scholarly studies of folklore. As an editor of the government cultural magazine *Majalle-ye musiqi*, he was at the center of the movement to study Iranian traditional culture: his name occurs frequently as a source in the folklore collections of his friend Fazlollah Mohtadi (who wrote under the name Sobhi), and Mojteba Minovi recalls that Hedayat was a major anonymous contributor to Dehkhoda's monumental dictionary of Persian proverbs (*AA* 108). This is the period of his interest in Sartre and his fascination with Kafka. The Hedayat of this period is the figure described in the eulogies and memoirs of acquaintances: the aristocrat who has resisted the temptations to compromise with a vulgar and corrupt regime,[38] the *flâneur* who is a common sight at the popular cafés, a vegetarian, at once gregarious and reclusive, apparently homosexual,[39] who continues to live alone in a room in his parents' house throughout his adult life. The works of this period are not among his most well known. There is a fourth collection of short stories, *Sag-e velgard* (The stray dog, 1942), the title story of which is much admired, but by and large the recurrent themes of the first three collections have hardened into formulas.

In the years of relative political freedom between Reza Shah's abdication in 1941 (shortly after which *The Blind Owl* is first published in Iran) and the withdrawal of the Soviets from Azerbaijan in 1946, Hedayat experimented with politically engaged styles. "Ab-e zendegi" (The water of life, 1944), a political parable in the form of a children's folktale, has been an influential genre. *Hâjji Aqâ* (1943), the satirical study of a hypocritical and sycophantic reactionary businessman (the book whose political naiveté Gianroberto Scarcia articulates in his 1958 article), is the only other extended narrative of a length comparable to that of *The Blind Owl*.[40] "Fardâ" (Tomorrow, 1946)[41] is an experiment in stream-of-consciousness form in which we follow the thoughts of two workers as they drift asleep at night. Though the influence of Joyce is clear (Mostafa Farzaneh cites more than one conversation in which Hedayat praises Joycean innovations; *ASH* 48, 275), the emphasis in "Fardâ" is not on formal technique but on the painful isolation between the two narrators and their complex thoughts about unionization.

The most successful work of this period, surprisingly, grows out of the buffoonish mode of discourse developed in the *qazâyâ* of *Vagh vagh Sâhâb*: it takes the form of a comic history of an inanimate object, a Tehran landmark called the Pearl Cannon, *Tup-e morvâri* (1947). It was not published in Hedayat's lifetime, though a year after his death his friend Hasan Qa'emyan managed to sneak a twenty-five-page excerpt past the censors in the form of a mammoth footnote to his translation of Vincent Monteil's biography of Hedayat.[42] *Tup-e morvâri* was not published in its entirety until May 1980, when it appeared in Tehran barely long enough to be rounded up and taken off the shelves again.[43] (The name on the 1980 title page was Hadi Sedaqat, evidently Hedayat's pen name on the manuscript; the public prosecutor of Tehran, it is said, not recognizing the pen name, attempted to sue him.) The historical Pearl Cannon was taken from the Portuguese at Hormoz in 1622; in Hedayat's version the Portuguese get it from Columbus—portrayed as a caricature of an American *miles gloriosus*—who has stolen it from the natives on the island of San Salvador. It is a scurrilous and surreal performance, which may finally rank with *The Blind Owl* as Hedayat's most inventive, polysemous, and exuberant creation.

Political and personal misfortunes combined near the end of his life in such a way that his departure for France (5 December 1950) and suicide in Paris (9 April 1951) seem overdetermined. The assassination of his brother-in-law, the prime minister Ali Razmara (7 March 1951), would have represented the violence of history striking close to home. Hedayat had arranged to visit his friend Shahid Nura'i, who worked at the consulate in Paris, but between the time the plans were made and the time of Hedayat's arrival in Paris Nura'i had become terminally ill. Mostafa Farzaneh, who was a student

in Paris during those months, recalls an excursion with Hedayat to visit a pension outside of Paris, in Cachan, where Hedayat had lived in his student days: in a sinister inversion of
the homecoming scene in "Tonio Kröger" they found in its
place an insane asylum (*ASH* 339–43). Farzaneh's moving account of Hedayat's last days is the most complete. The physical scene is itself melancholy: frequent moves from one cheap
hotel to another; hopeful visits to old haunts that, like the pension in Cachan, have changed; the constant beaureaucratic
limitation of his three-month visa; and the haunting additional detail that one side of the frames of his glasses had broken, forcing him to hold them up with his hand. He mends
them perfunctorily with tape, as if acknowledging that he
won't need them much longer (*ASH* 374–75). Finally there is
the wire basket in his apartment in which Farzaneh sees the
torn fragments of unpublished manuscripts, suggesting that
Hedayat killed himself in parts before committing the final act
(*ASH* 382–84).[44]

Al-e Ahmad's essay on Hedayat observes that while he was
alive, no matter how much he wrote and spoke about death,
no one ever really took that fascination seriously, with the result that now, when he is gone, we have only the works to say
what he was like (*AA* 79–80; *FYA* 27–29). This is the paradox
of suicide as a statement: before the act has actually taken
place, statements of despair lack the final authority. Serious
intentions, while the future suicide is alive, take on the appearance of art. Hedayat's suicide is in a sense a protest
against his own art—for failing to possess the authority of reality—and the destruction of his manuscripts is a reduplication of the final act. And paradoxically the author's suicide
creates a new power in what he wrote.

Hedayat was a controversial writer during his life, and the
nature of his death (in a country where suicide is a rarer phenomenon than it is in the West, though the value placed on
martyrdom was a central part of Iranian life long before the
revolution) intensified that aspect of his reputation. For those
who wished to attack him, the manner of his death became
evidence that his personality was unbalanced, an excuse for

discounting the pessimism expressed in his stories. For those of the opposite persuasion, his suicide was used to give validity to the pain we encounter in his work, and the cult that grew around his name—with its eulogies and commemorative publications, even a commemorative medal on the tenth anniversary of his death[45]—displays an intensity that sometimes surprises Western observers. We might compare the reaction to Sylvia Plath's suicide, or to the death of Camus.

What particularly marks the enthusiasm for Hedayat in the popular press, however, is morbid curiosity. In general, there is an openness about the physical details of death that may strike the Westerner as morbid and unhealthy. The frontispiece of a popular book may show a picture of the author and a verse that explains that the picture will remain when the writer has turned to dust. In the introduction to a posthumous edition of children's folk stories collected by Hedayat's friend the radio personality Sobhi, there is a (to Western eyes) horrifying photograph of the collector recently expired on his deathbed, with the caption "Khodâ hâfez-e shomâ" (roughly, "Good-bye, everybody"). Esma'il Jamshidi's *Khodkoshi-ye Sâdeq-e Hedâyat* (Sadeq Hedayat's suicide) concludes with seven photographs taken by Rahmatollah Moqaddam, then a student in Paris, of Hedayat's corpse in the rue Championnet apartment where he died and in the coffin before his interment in Père Lachaise Cemetery. They are fuzzy, amateur pictures and the text notes with irony that the developers in Paris thought they were not worth printing. "These photos," it comments, "upset us, shook us, and made us cry. How about you?" (98).

Hedayat's suicide did more than appeal to an idiosyncratic Iranian attitude toward death: it made it inevitable for him to be identified with a vision of the artist (a vision by no means restricted to Iranian culture) as a communicant with a higher world, the myth of the poet-hero who is only briefly among us because his real home is elsewhere. Significantly, the collection of essays and remembrances dedicated to Hedayat on the occasion of the sixth anniversary of his death includes a translation into Persian of Shelley's "To a Skylark."[46] Birds enter frequently into Hedayat's writing, as they do into the eulogies to him. Hedayat's friend Parviz Natel Khanlari, who worked with Hedayat on the journal *Sokhan* during the forties, dedicated a poem entitled " 'Oqâb" (The eagle) to him,[47] a poem that since Hedayat's death seems almost prophetic. In it, the eagle asks the raven why ravens live so long. The answer, which is the raven's diet of filth and carrion, has an obvious political interpretation—the raven's diet is the course of flattery and hypocrisy—and the eagle's response, which is to disappear into the sky, becomes an image for Hedayat's modesty in life; it is also an image for his death.

The potential fallacy of the tragic myth of the poet's life is that by giving us a single standard for his art and his biography it implies that the artist's life is purposely and consciously shaped toward an inevitable end. One elevates the poet at the expense of making his suffering seem less real. To elevate is to distance. A successful suicide, after all, is by definition someone who has experienced thoughts and feelings we have not, someone from a different world. This danger is compounded by the circumstance that Hedayat, even in his life, ran the risk of being read as a curiosity. He consistently—in his vegetarianism, in his opposition to Islam—took extreme positions and made no visible attempt to accommodate himself or his fictional narrators to public opinion. But a writer's estrangement and indifference to society exist in relative terms: there is a contradiction between Hedayat's esthetics of isolation and the public nature of the medium of literature. This contradiction is at the heart of his biography, as it is at the heart of his works. In one sense the cult that grew around the fact of his death would have been the last thing he wanted; in another, of course, he courted it simply by being a writer.

Another response to the same dichotomy between public and private is to interpret his death as a commentary on the society in which he was forced to exist. Monteil suggests this tentatively and archly: "Is the drama of Sadeq Hedayat simply the individual case of a soul pledged from the start to the angel of Suicide, or is it simply a symptom of disorder, of the evil of the generation which suffocates in the confining shadows of a cul-de-sac?" (Monteil, 48). Al-e Ahmad says the same thing explicitly: "Hedayat was a child of the Constitutional period and a writer during the time of the dictatorship. . . . During his life he was witness either to political anarchy or to stifling dictatorship. The prevailing reality in Iran throughout the forty and some odd years of his life was one only of meanness, lies, deceit—nothing but wretchedness and misery [*faqr va maskanat*]" (*AA* 86). Al-e Ahmad interprets the seclusion and withdrawal of the speaker in *The Blind Owl*, and his hostility to the reality outside his four walls, as a symbol for the response of honest Iranians to the reign of Reza Shah. Withdrawal was the only reaction at a time when "a man is scared to express his true thoughts to his friends, to his wife, to his colleagues or anyone else, when he is reduced 'to being able to talk freely only with his own shadow.' Its artistic value aside, *The Blind Owl* is a social document" (*AA* 87).

In the 1960s and 1970s the hypothesis that the response of an honest man to tyranny is withdrawal was more frequently called into question, and Iranians who were involved in opposition politics, but who admired Hedayat, often felt it necessary to explain his isolation with reference to biographical evidence. His possible addiction to opium is often cited in this regard as an excuse for his supposed refusal of political commitment. Bozorg Alavi was the first writer to mention it in print, in his preface to a German translation of *The Blind Owl* (Kamshad, 179–80), but it was for years the most popular piece of folk wisdom about Hedayat. As an explanation of his career, however, it does not work out chronologically: the most self-contained and involuted of Hedayat's works, and the one that presents itself as an opium dream explicitly, is *The Blind Owl*, and that is a work of the 1930s, written during a period of prolific publication. If addiction were somehow the "cause" of Hedayat's obscure style, he must have cured himself in the 1940s, because his engaged writings of that period are as public and accessible as Gorki's or Bozorg Alavi's.

The author of *The Blind Owl* is obviously someone who has smoked opium. In fact, to judge from the two authoritative studies of opium and its effects on writers of the Romantic period, Althea Hayter's *Opium and the Romantic Imagination* and M. H. Abrams's *Milk of Paradise*,[48] it seems likely that a useful study of *The Blind Owl* could examine the ways in which its imagery is characteristic of the imagination under the influence of opium. Abrams lists as characteristic images of opium users many of the most striking features of *The Blind Owl*: "enormous extension of space and time" (Abrams, 8), a persecution theme often manifested as consciousness of having committed an unforgivable crime (40, 75–76, and passim), the image of accusing eyes (26, 44, and 71–72) and heightening of auditory perception (25–26), all of which are images and themes we shall discuss in other contexts in the chapters that follow. Francis Thompson's "Finis Coronat Opus," a short prose narrative that Abrams appends to the paperback edition, is so like *The Blind Owl* in tone and imagery that one might suspect it to be a possible source if there were not already an overabundance of sources in Western literature.

Althea Hayter adds to the list of common themes two characters commonly encountered: "pariahs" (like the Malay traveler who haunts De Quincey's fantasies or the recurring figures of the old man in *The Blind Owl*) and harlot ogresses (like the "female fiend" in George Crabbe's "The World of Dreams" or the wife in *The Blind Owl*; Hayter, 337). The extraordinary tour de force with which her study concludes, in which she combines the features of opium writing in a single imaginary monologue (Hayter, 337–41) is again so like *The Blind Owl* that the astute critic would be tempted to label it a source if it had not been written after Hedayat's death.

Chapter Two

THE BOOK OF LOVE: DANTE AS TEMPLATE

I

THE form of *The Blind Owl* is above all that of a love story, in fact a highly conventional love story after the manner of romances that have become classical in our tradition. If we do not often speak of it in those terms, one reason may be Hedayat's solitary life, which leads us to anticipate a solitary, companionless fiction. Another reason might be the way the book opens, with a bravura overture that seems almost to stand alone.

The opening sentence of *The Blind Owl* is one of the best-known and most frequently recited passages of modern Persian, perhaps as well known to literate Iranians as the opening lines of Iraj Mirza's homiletic poem "Mother" or Forugh Farrokhzad's "Those Days." We remember the opening sentence separately from the rest of the book (a property it shares with the title), as if its authority were distinct from or even contrary to the narrative that follows it.

> *Dar zendegi zakhm-hâ-i hast ke mesl-e khure ruh-râ âheste dar enzevâ mikhurad va mitarâshad.* (1/9)

> There are sores which slowly erode the mind in solitude like a kind of canker. (Costello)

Someone is talking to us. He sounds reasonable enough. The sentiment has the kind of generality we assent to uncritically in proverbs. And as in proverbs there is a disjunction between the seeming universality of the proposition and the specificity of the images that convey it. The claim to universality is clearer in Persian because the translation omits the opening phrase, "in life," to our ears pleonastic, which at once expands and trivializes the field of reference. As for its specificity of diction, M. Y. Qotbi, in his extended reading of *The Blind Owl*, points out justly that the word *dard* (pain) would sound more normal in the place of *zakhm* (wound), the word Costello translates as "sores." *Zakhm* is at once more specific than *dard*, more concrete and urgent, and not a recognized expression in this context.[1]

Qotbi also calls attention to an aural effect centering on the *kh* sound in *zakhm* that is worth expansion: a series of consonants formed at the front of the mouth (*d*, a rolled *r*, *z*, *n*) is interrupted by a scraping guttural, which will be echoed in the accented words that follow, *khure* and *mikhurad*. There is a level on which the subject of the sentence is the letter *khâ'* seen as the letter of penetration (in *khordan*, to eat), of desire (*khâstan*, to wish, want), of intimacy (*khod*, self). Phonetically, the word *zakhm* sums it up by moving back into the throat and out again, a miniature wedge shape that can be said to mimic its meaning.

The first four words (literally, "in life there are wounds") can be seen as another such wedge shape narrowing from general to specific. And as the relative clause modifying *zakhm-hâ* continues, Hedayat's characteristic tendency to juxtapose the intangible and the material intensifies. The sense of materiality and precision is furthered by a simple, direct vocabulary that the English cannot reproduce. Words such as "erode" and "solitude" have an elevated, Latinate quality that conveys the significance but not the plainness and simplicity of the Persian: "erode" renders two common verbs, *khordan* (to eat, wear away) and *tarâshidan* (to wear down, grind, grate, shave). *Khure* (leprosy) is hardly a household word, but its proximity to the verb *mikhurad* (from *khordan*) suggests its simple root meaning "that which eats, wears away." Costello's word, "canker," is strictly speaking a mistranslation, but a purposeful one (he translates *khure* as "gangrene" later in the text, 47/47). The archaic field of semantic reference for English "canker" covered any eating or spreading sore, thus suggesting the root meaning of *khure*. (For most readers the term "canker sore," which looms behind the English text, is too domestic and homely.)

Simple vocabulary and a sense of mathematical precision have a contrary effect buried within them, a central conceptual hole that the relative clause modifying *zakhm* leaves open despite its narrowing field of reference. It opens with *ruh-râ* (the soul, accusative case), which tells us that whatever the *zakm-hâ* do the soul is the object of it. (*Ruh* is, in fact, the only word that tells us we are not dealing with a physical disease.) The tentative metaphor of life as body (a life in which there are "wounds") shifts into a similar metaphor, mildly paradoxical: soul as body (a soul in which there are wounds). There follow an adverb and an adverbial phrase, one temporal, one spatial: *âheste* (slowly, gradually) and *dar enzevâ* (in solitude). (The long *a* sound that opens and closes the phrase sets it off, isolates it like a pair of parentheses.) The pair of adverbs is followed by a pair of verbs, unmistakably physical in nature. Meanwhile the caesuras that accumulate toward the end of the sentence isolate the violence of the verbs. (*Âheste* and *dar enzevâ* are gentle, seemingly positive terms in contrast with *mikhurad* and *mitarâshad*, which they delay and, by contrast, emphasize.) This pairing of doubles functions as more than an ornamental rhetorical device: the process of erosion seems to rest and then take another bite between the two verbs, giving the sentence an additional sense of closure. What is missing is the antecedent of the figure *zakhm-hâ*.

It is now clear enough that the wounds are other than physical, but if we write the equation out like the category of metaphor Aristotle calls analogy, there is a missing part: X is to "soul" as wound is to (unstated) body, the unknown entity being described only by what it does. The occultation of signified in effect makes form copy content, as if the absence that gnaws away at the body in the vehicle of the metaphor, and at the soul in the tenor, had also gnawed away at the sentence.

It is not only the theme of insistent pain that foreshadows later developments in *The Blind Owl*. The absent or veiled subject of the opening statement (veiled by the figure "wounds," itself a kind of absence) merges with the invisible agent whose influence we intuit behind or within the speaker as the book unfolds, the gaps and blindnesses of his madness. This foreshadowing exists, but it may obscure a fact that separates the opening from the rest of the narrative: that we have not had, and will not have for some pages, any indication that the narrator is insane. Compare the opening of the short story "Three Drops of Blood," where the speaker's disjointed account of his surroundings tips us off immediately to his condition. The difference is striking: whereas "Three Drops of Blood" remains a tour de force, *The Blind Owl* unrolls a complex succession of voices that is various and symphonic. The subtlety of this technical feat is so thorough that many readers still refuse to see *The Blind Owl* as an insane monologue. An impersonal, seemingly scientific voice ushers us so uncritically into the action that we are not even aware we are hearing a first-person narrator until the second page ("I propose to deal with only one case. . . . It concerned me personally"—2/9), and the discovery that he is mad is postponed through a long process of sorting out the unexpected repetitions of his discourse. This involves us in his madness, forcing us to participate in it as readers.

We have been analyzing the first sentence. The second sentence establishes a new voice:

In dard-hâ-râ nemishavad be-kesi ezhâr kard, chun. . . .

> It is impossible to convey a just idea of the agony which this disease can inflict.

The aphoristic authority of the opening sentence has given way to a drier, more distant style. This is not a famous sentence. The voice speaking to us is still reasonable, but less interesting, less engaging. The entire phrase "the agony which this disease can inflict" is Costello's interpolation, and yet it carries the feeling of rhetorical inflation that exists in the original. The equivalent of "the agony" is *dard-hâ*, the relatively colorless word Qotbi cited as the usual term we expected in the place of *zakhm*. The verb *ezhâr kardan*, itself a colorless newspaper word, in the colorless and impersonal form (a for-

mal and slightly evasive construction like the French use of
on), conveys a paradoxical force that none of the translations
captures. Is it that these pains cannot be expressed because
people won't believe them, or that they are simply too intense
for expression? Presumably the project of the book is exactly
this, *ezhâr kardan*, the act of expression declared impossible.

The experience of the book will be that the speaker's blindness is the obstacle to expression; the long phrase that follows
blames an uncomprehending audience:

> In general, people are apt to relegate such inconceivable suffer-
> ings to the category of the incredible [the last four words are, in
> Persian, two pairs of synonyms, *ettefâqât va pishâmad-hâ-ye nâ-
> der va 'ajib*]. Any mention of them in conversation or in writing
> is considered in the light of current beliefs, the individual's per-
> sonal beliefs in particular [*bar sabil-e 'aqâyed-e jâri va 'aqâyed-
> e khodeshân*], and tends to provoke a smile of incredulity and
> derision [*labkhand-e shakkâk va tamaskhor-âmiz*].   (1/9)

In one sense this passage is stylistically typical of Persian writing, if not of *The Blind Owl*. There are privileged Hedayatian
terms such as *bâvar na-kardani* (incredible, Costello's "incon-
ceivable") and *tamaskhor-âmiz* (derisive, mocking),[2] but on
the whole the diction has an elevated and formal quality that
is unlike Hedayat and unlike the rest of the book. The reasonable voice of the opening sentence has modulated into that of
a textbook or a newspaper columnist, if not for its content at
least for its long-windedness. Costello has split the above passage into two sentences: in Persian it is a long and complex
phrase that is part of a longer period, one of those conglom-
erates of what would be, in English, numerous sentences, con-
glomerates that are the despair of students learning Persian as
they cast their eyes down the page looking for punctuation.
The passage, which is Costello's second paragraph in the
translation, is one such conglomerate sentence in the original.
Costello's second sentence is in Persian a phrase ending with
the loose connective *chun* (because, since, as); the passage
above, following *chun*, ends in Persian with a dash followed
by the word *zirâ* (*chun*) and another stream of words.

The incessant pairing of complementary terms and synonyms ("in conversation or in writing," *nâder* and *'ajib, 'aqâyed-e jâri* and *'aqâyed-e khodeshân, shakkâk* and *tamaskhor-âmiz*) is the most common of rhetorical devices. It is not the sign of careful writing: when it does not draw a real distinction it seems to imply that neither word was quite what the writer wanted. (It may be significant that the same Hedayat who elsewhere purged his writing of this device on a stylistic level is so taken on the level of plot with doubling and repetition.) We could argue that this sentence is a regrettable lapse from Hedayat's usually careful and unadorned style; we may read it also as a style approaching parody, part of the gradual transition from the opening voice to the personalized monologue of *The Blind Owl* proper.

We move from the proverbial authority of the opening sentence to the colorless authority of traditional elevated writing (as if to say, this is the style that convinces you; I may as well try it) in the course of which *zakhm* disappears (it will not return), to be replaced by *dard* and the still more colorless *ettefâqât* and *pish-âmad-hâ* (events, occurrences). In the next sentence it is *ettefâqât-e mâvarâ tabi'i*, "events which are extraordinary" or "beyond the natural" (Costello's "this disease which transcends ordinary experience"), which introduces the sense of the supernatural we find pervading the first episodes. (The Arabic translation by Ibrahim Desouqi Shitta raises an unusual translator's dilemma here, *al-ittifâqâtu al-mitâfiziqiyyatu*, bringing in a Western loan word whose Greek stems *meta* and *physikalis* echo *mâvarâ* [beyond] and *tabi'i* [natural, physical], but whose total effect is altogether alien to the Persian text's deliberate avoidance of loan words.)[3]

The remainder of the opening section may be construed as increasingly more personal fragments: a paragraph on opium as a temporary, unsuccessful palliative, the statement of intention to recount the speaker's own story, his statement of his own alienation from the rest of humankind, all of which serve increasingly to individualize the speaker. It modulates gradually into a speaking voice: the periods become shorter and marked with exclamations ("but no, that is too much to expect"—2/10) and a series of rhetorical questions. The passage marking the terminal point in that process is marked by another frequently quoted passage:

> In the course of my life I have discovered that a fearful abyss [*varte-ye hulnâki*] lies between me and other people and have realized that my best course is to remain silent and keep my thoughts to myself for as long as I can. If I have now made up my mind to write it is only in order to reveal myself [*mo'arrefi bekonam*] to my shadow which at this moment is stretched [*khamide*] across the wall in the attitude of one devouring with insatiable appetite each word I write.   (2/10)

The speaker is not only personalized, but in the same gesture of solidification, made an outsider from society—indeed made into two distinct parts, self and shadow.

The transition from anonymous to personal speaker is comparable to the transition from exposition to narrative, which takes place more conspicuously, marked by a typographical break. It has the effect of a second beginning:

> *Dar in donyâ-ye past-e por az faqr va maskanat, barâye nokhostin bar gomân kardam ke dar zendegi-ye man yek sha'â'-e âftâb darâkhshad, ammâ. . . .*
>
> In this mean world of wretchedness and misery I thought that for once a ray of sunlight had broken upon my life.   (4/10–11)

The second beginning, like the first, speaks in totalities—*dar in donyâ*, "in this world"; *dar zendegi-ye man*, "in my life"—but the totalities have been given specifying modifiers. Instead of "life" as in the first sentence we have "my life." The world is *in donyâ* (this world), suggesting perhaps that there are others, perhaps that "this world" is simply the environment of the speaker, as we say "my world" or the "world" of the narrative. The words *faqr* and *maskanat* will interest us later, in Chapter Four, but at this point the possibility of an explicit social context must occur to us. Numerous critics have observed that Iran in the thirties, and since, has been in fact a vista of poverty and deprivation; *faqr* and *maskanat* denote more strictly economic suffering than the English "wretchedness" and "misery," suggesting that for a moment the speaker's personal vision is aligned with a political observation before it drifts off into a narrative whose dimensions are personal and psychological. As a glimpse of a realistic world, however, it is momentary: the characteristic focus of *The Blind Owl* is not on the degrees of shading we associate with narrative realism but on a subjective world. The scenario of intense desire allows for a portrayal of polarities, of terminal points: a world cut off, characterized by absence and poverty, and a higher world characterized by plenitude and light. It is a style of outline rather than color, in which it is appropriate that the central recurring figure should be the narrator's shadow projected against the wall.

Whoever is speaking to us is now speaking from a scene—not yet particularized except by mood, but unmistakably it is a scene—and as a character is defined only by affect. We need not read any further to guess that the light in the passage will be characterized as star, woman and angel to see that the next step is for the narrative to become a love story.

II

We could in fact summarize the plot of *The Blind Owl* as a series of love stories. The book divides into two parts: in the first (1–43/9–43) the speaker describes himself as a solitary painter who, after a glimpse of a beautiful woman resembling the subject of his own obsessive paintings, searches for her hopelessly in the countryside around his house. The woman comes to him again, unexpectedly and wordlessly, walks into his house, lies down on his bed, and mysteriously dies. He paints a portrait of her face. In a series of unmotivated, ritualistic scenes he dismembers her body, carries it to a nearby river helped by a mysterious old man with a carriage, and finds in the burial site a vase. He returns home, smokes opium, and contemplates the vase, on which he finds a portrait identical to the picture he has painted of the ethereal woman.

In part two (44–130/45–116) the speaker describes himself

as a convalescent in an urban setting. An extended autobiographical introduction includes the narrative of his parents, itself a second love story (54–59/54–57). His mother, a temple attendant in India, is seduced by a traveling Iranian merchant, the speaker's father. The merchant's twin brother, the speaker's uncle, takes advantage of his resemblance in order to seduce her as well, and the mother insists that they undergo "trial by cobra" in which they are enclosed in a pit with a cobra, the survivor to marry her. The trial is inconclusive because the survivor is rendered insane by the ordeal, so no one can be sure of his identity. The child (our narrator) is sent to be raised in Iran.

The plot of part two is less obviously a love story, but it turns on the speaker's unhappy marriage to the daughter of the household in which he was raised. He emphasizes the hostility between them: they have, he insists, never consummated the marriage, and he refuses to name her except as "the bitch" (*lakkâte*). On the other hand, he portrays himself as hopelessly drawn to her with physical desire. The only "event" of part two, except for a walk outside of town, is the concluding scene. He goes to kill her, armed with a knife, and in the course of a remarkably intense love scene, kills her—supposedly by accident.

The love stories are, as we shall see, more or less the same story, but readers, before assembling the parts of the text into a coherent reading, see them intertextually. We perceive the novel's traditional elements early in the first love story, before we are able to make sense of its peculiarities as a text, and we fit it into a pattern. It is the love story that acclimatizes us, since, whatever the strangeness of the plot, we all know how romance works. And for the Western reader it is not only romance but a particular form of romance. The wretchedness of the lover, the mysterious nature of the love object, the obsessive focus on his complex reactions to her appearances—all are typical of the literary conventions of courtly love. Courtly love is of course as much a part of Islamic tradition as of ours: the story of Qais and Layla, or in Iran Layla and Majnun ("the crazed one"), is at the heart of Islamic literature. *The Blind*

Owl, however, suggests analogies not so much with Islamic epic accounts of fated and ill-starred love, or even with the lyric monologues of ghazal poetry, which often allude to those narratives, as it suggests the self-conscious deification of Beatrice in Dante's *Vita nuova*.

At this point, since we are going to pursue the analogy further, we should acknowledge that comparisons with Dante are always a little suspicious. Dante has so frequently been put in a tutelary position to contemporary writers that any work with apocalyptic overtones, or even any work with conspicuous patterning, really any work that can be divided into three parts like the Divine Comedy, runs the risk of the Danteian embrace.[4] For this reason I emphasize at the outset that the specific set of analogies I wish to isolate does not argue for an affinity of sensibility between Hedayat and Dante. If they resemble each other, it is because the genre has its own peculiar logic. Still, the accidental resemblances produce a kind of symmetry: Hedayat is, like Dante, a pioneer in the use of his demotic language. The *Vita nuova* stands at the beginning of courtly love traditions (150 years after the first Provençal poems by Dante's own count in *VN* 25.4),[5] which may have been influenced by Islamic traditions. Hedayat, writing from within in Islamic culture, operates under the influence of relatively new European narrative styles.

The possibility does exist that we may by talking about direct, conscious influence, since Hedayat can be shown to know at least by reputation the usual details about Dante's works. In his 1928 essay "La magie en Perse," published in the French periodical *Le voile d'Isis*, Hedayat compares the angels of death in Zoroastrian tradition to Beatrice: "If he has deserved a reward, he is led by the Yzeds to the summit of the sacred mountain, and sees the great passage open before him. A charming, smiling face presents itself in front of him, and as Beatrice to Dante, she takes his arm and draws him near."[6] There is not a trace in that reference of the irony with which he treats comparable Islamic mystical poetry in his 1932 story "Mardi-ke nafs-ash-râ kosht" (The man who killed his "self") or his 1933 essay on Omar Khayyam. It is not impossible, though it seems unlikely, that *The Blind Owl* was conceived as a specific parody of Dante. But whatever Hedayat's attitude toward Dante, the *Vita nuova* provides the romance pattern in its broadest outlines, and juxtaposing the two provides us with a logical first step in tracing the traditional structure, the romance grain of *The Blind Owl*.

The *Vita nuova* is a founding text of European culture, but it has not exerted its influence over an unbroken chain of transmission. It was not much read in the generations following Dante's,[7] but the extraordinarily fruitful influence in all the European languages of Petrarch's obsessed persona in the sonnets to Laura, undoubtedly influenced by the Dante of the *Vita nuova*, carried it forth in more schematic, less spiritual form. The coherence of the tradition is so great that it is as if we could extrapolate our way to the premises of the *Vita nuova* without knowing it, simply because it occupies the originating center of the tradition. Seen side by side with *The Blind Owl* we might expect it to articulate the romance tradition in pure form, relatively free from irony, whereas we might expect *The Blind Owl* to run through the same themes in a brutal parody, exemplifying the angle of vision Harold Bloom calls belatedness, what Northrop Frye calls the ironic mode. On the other hand, the *Vita nuova* was shocking to its contemporaries, perhaps no less uncanny and unsettling than *The Blind Owl*. Erich Auerbach, always aware of realism behind conventional expression, summarizes the poems of the *Vita nuova* in his 1929 study of Dante in terms that have not, I think, been echoed in the critical tradition:

> Seldom does one of the customary poetic ornaments appear; and when it does, it is not introduced with taste and charm, but is so immoderately exaggerated, so earnestly transposed into the realm of reality as to frighten and repel Dante's contemporaries. By its insistence on the concrete, unique situation, by its unabashed disclosure of personal feeling the poem takes on such an intensity that those who were not prepared to commit themselves with passion felt wounded and alarmed.[8]

It may be that Hedayat's innovations are already latent in the tradition, from the speaker's monomania to its seemingly modern focus on textuality, even its obsessed focus on the death of the love object. The moral issues raised by the attitude toward women in *The Blind Owl* are also present in Dante.[9]

Both narratives demonstrate hesitation to specify, a suppression of visual detail, and an unwillingness to name characters, all of which suggest an inward focus. Both are texts in which an observer watches his own reactions, and both portray themselves as artists commenting on their creations. The narrator of *The Blind Owl*, as he represents himself in the opening episode, is a young painter (as the young Dante is a beginning poet), or more accurately a hack artist who decorates *qalam-dân*'s, pen cases, evidently those Qajar papier-mâché pen cases that were briefly in demand in antique auctions during the seventies. His theme is a single obsessive picture, always identical, which will be taken to India and sold by his paternal uncle:

> For some reason unknown to me the subject of all my paintings was from the very beginning one and the same. It consisted always of a cypress tree at the foot of which was squatting a bent old man like an Indian fakir. He had a long cloak wrapped about him and wore a turban [*shâlme*] on his head.[10] The index finger of his left hand was pressed to his lips in a gesture of surprise. Before him stood a girl in a long black dress, leaning towards him and offering him a flower of morning glory [*gol-e nilufar*]. Between them ran a little stream. Had I seen the subject of this picture at some time in the past?   (6/12–13)

This scene is refracted, hauntingly, throughout the narrative. Though the paintings cannot, like Dante's poems, be separated from the narrative settings, the scene develops a substantiality of its own. In fact they work to generate the action. Dante tells us that he had tried his hand at writing poems before zeroing in on Beatrice as a subject (*VN* 3.9), and with Hedayat's hero, too, the art precedes its romantic application, since he does not recognize the woman in his picture as his inspiring angel until she appears to him in a vision. (In fact we are not told explicitly whether he has ever made the connection that the subject of his drawings and the figures of his vi-

sion are the same.) The occasion of her first visionary appearance is a visit by his uncle, who sells the pen cases in India,
and who also resembles both the old man in the picture and
the vision. The narrator looks for something suitable to offer
the guest and finds a forgotten bottle of wine (later we learn
that it was laid down at his birth,[11] and that it is poisoned) on
the shelf in his closet. Standing on a stool to get the wine
down, he glances out at a ventilation hole to the desert outside
and sees the scene of his paintings:

> As I reached toward the bottle, I chanced to look out through
> the ventilation-hole [surâkh-e havâ-khowr] above the shelf. On
> the open ground outside my room I saw a bent old man sitting
> at the foot of a cypress tree with a young girl—no, an angel from
> heaven—standing before him. She was leaning forward and with
> her right hand was offering him a blue flower of morning glory
> [gol-e nilufar-e kabudi]. The old man was biting the nail of the
> index finger of his left hand.   (8/14)

The absence of affect in the initial picture breaks down in the
passage that follows, giving way to a long, sensual description
of the woman, not only sensual but mesmeric: the leisurely,
paratactic catalogue of her features, in contrast with the hur-
ried narration of events preceding it, produces the effect of a
tableau vivant, or of stopped time, rather than a scene from
life. The catalogue of features follows the order of items that
is standard in polite depictions of literary love objects: smile,
eyes (here for eight lines the camera lingers), the shape of her
face, her eyebrows, but it concludes by giving the list an erotic
turn that leaves us no doubt what it is in the vision that was
missing in the paintings:

> Her lips were full and half-open as though they had broken
> away only a moment before from a long, passionate kiss and
> were not yet sated. . . . It seemed to me as I gazed at her long,
> slender form, with its harmonious lines of shoulder, arms,
> breast, waist, buttocks and legs, that she had been torn [jodâ
> shod] from her husband's embrace, that she was like the female
> mandrake which has been plucked from the arms of its mate.

She was wearing a black pleated dress which clung tightly to her body [*ke qâleb va chashb-e tan-ash bud*]. Gazing at her, I was certain she wished to leap across the stream which separated her from the old man but that she was unable to do so.

(9–10/15)

The sensuous prose rhythm is even clearer in Persian than in the English translation, but in English, too, the sense of objectification of the figure into a warm, meaty object redefines the surrounding narrative with its latent, submerged sensuality. This passage provides us with the clue, verified later, that the obsession is physical.

Dante's Beatrice has not impressed readers as a sensual figure, but an analogous sensual tableau in the *Vita nuova* is not hard to find. As Etienne Gilson remarks in *Dante the Philosopher*, "I believe that in the whole of Dante's work not a single case can be found in which the salutary intercession of Beatrice does not owe something of its efficacy to the sight or memory of her bodily beauty."[12] In the vision of Beatrice described in chapter 3 (subject of the sonnet "A ciascun'alma presa e gentil core"), again a vision of a young woman with an older man, there is an analogue in foreshortened form of the vision through the ventilation hole in *The Blind Owl*. The tableau in *The Blind Owl* was both picture and hallucination, neither one of which takes priority. Here the relation and sequence are clear: it is a dream that becomes a poem, which in turn generates a prose *ragione* or explication. As a dream it is already equivocal: "In his arms it seemed to me that a person was sleeping covered only with a blood-colored cloth [*nuda, salvo che involta mi parea in un drappo sanguigno leggeramente*] upon whom looking very attentively, I knew that it was the lady of the salutation who had deigned the day before to salute me" (*VN* 3.4/Rossetti, 549–50).[13] The vision is more appropriate to the dreams of an adolescent of eighteen years than the scholiasts have acknowledged, and the voyeuristic nature of the scene is emphasized by the woman's ignorance of her admirer, Beatrice because she is (at the outset) asleep, the other for unspecified reasons: "The girl was directly op-

posite me but she appeared to be quite unaware of her surroundings. She was gazing straight ahead without looking at
anything in particular" (8–9/14). An effect not unlike that of
the paratactic catalogue in *The Blind Owl* grows out of the
two phrases between the word *nuda* and our recognition of
the sleeping figure's identity. The effect is that the reader's
voyeuristic curiosity merges with Dante's for the space of that
syntactic suspension.

Meanwhile the color red (traditionally glossed as a sign of
nobility) reinforces the images of fire (the flame-colored cloud
in which the two figures appear) and blood (his heart, which
the old man has in his hand). Both images have traditionally
violent and sexual connotations, and the sequel in which she
is forced to eat his heart combines them in a way that reminds
us more of the conclusion of *The Blind Owl* than of anything
in the remainder of the *Vita nuova*. "But when he had remained with me a little while, I thought that he set himself to
awaken her that slept; after . . . which he made her to eat that
thing which flamed in his hand; and she ate as one fearing
[*dubitosamente*]" (*VN* 3.6/Rossetti, 550). Later in the history
of courtly love the image of the lover's heart in the woman's
breast, or the hearts exchanged, would become a commonplace (as in Donne's "The Legacy"), but this image is likely to
have been as grotesque to Dante's contemporaries as it is to
us. The poet Giovanni Pascoli has suggested, apropos of Cavalcanti's sonnet "Vedesti il mio parere ogni valore," which
answers Dante's sonnet describing this vision ("A ciascun-
'alma presa e gentil core"), "He succeeds only in demonstrat-
ing that the dream has no reasonable meaning and is therefore
a real dream after all."[14] A contemporary, Dante da Maiano,
replied to "A ciascun'alma presa e gentil core") with the cyn-
ical suggestion that all further commentary of the dream be
postponed until after a general purge and urinalysis.[15] I believe
the first commentator to say the obvious about this dream
(that "the vision in question resembles a wet dream") has been
Gayatri Spivak (in "Finding Feminist Readings," 78). Dante
would at least have agreed that it is the most explicitly erotic
episode of the *Vita nuova*, and might have added that this is

why it occurs at the beginning. It may be a fantasy of sexual initiation (heart and mouth transposed from sexual organs),[16] but Dante's point is that he outgrows it.

Both passages end the same way, with a voice that dispels the reverie. In Dante's vision it is the bitter weeping (*amarissimo pianto*) that replaces Love's initial gaiety (*letizia*). The contrast is emphasized in the sestet of "A ciascun'alma presa e gentil core," which begins with the word *allegro* and concludes with *piangendo*. The speaker takes up this crying himself, and it becomes the spiritual exercise by which he will purge himself of guilt after Beatrice's death (chapter 39). Crying, as an act that is devotional and humbling to the self, is appropriate to the mood of the *Vita nuova*. The laughter that brings to an end the vision through the air hole in *The Blind Owl* is similarly characteristic: "All at once the old man burst into laughter. It was a hollow grating laughter [*khande-ye khoshk va zanande*] of a quality to make the hairs of one's body stand on end: a harsh, sinister, mocking laughter. And yet the expression of his face did not change. It was as though the laughter was echoing from somewhere deep within his body" (10/15–16). As in the *Vita nuova* there is a disjunction between the content of the vision and the sound that ends it. Here the stillness of the picture, embodied in the mesmeric rhythm and the unchanging expression of the old man, implies an attempt to disassociate the physical reaction from himself, a withdrawal of affect seen later to be characteristic of this speaker. The sound itself is an appropriate leitmotif for the book, as the tears are appropriate to the *Vita nuova*: the laugh comes to characterize the speaker's bitterness and hostility to the world, which separates him from the desired object. Between its first occurrence, when he hears it coming from a seemingly motionless figure, and the conclusion, when he produces the same sound involuntarily (115/103–4, 122/109, 127–28/114), it is distributed among various other figures (the gravedigger, the father/uncle in the story of the parents in India, the wife's father [61/59] and the odds-and-ends man).

Without broaching the argument of the next chapter, which is concerned with the identity of the characters who produce that laugh, it is enough to point out that laughter and the erotic themes of *The Blind Owl* are connected. The frightening nature of the laughter of witches and ghouls in horror stories and films lies in the fact that they are broken language, the voice without articulation, sounds that do not communicate: they represent the human voice out of control. The rising hairs of the imagined listener's body (*mu-ye tan-e âdam*), like a parody of tumescence, suggests that the laughter is directed at the speaker's sexual excitement as he looks at the woman in the tableau.

The path from the initiating vision through the mysterious voice is in Dante direct and transparent. The dream is perceived immediately as a message with significance, transcribed as a sonnet, and circulated among fellow poets for interpretation. The speaker in *The Blind Owl* faints in terror at the sound of the mirthless laugh, wakes to find his uncle gone, and only after three days overcomes his fear sufficiently to look for the vision again. Everything is designed as if to distract the reader from the question of the tableau's significance: from the marvelous detail that when he looks again there is no ventilation hole, to the first complication in the plot, his elegaic search for the woman in the outside world. She is reduced to simple undifferentiated desire.

> Could I abandon the hope of ever seeing her again? It was not within my power to do so. Henceforth I lived like a soul in torment. All my waiting, watching, and seeking were in vain. I trod every hand's-breadth of ground in the neighborhood of my house. . . . I came to know every stone and every pebble in the neighborhood but I found no trace of the cypress tree, of the little stream or of the two people which I had seen there.
>
> (12/17–18)

As it turns out, the outside landscape will not serve as an intermediary between him and the woman in the vision; she appears spontaneously, at his doorway waiting for him as he returns from a day of searching, and when she appears she goes directly to his room and lies down on his bed. But the initial portions of his search resemble the reactions of the nine-year-old Dante at his first sight of Beatrice in the streets of Florence: "He [Love] oftentimes commanded me to seek if I might see this youngest of the angels: wherefore I in my boyhood often went in search of her, and found her so noble and praiseworthy that certainly of her might it have been said those words of the poet Homer, 'She seemed not to be the daughter of a mortal but of God' " (Rossetti, 548).[17]

The search in *The Blind Owl* leads to a similar conclusion for opposite reasons—the lack of information to the contrary: "In the end I understood that all my efforts were useless, because it was not possible that she would be connected in any way with the things of this world: the water in which she washed her hair came from some unique, unknown spring; her dress was not woven of ordinary stuff and had not been fashioned by material of human hands. She was a creature apart [*yek vojud-e bar-gozide bud*]" (13–18). In both cases the act of deification concludes with an avowal of Platonic love, stated overtly in the *Vita nuova* during the conversation with the women in chapter 18 and for Hedayat in the denouement of the vision ("At no time did I desire to touch her"—11/14).

Before proceeding it may be well to remind ourselves of the differences, lest obsessed narration give way to obsessed criticism. The distinction between a sensibility that praises the love object by reference to a literary tradition—by aligning his discourse with a citation from Homer—and the self-enclosed, comic, ultimately parodic bathos that, in attempting to elevate the love object, comes up only with additional sensual details about her hair and dress is one way to clock the differences. The motion of the narrative repeats the difference on another scale. For Dante the projects of searching out and deifying Beatrice break down into a series of stages in the sublimation of his desire, unfolding metonymically, while the events of *The Blind Owl* repeat one another, folding inward in jumps we might call metaphorical. For Dante the narrative motion is one of expansion, to higher worlds that are also wider orbits, the final image of the *Vita nuova* being the sigh that passes beyond the farthest heavenly sphere. For Hedayat, who insists on the imagery of walls and enclosures as a symbol of the hu man condition, that trajectory is not an option. The increasing spiritualization of his narrator's love is an index of his madness, and the events that follow the air-hole vision reproduce it rather than pass beyond it: instead of expanding vistas, mirror images.

The tradition that love is a force independent of the will suggests a logic that subdivides the character of the lover. The fragmentation of speaking selves, made plausible for Dante by the compartmentalization of mental faculties in Thomistic moral philosophy (a habit of mind congenial to psychological allegory) and for Hedayat by a contemporary psychology that puts into question the unity of the self, is at the heart of what makes Dante sound modern to us. It has become a standard critical device in the reading of the *Vita nuova* to acknowledge multiple narrating Dantes: the Dante who wrote the original "libro de la mia memoria" from which the poems are drawn (evidently a term for a commonplace book or diary); the Dante who is transcribing it, or epitomizing it, in the book we read; the Dante who observes critically the younger self participating in the events of the narrative. Much of the criticism is predicated on the search for a specific point of view, like a vanishing point in perspective, which will act as an unchanging *point d'appui* for the deviating voices. In Mark Musa's formulation: "That the exposure of Dante the protagonist was a constant (if not the only) preoccupation of Dante, the author of the *Vita nuova*, I am convinced."[18] It does not seem to me that a consistent attitude flows uniformly from early narrators to the final redactor. Dante is obviously proud of some of the poems the early episodes of his obsession have produced; in any event his obsession has led him to where he is at the time of transcription, the threshhold of the *Divine Comedy*. The analogous problem in *The Blind Owl* is even more complex; it may be the single problem that contains all the others.

One result of the textual gap is registered on a syntactic level. In *The Blind Owl* the fragmented self is visible stylistically in the unusual frequency of such terms as *be-fekr-am resid ke* (it occurred to me, rather than *fekr kardam* or *gomân kardam*, I thought) and *be nazar-am âmad ke* (it came to my mind that), which suggest a conception of mental life in which the speaker witnesses his own mind as an object, a field of entities separate from his own identity. In the *Vita nuova* comparable turns of speech become particularly frequent after the crisis of chapter 10 in which Beatrice refuses her greeting: "mi giunse tanto dolore" (12.1), "mi giunse uno pensamento forte" (15.1), "mi mosse tanta volontade di dire" (19.1), "vennemi volontade di volere dire" (21.1). We have also discussions between components of the speaker's mind—not only the poetic conversations of chapters 37 and 38, of eyes and heart with *anima*, "soul," but on a literal level of conflicting thoughts described in chapter 13, referred to (perhaps comically) as "la battaglia de li diversi pensieri" (the battle of differing thoughts—14.1), and the three *spiriti* in Dante's body who comment in Latin at first sight of Beatrice in chapter 2.

III

Romance narrative concludes traditionally with a marriage. It celebrates a social institution, or a sacrament. Both the *Vita nuova* and *The Blind Owl* open with promising romance confrontations, and both deny the traditional resolution. In the *Vita nuova* we have the tradition that love is unconsummated, but the plot that bypasses the traditional union of romance is also present in the narrative of the divine plan as interpreted in medieval theology.[19] One way to ground the Danteian use of romance tradition in social realities would be, like those schools of myth that looked beyond each text to a ritual that generated it, to see them against the practices of courtship. We could, for instance, locate sources of Dante's variation of romance forms in marriage customs of thirteenth-century Florence. We would be carrying out something like the biographical criticism that lies beyond our analysis of Hedayat. In Dante's case, however, there is a component of the narrative that alludes to an outside world explicitly.

We infer from the *Vita nuova* a world in which the poet's

apprenticeship begins with service to an individual woman; praising her is the project that propels his craft. This is of course a deflection of courtship ritual properly speaking, since marriage with the love object is not part of the convention. It seems clear that becoming a poet in Dante's generation meant to some extent acting out the convention in real life—what we now recognize as a kind of Don Quixote gesture—choosing real women for courtly love objects and circulating poems that praise them. Dante may have lived this conventional scenario out more seriously, with less irony, than any of his contemporaries, exposing the latent dialectic tension more clearly than in any other poetic oeuvre. The tension is one of public and private. Poems, more than prose, are public acts: more easily memorized, easier to circulate, more portable. We know of course that Dante's poems were circulated publicly because we have answers to "A ciascun'alma presa e gentil core"; allusion to the audience is explicit in "Donne ch'avete intelletto d'Amore," where the speaker urges the poem not to waste time with *gente villana*, an eventuality against which there is in reality no insurance (as the existence of this chapter may prove).

After Beatrice's death Dante seems to have addressed a letter to men of rank (*li principe de la terra* [VN 30.1], which Musa translates "the princes of the land," clearly a public context) advising them of his grief. But the public act projects a private passion that potentially compromises its object. A successful poem widens the circumference of the poet's reputation; it is tested in society, made a valid esthetic act by its visibility. Dante seems proud of having kept Beatrice's identity a secret in his poems up to her death (though in the sonnet of chapter 24, "Io mi senti' svegliar dentro a lo core," for some reason he does refer to her by a transparent nickname), evidently because a respectable woman had cause to resent being the subject of a poem. Behind the protestations that the woman's identity is hidden, or that the poem is to be read only by the enlightened, is the reality of praise as scandalous, even as an act of defilement. The reason for Beatrice's refusal of her greeting in chapter 10 is not explicitly stated, simply that it has to do with the second screen woman (the one designated in chapter 9) and the calumny of observers, but it seems likely that what annoyed her was his poems. Love's advice in chapter 12 suggests this indirectly: " 'Our Beatrice hath heard from certain persons, that the lady whom I named to thee while thou journeydst full of sighs, is sorely disquieted by thy solicitations [*ricevea da te alcuna noia*]: and therefore this most gracious creature, who is the enemy of all disquiet [*tutte le noie*], being fearful of such disquiet, refused to salute thee' " (*VN* 12.6 Rossetti, 561). Rossetti's translation makes the term *alcuna noia* more concrete than the Italian, but only slightly, and the *ballata* that follows ("Ballata, i'voi che tu ritrovi Amore"), by personifying Love and the poem as characters in danger of separating, seems to support that interpretive translation.

The theme of the amoral nature of poetry is never explicit, but it seems to lie behind many of the scenes in which the poet questions his own motives. (We might see this as a counterbalance to what Mark Musa calls the theme of mockery in the *Vita nuova*.) It may be conventional for the poet in love to be unfit for society, but there is always another, crucial sense in which the poet is in control within the world of the poem.[20]

To return to Dante's most Hedayatian moment, the dream vision quoted above where Love feeds Beatrice the poet's heart: we left unmentioned a discordant detail, left untranslated by Rossetti, that Love forces her to eat it "cunningly" (Musa's word): "tanto si sforzava per suo ingegno, che le facea mangiare" (*VN* 3.6). With the words *per suo ingegno* a sliver of affect is dislodged in a scene that is otherwise distanced and dreamlike. Beyond the equivocal significance we glossed above, there is a moment of intersubjective contact above what we expect in a dream vision. The word *ingegno* for Dante frequently means "guile," which is sufficiently unsettling for a completely ethereal reading of the relationship between Beatrice and Love; but Dante also uses the word in its modern sense of artistic skill or genius twice in prominent passages of the *Inferno* (2.7, in the dedication to the Muse, and 10.59, in the confrontation with Cavalcante de' Cavalcanti, father of Guido). To what extent does *ingegno* suggest a dream of the young Dante forcing Beatrice to his will by means of his persuasive skill as a poet? Enough so that we can speak of an unaccented but unmistakable theme of poetry as not only an amoral force but as a kind of aggression. It will not be until chapters 5 and 6 that we will deal fully with the circulation of works of art in the world of *The Blind Owl*, or the equivalent alignment of art and aggression there, but it may be enough to say that love stories and guilt are embedded early in the patterns of romance tradition.

A faint implicit theme in the early episodes of the *Vita nuova*, a sense of aggression directed, perhaps unwittingly, against the living Beatrice, has a more tangible counterpart in the sequel. The image of Beatrice dead is more than a theme; it is the pivotal event of the work. Her death and the creation of the work are patently connected, though a logical link is not part of the story. Any number of contexts could be put between them, for one the guilt that the historical Dante seems to have felt after her death—whether we ascribe that guilt to the affair with the *donna gentile* of chapters 35 to 38, to heretical beliefs as suggested in the *Convivio*, or to a period of profligacy mentioned in Guido Cavalcanti's sonnet "Io vengo il giorno a te infinite volte." Dante might even have agreed that someone who has foreseen the death of the object of love in dreams and premonitions cannot avoid a feeling of guilt when the event comes about.

The juxtaposition of Hedayat and Dante is, in part, a device we use to force an overview, an occasion to sketch the plot of *The Blind Owl* and keep big issues momentarily at bay, but big issues can swim into place in the process, unsummoned. The fact that *The Blind Owl* concludes with the murder of the woman may make the centrality of Beatrice's death look different, and it may make peripheral elements of Dante's narrative more prominent. For instance, the scene in chapter 18 where Dante's speaker is teased by women (who ask the sensible question what is the point of his love if he cannot bear to be in her presence): it articulates the paradoxical nature of the poet's desire, but it also gives us a glimpse of women's society and women's use of language, which is not concerned with

Dante's obsessive quest. Their question, unemphasized in the text, sums it up. The poet's quest is not a practical one; his project (to praise Beatrice, to substitute writing for her absence) makes no sense in logical terms. On the other hand, there is no logical reason that the two perspectives cannot coexist (as in Dante's life, which includes a marriage and children as well as his Beatrician obsession), but the effect of the text is to suggest that the two are incompatible worlds, that Dante's task is to escape, transcend, negate theirs. Later what magnifies his love is the status of the love object, a dead woman. (The logic of the text seems to say that being dead is the next step after being beautiful.)

Philippe Sollers, in his essay on Dante, insists on a Beatrice whose biographical identity does not matter to the reader, but who is still not an allegory. Her significance seems to lie in relations of meaning between biography and allegory:

> for Dante her reality is that which distance and death render certain. To the extent that the object of his desire is not simply a mortal object but rather comes to life only within a continual death, a luminous point made all the more fiery by that darkness in which it can only assert itself, the identity of this object (irreducible to the status of the object, but a subject *other*, increasingly other) is posited as destroying the representation of social identities.[21]

Sollers's translation of thirteenth-century language into Lacanian terms is more than an exercise imposing anachronistic terminology on its subject: it maps out a big issue, the problematic corner of romance tradition where textuality interferes, where the poet's heroic suffering becomes paradoxical, where the same gesture that declares his love also celebrates his access to the (male) realm of language.

> This, it seems to us, is how the secret poetics (the *"trobar cluz,"* the *"senhàl"*) of the troubadors and the *"fedeli d'amore"* is to be understood; not as the illusory idealization of a real being, but as the concrete, erotic relation maintained between the indestructability of desire and death. In general, we can say that woman (whence we come) is the sole sign capable of eliciting a

limitless desire. She is the site of the law (of reproduction), and
at the same time she maintains the material (biological) power
to recognize its transgression. It would seem that a man's death
is open to recuperation, and so may afford an impression of fi-
nality and necessity, a group of clear, definite sentiments. A
woman's death, on the other hand, leaves us unsatisfied. It maintains a hidden, delusive side that summons [*qui appelle*].
Whence the necessity of pursuing this death, of playing out its
inexhaustible game, foreign to all reason, the source of an unknown writing and visibility.

                    (Sollers, 30/Barnard and Hayman trans., 26)

Dante's icon of the dead woman, in other words, suggests not
the baroque archetype of beauty undergoing corruption but
rather the persistence of affect in the absence of its object.
Death is a figure for the metonymic passage of signs from the
original (maternal) site of desire. (Sollers shows us a Dante
who is at the stage exemplified by the character of Manuchehr
in Hedayat's "Masks.")

The *Blind Owl* is also marked by the persistence of affect.
If there is a counterpart to Dante's sense of initiation into a
higher awareness, a vision from outside that expands his narrator's frame of reference, it is the discovery of the ancient jar
in the grave of the ethereal visitant. The narrator of *The Blind
Owl* no sooner buries her, that is, than he finds her image rendered into art. Dante's communication from outside leads him
upward; this message is from underground, presumably from
the past. The portrait on the jar is identical to the one he himself has just painted at her deathbed, and the opium dream he
undergoes while contemplating it is, we gather, simply a vision
of his own life. The effect is to close off the possibility of an
intersubjective world like Dante's, which, despite its self-ab-
sorption, includes readers and other writers.

The *Vita nuova* concludes by promising the audience a
larger vision and refusing to describe it further until the sequel. We are willing to believe that Dante's vision in fact occurred, but that hint of a larger vision is also an accepted and
catalogued rhetorical figure. The *Rhetorica ad Herrenium*
calls it *occultatio* (*IV.27*), a figure that alludes to its object by

refusing to describe it; medieval rhetoricians also refer to it as *occupatio* (Greek *paraleipsis*), useful as a topos of humility before scenes of grandeur. It is a stock device of praise (the "non si pò dicer nè tener a mente" [one can neither describe it nor hold it in thought] describing Beatrice's smile in the sonnet of chapter 21), but Dante also uses it as an instrument of deferment, as in chapter 8, where he declines to treat the subject of Beatrice's death because he is not yet capable of doing so properly. At times it is even used in the service of a whimsical boast on the potential power of his subject, as in the poem "Deh peregrini" (chapter 40), where he tells the pilgrims that he could make them cry if he wanted ("e le parole ch'om di lei pò dire / Hanno vertù di far piangere altrui"). *Occultatio* is also the device that most characterizes the closing pages of *Paradiso*, in the vision that follows Saint Bernard's prayer. It is also a characteristically modern device, notorious in Mallarmé, and this indirection is the source of what Philippe Sollers calls Dante's modernity.

The modernity of *The Blind Owl* is not founded on the allusion to an unsayable beyond. Instead it places its speaker in a world below ours, a world represented by the metaphor of the sky as a tent, the stars as holes in the canvas ceiling (90/ 83). Above it is our world, the world of shared vision. The narrative itself acts as a kind of nondirected therapy in which the speaker reveals to himself his own unacknowledged memories. It is as if the act of writing, the sequentiality of word after word, itself worked to conquer the narrator's habit of repeating the same episode endlessly varied. The focus falls not on the inexpressible but on the relationship between repetitions. *The Blind Owl* is also characterized by a classical rhetorical device, again a figure that calls attention to textuality: *correctio* (Greek *epanorthosis*), which the *Ad Herrenium* lists together with *occultatio*. In *correctio* the writer stops to examine what he has just said in order to revise it. Thus, "It is three months—no, it is two months and four days—since I lost her from sight" (4/12). And thus we pass from the episodes of fantasy to versions nearer the speaker's reality, a pattern that allows us to read part two as a revision of part one.

Chapter Three

CHAPTER ONE SAYS YOU LOVE HER

I

THERE is a transitional passage in the second part of *The Blind Owl* where the speaker, having described the story of the parents and the introductory narrative of his own marriage, sums things up with an uncharacteristically authoritative judgment of his own mode of seeing: "It seemed to me that until now I had not known myself and that the world as I had conceived it hitherto had lost all significance and validity and had been replaced by the darkness of night. For I had not been taught to gaze at and to love the night [*chun be-man nay-âmukhte budand ke be-shab negâh konam va shab-râ dust dâshte bâsham*]" (70/66). It is a unique moment when the narrator speaks of his own sensibility as an entity molded by an outside world, rather than the hard, already complete kernel of self we have seen reacting throughout the narrative. His regret that he has not been taught to appreciate the darkness may seem a perverse act of self-analysis, since darkness and night seem such ready images for his insanity, the world of pain in which he is trapped. As a commentary on the text of *The Blind Owl*, in which he is also trapped, it isolates the imagery of light and darkness that is the stuff of the book's central motif, the place where it is most evidently informed by Western tradition. There are two different systems of imagery that allow us to trace that motif as a literary inheritance: one is the poetry of Omar Khayyam, which supplies a repertoire of images, and the other is the imagery of psychoanalysis, which is traceable less through isolated references than through the book's unfolding narrative pattern.

With the imagery of light as with romance, the Western tradition that informs Hedayat is common to Europe and the Islamic world; the metaphor of consciousness represented as light is deeply embedded in the metaphysics of both. Dante's photology[1] is summed up in his final vision through the mystic rose at the top and center of Heaven, where his concluding gift is a glimpse of pure light. The point at which the language of the Koran most clearly overlaps with the rhetoric of poetry is in the passage in the Sura of Light where God is compared to a lamp in a niche (24.35, the "Mishkât al-anwâr"). When God shows himself in the Koran that act is represented with a verb (*tajalla*) that denotes light (Koran 7.143; see also 92.2, where the day *tajalla*). In its nominal form, *al-tajalli*, it becomes a Sufic term for unveiling, revelation. The Persian equivalent, *tajalli kardan*, is the verb Hedayat uses to describe the visitation of the ethereal woman ("it was not sunlight, but a passing gleam, a falling star, which flashed upon me"—4/11). The analogy that gives us terms such as "illumination" and "enlightenment" is equally central to the idiom Hedayat adopts throughout *The Blind Owl*. The parallels between the speaker's language and the terminology of Sufism may be construed ironically, but the photological imagery that underlines it is so pervasive and fundamental that it is not easily reversed or eroded.

   M. Y. Qotbi's 1973 study *In-ast Buf-e Kur* (This is "The blind owl") offers a series of allegorical readings for the stage properties of the narrative that fit into this complex of images.[2] The house, he suggests, is the speaker's *'aql* (intelligence); the lamp represents *manteq* (logic); the closet his subconscious (Qotbi, 33, 49). Qotbi carries the analogy farther than it will go for most readers, adding that the cypress tree under which the old man appears stands for freedom of thought (64), the bottle of wine represents confusion, and that this explains why the old man "refuses" it (49), whereas opium represents clarity of thought (132); but the hint that a psychomachic dimension is at work to guide our reading is a convincing one. It we take the room as an image of his mind, a device for representing schematically the notion of character developed narratively in the story (like the schematic representation of Spenser's Castle of Alma or Poe's poem "The

Haunted Castle"), the sputtering flame of his oil lamp (*pie-suz*, "oil burner"—by using this instead of the less specific word *cherâq*, "lamp," he emphasizes the transitory nature of its light) seems to represent a frail animating spirit. The narrator speaks of his life as a burning object—a green log (50/50) contrasted with a neatly burning lamp (84/78, 98/90)—and his world as the shadows that lamp throws on his wall. We might include burning opium in the same category, since as a fire with a delusive interior light it, too, throws shadows in the form of images that are confused with reality. The opium brazier itself becomes a kind of parodic duplication of the *pie-suz*, and the burnt-out coals in the epilogue are linked explicitly with the speaker's mind: "The charcoal in the brazier beside me had burnt to cold ashes which I could have blown away with a single breath. I felt that my mind had become hollow and ashy like the coals and was at the mercy of a single breath" (129/115).

We may regard the two fires, opium and oil lamp, as rival forms of illumination, so much so that either context can be seen as the frame for the other. We can see the relatively realistic world of part two as the scene from which the vision of part one deviates; we can also see part two as an opium dream, a narrative whose writing is contained by the events of part one, since the coals in the epilogue are evidently the same coals that lit the opium the narrator began to smoke at the end of part one, creating a pattern like the famous dream of the Chinese philosopher Chang-tsu, that he was a butterfly dreaming to be Chang-tsu.

As an adjunct to the outer fire of the *pie-suz*, by which he writes the story, and the inner fire of the opium is the proliferation of shadows and images on surfaces that pervade the book. His shadow on his wall, on the bathhouse wall, and his image on the mirror are obvious examples. But the picture on the pen case is also an image on the surface on a rectangular object. Pen cases are shaped like coffins, and the narrator speaks of his room as a coffin, so in a sense he is decorating his own life in miniature. (Since a pen case also holds pens, the fantasy vocation of painter is at only one remove from the narrator's role as a writer of his history.)[3] Perhaps the crowning example of mirroring in *The Blind Owl* is the quickening demonic refrain of the drunken policemen in the closing pages of the story. The policemen represent to the speaker the essence of what he calls the rabble, everything that he most detests in society, and yet the message of their song ("Come, let us go and drink wine") is identical to his, though his drunkenness is from opium instead of alcohol. It is as if, at the boundaries of his subjective vision, where we might expect an objective reality to start up, we see only his own obsessions reflected again.

Devices of mirroring and doubling are so common with Hedayat that they suggest a natural reflex rather than a philosophical program. Occasionally that device is so gratuitous that it seems a commentary on his own style. In the mad discourse of "Three Drops of Blood," for example, a text already much given to splitting and pairing, when the speaker's friend Siavosh describes his cat, the last detail is like a concretion of the story's narrative pattern, doubly apt for its mad narrator because it alludes obliquely to a Rorschach design: "There was a symmetrical [*morattab*] pattern on her back, as if someone had poured ink on a piece of blotter paper and folded it in two" (*SQKh* 21). In a painting dated 1930 Hedayat draws a table with symbols of dissipation scattered on it: a wineglass and bottle, a burning candle and cigarette, a pistol. Two hands reach at the table, one to pick up the wineglass and the other to pick up the pistol. The reflection of a (purposely?) distorted face is in the bowl of the glass, and the inscription is a line from Hafez: "Mâ dar piâle 'aks-e rokh-e yâr dide-im" (We have seen the beloved's face reflected in the cup).[4] Theme and execution are juvenile, but the conceptual balance is remarkable. The objects, from glass to bottle to cigarette to candle to gun, are like a free association of ideas leading clockwise from love to death. The symmetry of imagistic reference (liquid on the left, objects related to fire on the right, the similar shape of the wineglass and the candle holder) is like a paradigm of Hedayat's habits of thought. Perhaps one reason *The Blind Owl* carries a unique authority among his works is that, through

the device of the mad narrator, the metaphor of light and reflection allows his characteristic doubling freer reign; there is
a more frequent use of those devices, and more than in any
other Hedayatian text they are accounted for and made to fit.

II

Even some of the details of Hedayat's mirror imagery can be
found in Persian classical writing. The imagery of Persian
verse narrative contains a considerable tradition of tapestries,
carpets, portraits, and paintings, which reflect, summarize,
comment on, or enter into the action of the poem, culminating
in the extraordinary, hallucinatory scene in Jami's fifteenth-
century verse romance *Yusof and Zuleikha* (from the collection called the *Haft Awrang* or "Seven Thrones"), where Zuleikha, in her attempt to seduce the prophet Joseph, takes him
to a room decorated with painted and woven scenes showing
Yusof and Zuleikha making love wherever the eye can rest.[5]
Hedayat would not have been an admirer of Jami, but Hedayat's much discussed relationship with Omar Khayyam could
have taught him the same device.

The collaboration between Hedayat and Omar Khayyam
may be as profound as that between Omar Khayyam and Fitz-
Gerald. Both see in Khayyam the same skeptical, Lucretian
figure, and in fact it is difficult to see Hedayat's interest in
Omar Khayyam disconnected from the outsider's persona
through which Hedayat looked at traditional Iran in his fiction: Omar as the poet first discovered in the West, the poet
who unveiled an emptiness behind the pieties of mystical poetry, the only Persian poet Hedayat describes with unmixed
admiration. Reference to Khayyam in his writing is frequent,
if indirect. As Costello points out in a footnote to his translation of *The Blind Owl*, there is an oblique reference to a quatrain of Khayyam in one of the speaker's statements of doubt:
"I do not know where I am at this moment, whether the patch
of sky above my head and these few spans of ground on which
I am sitting belong to Nishapur or to Balkh or Benares" (48/
49). In Omar's quatrain (as it occurs in Hedayat's edition) the
cities named are Balkh and Baghdad:

Chun 'omr be-sar resad, che Baghdâd che Balkh,
Paymâne chu por shavad, che shirin-o che talkh,
Khosh bâsh ke ba'd az man-o to mâh basi
az talkh be ghorre âyad, az ghorre be salkh.[6]

Costello's translation, following Hedayat's paraphrase, substitutes Nishapur (the city associated with Khayyam) for
Baghdad:

> Since life passes, whether sweet or bitter,
> Since the soul must pass the lips, whether in Nishapur
>   or in Balkh,
> Drink wine, for after you and I are gone many a moon
> Will pass from old to new, from new to old.

Hedayat's juggling with place-names in this very oblique reference can be more easily comprehended if we view Fitz-
Gerald's translation as an intermediary:

> Whether at Naishapur or Babylon,
> Whether the Cup with sweet or bitter run,
> The Wine of Life keeps oozing drop by drop,
> The Leaves of Life are falling one by one.[7]

FitzGerald substitutes Nishapur for Balkh, Babylon for Baghdad. Hedayat characteristically omits the Arab capital and
adds an Indian one, Benares. It is also characteristic that the
remaining two cities, Nishapur and Balkh, refer as much to
FitzGerald's version as they do to Omar Khayyam.

Hedayat's language of light and dark is traceable in part to
his reading of the quatrains. Khayyam does not appeal to the
sun as an image of the good, but his Platonic imagery occasionally shows through the verse, notably in a quatrain that
compares the universe to a magic lantern:

> *In charkh-e falak ke mâ dar u hayrân-im*
> *fânus-e khayâl az u mesâli dânim;*
> *khorshid cherâgh dân-o 'âlam fânus:*
> *mâ chun sovar-im k'andar u gardân-im.*[8]

This is FitzGerald's "For in and out, above, about, below, /
'Tis nothing but a Magic Shadow-show" (1859 ed., stanza

46). A. J. Arberry provides a prose translation, which we paraphrase here:

> The vault of heaven at which we are bewildered
> we know to be a kind of shadow-lantern:
> consider the sun the lamp, the world a lantern,
> we are like the forms that revolve in it.[9]

The word *mesâl* in line 2 is so frequently used in Persian philosophical writing to refer to Plato's cave (*mesâl-e Eflâtûn*) that
it is very likely Khayyam consciously refers to that parable.
(His use of the term *fânus*, whose origin is the Greek *phanos*,
"lamp, torch, lantern," reinforces this likelihood.) Plato's parable as interpreted by Khayyam is ambiguous, as are most of
Khayyam's adaptations of traditional metaphysics: if we emphasize the existence of the sun, it can be taken as a mystical
parable of the two worlds. If we emphasize the shadows, the
point is simply the illusory nature of human life, regardless of
what lies behind it. In any case, the phenomenal world is at a
remove from the source of light, this being a relatively direct
statement of the idea embodied elsewhere in Khayyam's poetry in less strictly photological terms.

More visibly, Khayyamic influence is evident in the artifacts
and stage setting of *The Blind Owl*: the ruins, the wine, and
the clay jar, as well as the picturesque old man (the odds-and-
ends man) who used to be a potter (54/53). What Hedayat
admires most in Khayyam is not the homeliness of his imagery
but his cosmic outsider's perspective, which foreshortens and
elongates the complexities of individual experience. There are
moments in Hedayat's 1934 study of Khayyam when he seems
to commend the quatrains in modern terms for their compression of imagery, but what appeals to him in fact is, I think,
something more personal. We might call it Khayyam's allego-
rizing tendency, his device of taking what seem narrative situations (the lovers in garden settings, the drinkers, the polo
players) and exposing them to a universalizing or abstracting
context that makes them figures in an exemplum. The lovers
in the idylls, for instance, become allegorical figures in those
quatrains that speak of them as reincarnations, that reduce

them to repetition: other lovers have done this before, been in this place, said the same things, and this makes the flat scene suddenly throw its shadow onto another plane behind it. It is not so much that it is *carpe diem* poetry, but that the process of repetition gives the scene a kind of depth—not the depth of perspective, with its use of light to establish a stable point of reference, but a disorienting light that suddenly throws the scene open to its dizzying reflections, a *mise en abyme* that swallows up the individuality of the representation.

Hedayat seems to take very seriously the idea of an almost Nietzschean repetition suggested by such quatrains as the one FitzGerald translates "I sometimes think that never blows so red / The rose as where some buried Caesar bled" (stanza 18 in the 1859 edition). Human life continues into the next generation in the form of dust and flowers, which provide the stage setting for the next pair of lovers. (One thinks of the theme of the morning glories in *The Blind Owl*.)

A scene exposed to repetition becomes, then, a deceptive reflection of an *ur*-scene. Another more radical transformation common to Khayyam's poetry is the image in which human complexity is reduced to a simple clay receptacle, in the quatrains FitzGerald called the "Kuza-nama" (Book of Pots). FitzGerald's device of arranging the poems by theme instead of alphabetically by rhyme (the traditional order for all Islamic poetry) was a brilliant interpretive act. For the Persian reader it would make the collection a kind of encyclopedia of themes; for the reader unfamiliar with the themes as conventions it makes the potter quatrains seem a stage in an unfolding argument. With the concrete image of the pots a mock solution materializes; the intangible metaphysical question of being and nonbeing is made visible in the endless reshaping of the clay vessels, and that materialization of the question has the feel of a solution, though logically it succeeds only in restating the problem. The reader experiences the pot as a metaphor for human, but since it is the product of an artisan we also see it as a metaphor for the poem. An analogy with a missing fourth part looms somewhere outside the poem: jar is to human as quatrain is to some profound, almost graspable statement beyond mortal language.

The metaphor of light as an agent, a creating consciousness, and the metaphor of the jar as human are complementary, reciprocal analogies. One represents the body by the element of earth; the other represents the spirit with that of fire. (The metaphor of human as clay vessel even occurs in the Koran—55.14.) The jar as a miniature of creation has a mouth that may be analogized to the sky, the round space where light enters, making it in turn a topological variation of Plato's cave. The metaphors are complementary, but in some ways parallel too, since both suggest images of creation or representation, the edge or outline of a shadow image corresponding to the round, symmetrical image of the jar. The two are roughly equivalent models of the artistic process, or writing machines. The motive force of the shadow-image is the mystery of light; the force that creates the symmetry of the vase is the simple technology of the potter's wheel, which is its advantage for a materialist reader such as Hedayat.

Hedayat's fascination with the "Book of Pots" quatrains in his study of Khayyam is not so much with the metonymic association of pot and earth as with the metaphorical act that carries us from human to pot. In it he exploits the overlapping terminology for human and vase (most of which carries over into English) in a strangely enthusiastic passage: "Aren't all the parts of the little *kuze* parts of the human body: for example the mouth, the lip, the neck, the arm [*daste*, "handle"], the belly . . . and the wine inside the *kuze*, isn't that the spirit filled with [the body's] pleasure?" (*Tarâne-hâ-ye Khayyâm*, 46). That abrupt, almost violent foreshortening is very much at issue in *The Blind Owl*, where the metaphor of human and clay jar is never articulated but alluded to again and again.[10] The jar that recurs in the action of *The Blind Owl* is, in part one, not a *kuze* but a *gol-dân*, a vase for flowers, which thus combines two of the images of recurrence Hedayat spots as central in Khayyam—the flower nourished by graveyard soil and the potter's clay. (In part two the word translated "pot" is *kuze*.) And since Hedayat in a sense exchanges the ethereal woman's body for it, and since it bears the image of his portrait of her face, it represents her.

Earth is in the world of *The Blind Owl* the site of mysterious transformations that take place away from the light of the sun, the world of repetition and regeneration, a world at once fearsome and desirable, a feminine element. In this association the imagery of *The Blind Owl* is at one with the degrading phrases for intercourse that are attributed to the rabble, "shoving the donkey's hoof into the mud" (*dast-e khar tu lajan zadan*) and "giving the ground a thump" (*khâk tu sari kardan*—117/ 105).[11] Hedayat's study of Khayyam helps us spot the prehistory of the images in order to see the animistic myth that generates them. Meanwhile the imagery of creation through turning is never far absent, since the very fabric of *The Blind Owl* is its circling repetitions.

III

The imagery of light and darkness is perhaps most vividly present as a metaphorical system for modern readers in the popularized vision of psychoanalysis, where the subconscious is conceived as a dark subterranean force and the conscious is a daytime world associated with sun and air.

Psychoanalytic scrutiny has been applied to Hedayat occasionally in Iran already, usually as a mode of attack. As long as one ignores the possibility that he wrote purposely and with care, Hedayat's fiction seems particularly vulnerable to that approach. Two psychoanalytic studies that appeared at the height of Hedayat's popularity, Sorush Abadi's *Bar-rasi-ye Sâdeq-e Hedâyat az nazar-e ravânshenâsi* (An examination of Sadeq Hedayat from the point of view of psychology) and Hushang Paymani's *Râje' be Sâdeq-e Hedâyat sahih va dâneste qazâvat konim* (Let's judge Sadeq Hedayat accurately and learnedly are not particularly sympathetic.[12] Abadi cheerfully limits himself to three works in his search for the real Hedayat, but brings in every piece of outside evidence imaginable, including a discussion of the leptomorphic shape of the subject's head (an indication of potential schizophrenia, which is presently found in the works). Abadi's book is short and displays a certain enthusiasm, conceding eventually that madness and genius can be allied; Paymani's much longer treatise is more consistently on the attack, concluding with an impassioned warning of the effect Hedayat's works could have on young people. Neither has a strong sense of literary context (both write as if the stories were diary entries), and the French medical terms that accumulate in the footnotes seem more like spells to conjure with than instruments of thought.

In their wake appeared a more readable, sympathetic study (unfortunately less psychoanalytic) by Dr. Mohammad Ibrahim Shari'atmadari, *Sâdeq-e Hedâyat va ravânkâvi-ye âsârash* (Sadeq Hedayat and the psychoanalysis of his works),[13] which defends Hedayat by interpreting the mental disorders of his characters as fictional creations, reporting at length the ways in which his sketches of disturbed states of mind can be put to use by teachers of psychology. Shari'atmadari takes a direction that is logical for an apologist, but the result is to lessen the possibility that Hedayat wrote, especially in the short stories, as a social critic. He implies that Hedayat's stories are in essence imaginary clinical records and that his outcast protagonists are there simply for us to pity or to cure. Commenting on the passage in *The Blind Owl* where the speaker lists his childhood fears (101–2/92–93), Shari'atmadari seems to discover before our eyes the split between biographical and fictional subjects:

> His fears: from his fear of the rabble and his fear of the policemen, his fear of the old man in the shawl and the ground cloth full of odds and ends, to the fear that "the buttons of his trousers would turn into millstones" and that "the worms in the gutter of the courtyard pool would turn into Indian snakes"—he recounts all of them with irony and sarcasm, though the narrative tone is ingenuous and sincere [*va qiâfe-ye haqq be jâneb sokhan mirânad*]. (119)

Shari'atmadari's interpretation manages to portray a socially acceptable Hedayat, but it fails to account for the paradoxical sympathy the narrator of *The Blind Owl* elicits from us. He is, however, correct to ground his presentation in Hedayat's familiarity with Freud.

Qotbi's *In-ast Buf-e kur* (This is "The blind owl") also takes *The Blind Owl* to be a purposeful embodiment of psychoanalytic principles. His primarily allegorical reading is not incompatible with Freudian interpretation, though it is not itself psychoanalytical. He is explicit, however, about the importance of Freud for a comprehensive reading of the text. "It has been established," he says in his introduction, "that Hedayat's inspiration in writing *The Blind Owl* was first his deep studies in the ancient literature of Iran and India and then the two famous books of Freud entitled *Ta'bir-e khâb* [*The Interpretation of Dreams*] and *Ayande-ye yek pandâr* [*The Future of an Illusion*] and it is expected that readers will study, or have studied, these two books before going on to my commentary" (Qotbi, 3). Qotbi gives no reference to show how he knows this, but his suggestion is made likely by circumstantial evidence elsewhere in Hedayat's writing. One of the narratives in *Vagh vagh Sâhâb* (1933) is called "Qazie-ye Froidism" (The case of "Freudism," 61–66): it differs from the other selections in its serious tone, almost as if it were a simplified verse summary of the theory of repression rather than a satire of it, perhaps even an attempt to make it respectable on a popular level. (Recommendations to read Freud are a leitmotif of Mostafa Farzaneh's memoires of Hedayat; see particularly *ASH* 169, where Hedayat suggests that he likes Freud's interpretations individually but suspects the system.)

André Breton, when he reviewed Lescot's translation of *The Blind Owl*, saw it filling a particular place on the shelf: "A masterpiece if there ever was one! A book that should find its place next to Nerval's *Aurélia*, Jensen's *Gradiva*, Hamsun's *Mysteries*, a book that takes part in the phosphorescences of Berkeley Square and the shudders of 'Nosferatu.' "[14] Knut Hamsun's *Mysteries*, whose hero carries a vial of poison with him in case he should decide to end his life on short notice, has its distant relevance to *The Blind Owl*; and *Aurélia*, with its uncanny rhythmic resemblance,[15] would have been a good

subject for Sorush Abadi and Hushang Paymani (a much better subject than *The Blind Owl*).

Jensen's *Gradiva*, however, the subject of Freud's most extensive literary discussion, is the most astute suggestion. *Gradiva* does not resemble *The Blind Owl* much in style or mood,
and without Freud's attention there would have been little reason to read it today, but it represents a particular pattern of
romance narrative that Hedayat adapted and improvised on.
Moreover, the way to *Gradiva* is through Freud, since the logical means by which a French speaker would become familiar
with it is Freud's analysis of it in *Delusion and Dream*
(1906).[16] The plot: Norbert Hanold, a German archeologist,
a bachelor with no interest in the opposite sex, develops an
obsession with a bas-relief in a Roman museum. The sculpture
depicts a woman walking with an unusual gait. He dubs the
figure "Gradiva" (an epithet of Mars, which the English translation renders as "beautiful in walking"). His fascination with
the sculpture leads him to Pompeii, where he is confronted
with a living counterpart of the bas-relief, a mysterious
woman he believes to have been resurrected from the days before the eruption of Mount Vesuvius. The woman turns out to
be someone he has known all his life—his childhood sweetheart, Zoe Bertgang—but his obsession prevents him from
recognizing her. She gradually brings Hanold around to realize her actual identity, and to acknowledge that his obsession
was a substitute for erotic desire, a disguised searching for her,
with the predictable result that the childhood lovers become
lovers again.

In *The Blind Owl* we also have an obsession with a work of
art (the drawing on the pen case and later the portrait on the
vase), a materialization of the image into a human being, the
ethereal woman of part one. There are similarities of superficial detail as well. Norbert Hanold's walks around Pompeii,
like the narrator's walk outside of town in part two of *The
Blind Owl*, take place in a landscape of midday sun. The sun
in *The Blind Owl*, "like a golden knife, was steadily paring
away the edge of the shade beside the walls" (73/69); the sun
is visualized with a similar comparison in *Gradiva*: "As with

a golden eraser, [the sun] . . . effaced from the edges of the houses on the *semitae* and *crepidine viarum*, as the sidewalks were once called, every slight shadow" (*Delusion and Dream*, 176). The flower that the recurring figure of the woman carries in *The Blind Owl* has a counterpart in the leitmotif of the asphodel in *Gradiva*, which Zoe Bertgang is seen carrying. Hanold imagines his "Gradiva" to be a Greek among Romans; the woman in *The Blind Owl* is (if her eyes are an accurate indicator) a Turkmen among Iranians. Both stories take place on the site of a buried city, Pompeii and the ancient city of Rey, settings that Freud argues are appropriate for narratives of repressed desire (*Delusion and Dream*, 61, 73).

There are differences: Jensen's *Gradiva* is a narrative whose point is its charm, a popular, ephemeral romance. If it represents for Freud a study of delusion paralleling the insights of psychoanalysis before the letter, this is because for Freud a successful analysis resembles the pattern of romance.[17] *The Blind Owl* is, on the other hand, very much after the letter, and armed with a reading of Freud, Hedayat has the option of dealing with the obsession itself rather than its cure. And here is our most obvious difference: that the speaker of *The Blind Owl*, unlike Norbert Hanold, is never cured. As a result we are never explicitly told the identity of the mysterious woman who appears in part one of *The Blind Owl*, although we are able to tell from the repeated descriptions that she must be a fantasied distortion of the wife in part two (also, as in *Gradiva*, a kind of childhood sweetheart). By making the entire story the monologue of the obsessed, Hedayat denies us the opportunity of seeing him from outside. Instead, he has the speaker circle around a single repressed, guilty memory, gradually dredging up the fact that he is unwilling to admit, except momentarily, the fact (which he refers to twice as "that which should not have happened" [*ânche ke na-bâyad beshavad*]— 16/20, 46/47) that he has killed his wife. He describes it twice, once in the episode of part one where the ethereal woman drinks the poisoned wine and later at the conclusion of part two, where he describes the murder but portrays it as an accident. The absence of reconciliation makes *The Blind Owl* a different kind of romance, but a pattern like Jensen's is still recognizable, even though Hedayat's perspective urges us to focus on the split between realities.

The division of *The Blind Owl* into two narrative sections shows in formal terms the characteristic Hedayatian paradigm of doubling we have noticed on the level of content. An understanding of Hedayat's reliance on Freud begins with the diastema between the two: the speaker represents himself in radically different circumstances from the one to the other, beginning with the descriptions of his house. In part one he emphasizes its affinity with his own being and its separation from society: "I am fortunate in that the house where I live is situated beyond the edge of the city in a quiet district far from the noise and bustle of life. It is completely isolated and around it lie ruins. Only on the far side of the gully one can see a number of squat mud-brick houses which mark the extreme limit of the city" (5/12). The introduction to his new life after the opium dream, in the beginning of part two, also begins with the description of a house, but the location has altered: "The room itself has two windows facing out onto the world of the rabble. One of them looks onto our own courtyard, the other onto the street, forming thereby a link between me and the city of Rey" (51/51). At the end of the same paragraph we learn that he lives across the street from a butcher shop on a busy city street. The confining rooms in the first and second parts, then, are not the same. (Al-e Ahmad notes this briefly in his essay on Hedayat—*AA* 83; *FYA* 32.)

The speaker in the first part also imagines himself to be a painter of pen cases, but after the break in the narrative there is no mention of his being an artist, and in fact when he sees a pen case like that described in part one here is how it looks to him: "My life appeared to me just as strange, as unnatural, as inexplicable, as the picture on the pen-case that I am using this moment as I write. I feel that the design on the lid of this pen-case must have been drawn by an artist in the grip of some mad obsession" (104/95). If we are skeptical that the split extends to the narrator's very identity, there are a number of mutually exclusive memories between part one and part two that serve as further evidence. The uncle who appears on the thirteenth of Now Ruz at the opening of the story is at that point a mystery: "I seem to remember that he was a sea-captain" (7/13). He is given a detailed life history in the Bugam Dasi story, with which part two begins. Names of people and specific terms that have been repressed in the first section materialize in the second, such as the word *rajjâle* (rabble), which during the introduction to part two he abruptly announces is the word he has been looking for (49/50). The nickname *lakkâte* (bitch), which he uses for his wife, does not appear until just before the story of his Indian mother Bugam Dasi in part two.

The terms *lakkâte* and *rajjâle*, representing the wife and her lovers respectively, stand out from the text, and the reader tends to consider them together in an imagistic unit that underlines the triangular situation of the narrator's household. (His gratuitous use of the unusual word *taslis*, "trinity," in a different context, at the conclusion of the passage explaining why he calls her *lakkâte* [72/68], is perhaps meant to tip us off to the schematic nature of the dramatis personae.)[18] Indeed, besides the butcher and the nurse who brings him food in his room in part two, there scarcely seem to be more than three characters in the story. A figure Hedayat used in passing in his other extended narrative, *Hâjji Aqâ*, could be used to portray this technique: "Because Haji's porch had only four seats, his guests never exceeded three in number. That is to say, as soon as it became crowded, those present began to slip away, yielding their places to the new arrivals. It was as though someone was proposing to stage the drama of Haji's life, but for reasons of economy had confined the mise-en-scene to the porch" (Wickens translation, 33).[19]

Adaline Glasheen, describing the complex shifting characters in Joyce's *Finnegans Wake*, refers to a quotation from George Bernard Shaw about a Dublin stock company that brings the same analogy closer to our situation: "a readymade cast that had to fit all plays, from *Hamlet* down to the latest burlesque; and as it never fitted any of them completely, and seldom fitted at all, the casts were more or less grotesque misfits . . . each claimed . . . the part which came nearest to his or her specialty; and each played all his parts in exactly the same way."[20] Hedayat's family drama is, to be sure, simpler and more somber than Joyce's, and the parts assigned to the three players are much more limited, but the principle is the same. The ingenue of the troupe is clearly both the ethereal visitor and the girl in the picture. We know that from repeated descriptions. When the narrator describes his mother Bugam Dasi in part two, we may think we have a new actress: "a girl called Bugam Dasi, a dancer in a lingam temple. Besides performing the ritual dances before the great lingam idol she served as a temple attendant. She was a hot-blooded olive-skinned girl, with lemon-shaped breasts." But as we reach the end of the description we begin to see a familiar face behind the makeup, the face of the mysterious woman in the opening fantasy: "great slanting eyes and slender eyebrows which met in the middle" (55/54). Perhaps the wife's brother is a part for the same actress in drag, since she and he (like the father and the uncle—55/54) are as alike "as two halves of one apple" (77–78/73) and since his lips have the same bitter taste as the ethereal visitor's and the wife's. In any case, if part two is the reality from which part one diverges, the prototype for the ingenue figures can only be, as we have suggested, the speaker's wife.

The actress whom the speaker forces into the female roles is his wife, but there is evidence that the wife we meet in part two, whose courtship is described after the Bugam Dasi story, the wife who deserves the title *lakkâte*, is simply another role and not the actress herself. Most of her appearances are filtered through the speaker's selective memory, but on three occasions she does enter the room in which he writes, and in none of them does she confirm his characterization of her. The first, which is also the first actual event (after the long introduction) of part two, is the nocturnal visit described by the nurse: " 'My daughter'—she meant the bitch, my wife—'came to your bedside and took your head in her lap and rocked you like a baby' " (68/65). It is, significantly, at this point that we learn she is pregnant. In her second visit he merely glimpses her at the door of the room after he has upset his soup bowl and shrieked (85/78). In her third visit there is a sign of hostility toward the narrator, but it is only the tone of her voice: "She asked me in a sarcastic tone [*be ta'ne*], 'How are you feeling?' I replied, 'Aren't you perfectly free? Don't you do everything you feel like doing? What does my health matter to you?' She left the room, slamming the door behind her. She did not turn to look at me. It seems as though I have forgotten how to talk to the people of the world, to living people" (112/101). A lot rests on the words *be ta'ne*. The speaker's sudden change of tone after her departure and her return on the next page (as well as the detail that she is dressed in her best clothes [*haft qalam-e ârâyesh*]) indicate that he may have willfully misheard her. If we count the two visits he makes to her bedroom, there are five confrontations in all, one for each of the five days described in part two.[21] Although her reaction on the two occasions when he comes to her room indicates that she is waiting for someone to come sleep with her, there is evidence, to be dealt with presently, that she is waiting for him. In any event, the fact of her infidelity is put into question the harder we look at it, and the speaker's contradictions extend to fundamentals. At one point he refers to "all the things people said about her" (118/106); at another he speaks of her affairs as hidden: "No one knew the secret which existed between us. Even my nurse . . . used to reproach me—on account of the bitch" (65/62).

The nature of her sin depends, of course, on the identity of the old man who turns up as her ultimate lover. In the Gothic setting of part one he plays the visiting uncle and a humorous gravedigger; when in part two the mode switches to realism, he plays the odds-and-ends man. In India we see him momentarily young, but after his experience in the cobra pit he is the same old man again, complete with his fearful laugh, in the guise in which we first met him on the pen case: "a bent old man like an Indian fakir" (6/12). That he also plays the role of the wife's father we know from his fearful laugh in the "courting" scene by the bier of the *lakkâte*'s mother. If, to take the stage metaphor a step further, the old men break down into a single actor, that actor can only be the speaker himself. He says as much at the opening of part two, though he draws our attention away from it immediately afterward: "Whoever saw me yesterday saw a wasted, sickly young man. Today he would see a bent old man with white hair, burnt-out eyes and a hare-lip.[22] I am afraid to look out of the window of my room or to look at myself in the mirror for everywhere I see my own shadow multiplied indefinitely" (47–48/48). He draws our attention away from this in order to intensify the reader's shock at the climax of the story when, after twice producing the old man's laugh, the narrator looks into the mirror and sees his other self there ("I had become the old odds-and-ends man"—128/114).

These two direct statements are ballasted by numerous hints. In the vision through the ventilation hole in part one, the girl is clearly described as facing the old man; in the paragraph directly following, the narrator has put himself in the same position ("The girl was directly opposite me but she appeared quite unaware of her surroundings"—8–9/14). As his uncle the old man resembles him "in a remote, comical way like a reflection in a distorting mirror" (8/13). The odds-and-ends man squatting before the canvas sheet (*basât*) on which his articles are spread out for sale[23] is seen as "a sample and personification of the whole creation" (109/99); the speaker in front of his oil lamp (also on a *basât*) is "a miniature god" (123/110). The hearse driver's insistence that he knows where the speaker lives (32/34, 36/37) takes on in this light the humor of understatement.

The classic study of this motif is Otto Rank's *Double* (1914), which traces instances of doubling in fiction, folklore, and popular culture. (Popular culture is in fact his starting point, in a discussion of Paul Wegener's film *The Student of Prague*.) In his schema the double works as a personification of the reflected character's repressed desires:

> The most prominent symptom of the forms which the double takes is a powerful consciousness of guilt which forces the hero no longer to accept the responsibility for certain actions of his

ego, but to place it upon another ego, a double who is . . . [a] detached personification of instincts and desires which were once felt to be unacceptable, but which can be satisfied without responsibility in this indirect way.[24]

The figure of the old man functions to reproach (and thus remind) the speaker of his own sexuality, as well as to embody it. Frequently his role is to intrude between the narrator and the woman, literally as in the tableau and figuratively in such scenes as when he interrupts the embrace near the mother's coffin (60–61/86–87); he appears as if spontaneously called forth whenever a potentially erotic scene begins. In his role as the odds-and-ends man he does this in the most explicit way: "And, now I came to think of it, why was it that this man had been hanging about outside our house ever since I had got married?" (107–8/98).

The nature of the link between the figure of the old man and the narrator's sexual self is represented in terms that not only fit Rank's schema but act as a commentary on the speaker's own story. The story of the parents is, in other words, simply a variation of the speaker's. There, too, we find doubling of characters, in the two merchant brothers who are as alike "as two halves of one apple" (55/54). Again one of the two is transformed into the guise of a fearsome old man (we should add that the speaker has been the fearsome old man throughout the narrative), and the agent of that transformation is his exposure to the snake in the trial-by-cobra scene. If we speak of the cobra as a sexual image, we do not need recourse to the obvious explanation of its phallic shape. The trial by cobra is after all punishment for a sexual transgression, the seduction of Bugam Dasi, and it takes place at a lingam temple. The cobra kills one of the twins; it leaves the other insane and prematurely aged. Applying this parallel to the narrator's two selves elsewhere in the book, we can say in psychoanalytic terms that under the pressure of his own venomous sexual anxieties he represents himself as a split being, a self that feels he is a living corpse (*morde-ye motaharrek*—65/62 and passim) and another self who is the old man that haunts him.

Rank's earlier study, *The Myth of the Birth of the Hero* (1909), is similarly applicable to the Bugam Dasi story. The motif (of folklore, mythic history, romance) of the hero with two sets of parents—real parents who are respected and admired, plus false parents who are humble, perhaps threatening and sinister—is traced to the conflicting affect of Oedipal desire, ultimately to the child's discovery of the sexuality of the parents.[22] We do not have two full sets of parents in the Bugam Dasi story, but the device of giving the father a twin brother in effect creates two father figures, and the element that creates the difference between them is the cobra. Hedayat has so cunningly remodeled the folktale device that it applies to both self and father, so that the evil father and the double become the same figure. The speaker's guilt, in other words, stems from his imagined identity with his father, and this in turn is his sexuality, the bond that ties him to the world of generation. What he has undergone is not a trial by cobra, but the anxiety of his own marriage.

Hedayat may have used both of Rank's studies in the preparation of *The Blind Owl*. He almost certainly used *The Double* for it.[26] Mostafa Farzaneh, in his essay about Hedayat's last days in Paris in 1951, recalls going to a number of films at a film club. Hedayat, he says, introduced him to the classic films of German expressionism, including Paul Wegener's *Student of Prague*, "a description and analysis of which he had read in a book by some German psychoanalyst" (Jamshidi, *Khodkoshi-ye Sâdeq-e Hedâyat*, 56–57). This would be Rank's *Double*, which begins with a discussion of that film. In fact, Farzaneh in his later memoire has Hedayat citing *The Double* by name in response to a question about twinning in *The Blind Owl* (*ASH* 350). There is also a specific substantive relation between *The Double* and the text of *The Blind Owl*, since both allude to the superstition of the headless shadow ("if anyone cast a headless shadow . . . that person would die before the year was out"—79/74), Rank in a chapter on the double motif in anthropology (*The Double*, 49–50) and Hedayat in the scene where the narrator returns from his walk outside of town. What Rank very likely provided Hedayat was first an explanation for the motif of doubling in his own fiction, and this in turn would have allowed him to expand his use of it, to treat it as a device rather than a tic, consciously entering a literary tradition.

The Blind Owl can also be read as a gradual coming to consciousness, the growing materialization of the repressed memory of the murder. Even within the fantasy of part one the memory does not seem to be uniformly distant. The opening situation in part one represents a kind of stasis, in which the painting of the obsessive scene is (as in a dream image) both outlet and disguise for the repressed material. The events that begin with the uncle's visit set off a process of escalation after which the picture is no longer a sufficient outlet. We may take the vision through the ventilation hole as a more persistent version of the obsessive scene in the painting, though the world of that vision does not close in on him until the evening of the ethereal woman's visit. As more and more of the speaker's actual world is admitted to his consciousness, the hallucination of the old man (as something other than himself) looms tangibly on the scene. He is paradoxically the speaker's last refuge from what he has done, and as an odds-and-ends man he plays a role analogous to that of dream images in psychoanalysis: he offers an array of objects no one wants to buy, but which have a curious significance waiting to be fathomed. ("Those dead objects left a far deeper imprint upon my mind than living people could ever have done"—109/98.) Since among his wares is an old jar, apparently the one that was discovered when the grave was dug for the ethereal woman at the climax of part one, we may conclude that he is, like our dream life, offering for sale the key to unifying the two worlds. (Or, since we see the odds-and-ends man and his wares as a hallucination against the realistic backdrop of part two, we may speak of the jar as a nodal point within the hallucination, as it was a nodal point in the dream that we read in part one, but that the speaker does not recall.) If we consider the erotic associations that accompany the image of the jar, it is significant that the speaker's attempt to buy it took place on his own wedding day (108/98).

The process of growing self-awareness has its limits. The situation of the domestic triangle and the speaker's consequent rage at his wife are two delusions he cannot break through. Once he has translated his disgust toward his own sexuality into personal rage at his wife, the dilemma remains which side of the imagined triangle to remove. He could kill the wife's lover, but the wife's lover is secretly himself. The other answer, killing the wife, achieves only the retranslation of the problem into its original terms, because once she is gone his jealous rage is left without an object and turns back into guilt. Nor is it the kind of cathartic guilt we associate with Sophocles' Oedipus and his physical blindness. What it achieves for the reader is an understanding of the forces that led to the crime; for the speaker it achieves only the completion of the book. The epilogue leaves no doubt that he has relapsed into fantasy, for after having "become" the odds-and-ends man he wakes up "as if from a long deep sleep" (129/115), and the narration connects without a break to where the fantasy of part one left off. The fog on the window-pane suggests that the outside world is again blocked out, and again he is separated from the double, while the double disappears with the Rhages vase.

The narrator's relapse throws the responsibility for understanding his blindness on the reader. We have found the speaker to be at the center of a complex network of illusions, the specular world of the Lacanian imaginary, a prison of mirrors—mirrors because the illusions all reflect his own image, a prison because by the end of the book we are sure that the speaker cannot see beyond the reflections. Yet if we sense an inexplicable current of affirmation running through *The Blind Owl*, which cannot be accounted for by the events of the story, it is because the walls of the prison are transparent from outside; a complicity of knowledge has bypassed the narrator and reached us.

Perhaps a final example is in the title. The word *buf* does not appear in the text of the story, but its synonym *joghd* does in connection with the shadow: "My shadow on the wall had become exactly like an owl [*joghd*] and, leaning forward, read intently every word I wrote. Without doubt he understood perfectly. Only he was capable of understanding" (123–24/110–11). One of the most abused terms in Hedayat criticism is the often-quoted phrase that he is writing for his shadow, which is usually taken to imply that he is writing not for an audience but only for himself, or that he is accountable to no one but himself for his style. The owl of the title is commonly held to represent the speaker, but here it is clearly something other than the speaker himself, the dark shape that the fragile lamp of his reason throws against the surface of reality. But the shadow is not alone; we are reading the story too, and when we remember this the passage quoted becomes one of those disturbing moments in literature when the fictional creation seems almost to look out and see the reader's eye peering in at him. It reminds us that from outside the shadow is transparent and that the prison of mirrors is only a prison in its fictional interior.

IV

Exactly what happens in the epilogue of the story is a matter of some importance. As I see it, the growing somberness of the preceding episodes is summed up more powerfully by the seemingly trivial incident of the Rhages vase being stolen than it might have been by a more emotional summation. There is a reading, however, that I suspect is widely held, expressed in Leonardo Alishan's "The *Ménage à Trois* of The Blind Owl" (*FYA* 168–84), responding in part to the previous section of this book in an earlier form,[27] which argues for a kind of moral growth in the narrator, that dredging up the memory of the murder is not a momentary act of vision but an insight through which he cures himself of his insanity. It follows that the epilogue must be made to echo that note of affirmation.

From my point of view the speaker's relapse is indicated by a number of details beyond the mist and the coals ("I felt that my mind had become hollow and ashy like the coals"—129/115), which, as we suggested earlier, remind us of the opium preparation that concluded part one. "The first thing I looked for was the flower-vase of Rhages which the old hearse-driver had given me in the cemetery" (129/115): though there was a vase in part two (*kuze*), it was not recognized as the "flower vase of Rhages" (*gol-dân-e Rhâghe*) of part one. The hearse driver, we recall, was not a character in part two; the speaker of part two would remember him no more than he would "remember" being a painter. The vase, meanwhile, has accreted so many layers of significance over the course of the narrative that it would seem to cheapen it to affix a unique meaning to it and to its loss, but when we spoke of it as the key to the unification of the narrator's two worlds we might have added that it stands for a wholeness his life never quite achieves. The vision of the old man (which manifestation is not specified) running away with it adds a peculiarly characteristic Hedayatian concretion of that sense of loss. What the old man runs away with, wrapped in a grimy rag (the rag, *dastmâl*, is also from part one—36/37), is the wholeness readers may want to see reaffirmed. We as readers recognize part two as a world nearer our reality, but for the speaker the atmosphere of enclosure is like that of interlocking realities in an Escher fantasy or the dream of Chang-tsu.

Alishan argues that the epilogue takes place in a scene that combines the worlds of part one and two, arguing by implication that such a world would be more real than either alone. His evidence is the detail that when the old man escapes it is into the alley (*kuche*), which is part of the scene of part two, not the wasteland outside of town, which is the scene of part one. He might have added that the narrator's observation that he is covered with blood also puts him in a level of awareness we never saw in part one or its epilogue, and that the closing sentence of the narrative ("And on my chest I felt the weight of a woman's dead body") could be interpreted as an admission of guilt.

> The spatial and temporal contrast between the hearsedriver and the street (the former belonging to the first section and the latter to the second) proves that the narrator's two worlds have indeed merged and that the "dead weight" which he now feels upon his

chest is the recognized sense of guilt which he must face for the
rest of his short, natural life. (I say short because, in acknowledging the truth, he must answer to the law, which will probably
arrest and punish him for the murder of his wife, and also face
his consumptive condition.)   (*FYA* 183)

Alishan's point is well taken that the epilogue is a composite
scene, but I read the composite nature of the scene as the sign
of a lapse from reality. (We may picture the same narrator
relapsed into delusion but without the comforting fantasy of
the romantic environment of ruins.) We can imagine admis-
sions of guilt which are more direct. The weight of the corpse
that he imagines on his shoulders in the closing passage is unspecified, without identity, suggesting that he feels the guilt (as
the jar rested on his chest while he was riding in the hearse in
part one, "with the weight of a dead body"—37/38) without
knowing its origin, and suggesting that he is puzzled at the
sight of the blood and the insects. We do not need the specific
recollection of the murder to explain the feeling of weight on
his chest, since at the beginning of the opium dream that closes
part one he says, "I felt as though a heavy weight had been
removed from my chest, as though the law of gravity had
ceased to exist for me" (41/41–42), the conclusion of the
dream meaning the restoration of the weight.

    In any event, the climactic revelation of part two has been
the realization that the speaker is the old man. For the old man
to appear in the epilogue itself suggests a relapse: the flight of
the double is the self's loss. It is at any rate difficult to imagine
why, if the point is to emphasize the narrator's self-knowl-
edge, there should be an epilogue at all.[28]

    An argument like this forces us into the critical questions:
what does make a narrative seem real to us? What are the elements that elicit our trust in the fiction? A first-person narrator is always a potential complication; an insane narrator
carries the complication toward a kind of limit, *écriture*. Two
simultaneous blurrings accompany this phenomenon in *The
Blind Owl*. One is a fuzziness of setting. Even when the narrative is visually clear, it is not rooted in an identifiable society

or period of history, and when a reviewer says of it that "an educated Persian lives by decorating pencases in a frightful hovel on the outskirts of his native city" (*Times Literary Supplement*, 7 March 1958, 125), that bare summary falsifies the story by implying the existence of more social background than there is in fact. When Iraj Bashiri says that *The Blind Owl* is set in pre-Mongol times (on the evidence of the passage where the narrator speaks of his window as a link between himself and the city of Rey, "the city which they call the 'Bride of the World', with its thousand-fold web of winding streets"—51/51) and finds the existence of the suitcase in part one to be an amusing anachronism,[29] he infers a historical perspective the story fails to fulfill. Hedayat's friend Mojteba Minovi made the same suggestion, instancing opium, tobacco, and eyeglasses as anachronisms, and Hedayat corrected him in a letter.[30] We are also likely to feel that when the Soviet critic D. S. Komissarov thinks to praise *The Blind Owl* for its realistic portraits of Iranian merchants (quoting from the descriptions of the butcher and odds-and-ends man—Komissarov, 43–44),[31] he is reading with a certain insensitivity. I find Elton Daniel's summary of the problem in his essay "History as a Theme in *The Blind Owl*" a sensible one:

> it may be argued that the time frame of the novel is the late nineteenth or early twentieth century—that is, contemporary with Hedayat—and that the deliberate evocations of the medieval period are designed to tell the reader about the narrator's psychological aberrations, about his belligerent insistence that time has no meaning . . . rather than to serve as proof that the novel is set in pre-Mongol times. They are expressions of the narrator's overwhelming desire to believe that his situation is of universal as well as personal significance.   (*FYA* 81–82)

As setting blurs we may expect some compensatory element to become more concrete. It is not character. The speaker of *The Blind Owl* becomes, in the absence of a network of recognizable communal relations, not so much a personage with a particular identifiable psychological impairment as the embodiment of a psychological condition, a machine for inscribing processes we recognize as characteristic of derangement: repetition, reversal, displacement. (We recognize them from our own fantasy life if we do not know them clinically.) *The Blind Owl* is an extreme case of what Ortega y Gasset, in his essay "Notes on the Novel," calls "imaginary" rather than "real" psychology,[32] and whatever specificity it possesses is a specificity like that of allegory.

The process of reading seeks compensatory certainties in the consistency of his obsessions, ranking his perceptions as we find them, along an axis between shared and private worlds. We can be reasonably certain, for instance, that we will not find houses in fanciful geometric shapes on the road from Rey to the Shah 'Abd al-'Azim graveyard, even if we have never been there ourselves. Other distinctions, such as the question whether the narrator is in "fact" a painter of pen cases, follow a more complicated set of rankings and comparisons. I feel that we have solved that one too (he is not), but we should also acknowledge that the process of naturalization, or recuperation, which we have been using, taking part one as an internalized distortion of an external part two, will not solve all the problems. As Michael Hillmann has observed in a different context (*FYA* 7), much of what occurs in part two seems "equally internal." The pen-case design repeated in part one is evidently generated by the pen case he is using as he writes in part two (which "must have been drawn by an artist in the grip of some bad obsession"—104/95), with the additional detail that she is dancing (this relates her to the story of the parents) and has her hands bound; but we must add that the same scene is also present, seemingly unnecessarily, on the embroidered curtain he remembers from his childhood (82–83/77). The detail that the woman appears chewing her finger in the Persian gesture of surprise is given a kind of explanation through the nurse's recollection: "She told me how my wife from early childhood had a habit of biting the nails of her left hand and would sometimes gnaw them to the quick" (66/63). We may not want to take the nurse as a good authority, since she is also cited as the source of the story about the parents in India, and of course the old man is also pictured with his finger at his lips, so it could not be considered an efficient explanation.

Often enough events in part two explain details of part one, but sometimes they just restate them in naturalistic terms. What do we do with the jar (baghal) of wine on the shelf in part one, for instance, when it is mirrored in this scene of part two?

> Lying there in the transparent darkness I gazed steadily at the water-jug [kuze-ye âb] that stood on the topmost shelf [ke ru-ye raf bud]. I had an irrational fear that it was going to fall and decided that so long as it stood there I should be unable to fall asleep. I got up, intending to put the jug in a safe place, but by some obscure impulse [be vâsete-ye tahrik-e majhuli ke khodam moltafat na-budam] that had nothing to do with me my hand deliberately nudged it so that it fell and was smashed to pieces.   (80–81/75)

On other occasions the events of part two might be said to explain too much. This is, I think, the case with the theme of the wife's miscarriage. We observe that she is still pregnant in the scene where he upsets the soup ("I had a look at her belly. . . . No, she had not had the baby yet"—85/78). He imagines he hears her giving birth that night (90–91/83), but the nurse speaks of her as pregnant and in precarious health (zan-at lak dide bud—120/108), and the news of the miscarriage is brought to us by the wife's brother: "Mummy [the wife] said, 'If I hadn't had a miscarriage the whole house would have belonged to us' " (122/109). This is presented as if it might be the impetus that sends him to her room a final time, to murder her, thus giving us momentarily an economic undercurrent that restates the hostility of man and wife in terms of domestic power. As the producer of a son the wife would retain power over the household on the death of the husband. This gives us a concrete motivation for the murder, which is perhaps novelistically desirable, but the bulk of the preceding narrative has worked to give us a subtle motivation that makes the concrete one unnecessary, even contradictory.[33]

We said that the schema of the narrator's divided consciousness accounts for Hedayat's characteristic doubling, but it
doesn't explain it completely, since there are supplementary
instances of doubling that can't be explained as hallucina-
tions. The butcher shop, for instance, is a reflection of his
room in part two, since an Iranian butcher shop is simply an
empty room with a hook in it for hanging up the sheep, and
since the speaker's room too holds a hook for two carcasses in
the form of a "horse-shoe nail which at one time supported
the swinging cradle where my wife and I used to sleep" (50/
50). The horseshoe nail and slender hook from which he imagines himself suspended in the opium reverie that leads to part
two (43/42–43) form a connection between the two babies
and the two dead sheep, between birth and death, which is
reiterated when the narrator kills his wife in the manner of a
butcher killing his sheep. The connections are all thematically
appropriate, but the duplications are of a substantiality that
suggests splitting or mirroring that has taken place prior to the
novelistic act of representation, duplications not contained by
the premise of the speaker's delusion.

Our final example will lead us, I think, to an element of
compensatory certainty outside the certainties of the speaker's
reality. What are we to make of his walk to the river Suran in
part two? Is it the speaker's reality or another fantasy? It is
tempting to consider it the prototype of the trip to the graveyard in part one, but since he encounters on his way the same
houses in geometric shapes we met in part one and returns not
walking but in a dreamlike gliding motion (77/72), the entire
trip takes on by association an atmosphere of fantasy, or perhaps we are meant to see the trip as a "real" event interspersed
with visions. The apparition of the woman from the abandoned fortress (75–76/71) takes on greater significance if it is
a delusion within reality rather than a dream within a
dream,[34] and the childhood memory of the picnic (appropriately on the day of the first apparition in part one, the thirteenth day of Now Ruz, April 2) that took place at the scene
has itself the feeling of a central generating memory:

We played hide and seek together. Once when I was running
after the bitch on the bank of the Suran her foot slipped [*pâ-ye
u laghzid*] and she fell into the water. The others pulled her out
and took her behind the cypress tree to change her clothes. I
followed them. They hung up a woman's veil as a screen in front
of her but I furtively peeped from behind a tree and saw her
whole body. She was smiling and biting the nail of the index-
finger of her left hand. Then they wrapped her up in a white
cloak and spread out her fine-textured black silk dress to dry in
the sun.   (76–77/72)

Taken as a bedrock reality, this memory could account for the
cypress tree and the stream running between the two figures
in the tableau of part one, as well as the clinging nature of the
dress and the aura of sensuality that surrounds the tableau
(since it is suggested that the scene by the river is his first sight
of her naked). The veil behind which she changes (*châdor-e
namâz*) could then be taken as a prototype of numerous other
veils and barring surfaces in the text. (His gliding walk when
he returns home [the verb is *laghzidan*, to "slip, slide"] is evidently suggested by the use of the same verb in the scene of
her falling.)

I want to see this scene as a bedrock certainty in another
sense, though. The scene where he sits by the river remember-
ing the picnic is set off from the rest of the action by its momentarily serene, almost idyllic quality, set off even from the
rest of the book.

I stretched myself out at full length on the fine sand at the foot
of the old cypress tree. The babbling of the water reached my
ears like the staccato, unintelligible syllables [*harf-hâ-ye boride
boride va nâ-mafhumi*] murmured by a man who is dreaming. I
automatically thrust my hands into the warm, moist sand. I
squeezed the warm, moist sand in my fists. It felt like the firm
flesh of a girl who has fallen into the water and who has changed
her clothes.   (77/72)

The primordial tradition that associates sitting by a river and
daydreaming, or literary creation, becomes almost explicit, as

if the narrator were listening to his own narration in elemental form: language as water. Rivers are erotic as well. "Brooks," says the narrator of Ebrahim Golestan's novelization of his film *Esrâr-e ganj-e Darre-ye Jenni* (The secrets of the treasure of Possessed Valley, 1971), are "the site of all rural affairs in Iran," as barns and haystacks are the site of rural affairs in European tales and films.[35] The more characteristic element, however, is the element of earth invoked immediately after. The riverside setting, reminiscent of various Khayyamic scenes in which lovers picnic over the dust of their predecessors (FitzGerald's "And this delightful herb"), is eroticized with a gesture, his kneading the sand, which reminds us of the molding of potter's clay, linking us in turn with the erotic interest in the image of the vase. (The breaking of the water jug in part two, then, becomes a brief foreshadowing of the—also "accidental"—murder.) In Persian, seas and rivers, as well as vases, have lips (*lab*); we may picture the speaker here pondering the source of his own voice, looking into a stylized self as in the popular scenes often illustrating editions of FitzGerald's *Rubaiyat*, scenes in which a melancholy figure looks pensively into an enormous wine jar, or (if we extend the concept of a feminized landscape) into the womb.

It does not seem to me that we need to decide where we are grounded—in the realistic framework of the narrative, in the obsessions of the biographical Hedayat. We are in a space that comments on writing and where it comes from, a commentary on the negotiations writers, male writers anyway, perform between language and a vision of their nonlinguistic self. The scene is not a personal possession of Hedayat: there is a pair of similar images in Faulkner's *Sound and the Fury* where Caddy walks or falls into a river (once in the aftermath of an erotic controversy with Quentin, once as a child, in a scene that Faulkner later said was particularly charged with affect for him).[36] They are similar, and central to the narrative, in ways that suggest not influence but parallel derivation, a set of images that lie close at hand in the repository available to us in our reveries of writing and how it begins. (Writing is a vat of liquid in the improvisation that concludes Derrida's famous essay "Plato's Pharmacy.")[37]

We are not in the realm of communal images all the time, but we may feel that we are because the narrator never becomes a character so distinct that we can see him apart from his madness. To show him waking up, learning the difference between fantasy and reality in any concrete or final way, would drastically reduce the power of the fantasy images; this is why we experience them first, bewilderingly, as reality.

The reader's strategy that works in *The Blind Owl* is not like walking on solid ground; to continue the analogy above, it is more like swimming. This is because the effects that make it distinctive are often unrelated or opposed to the effects that give it its mimetic, realistic solidity: the same devices that are used to represent insanity (the strategies of defamiliarization, the symphonic leitmotifs, the repeated investment of everyday objects with talismanic significance) are also conventional literary devices, and the processes that alienate us from the narrator also draw us into the text. A gently mocking voice discernible behind the narrator's can frequently be heard operating independently of the growing schema of the narrator's derangement. As the speaker introduces himself in part one, for instance, the description passes through a series of ironic reversals that are neither sardonic nor pointed, but are unavoidably comic: in spite of his pain he has the consolation of his painting, but on the other hand he isn't really a painter because he has only one subject. But then, maybe he is, because there is a considerable international market for them. This mocking undercurrent persists in the most morbid passages: when the ethereal woman dies he realizes it in stages that begin with a rhetorical flight: "Then I thrust my fingers into her hair. It was cold and damp. Cold, utterly cold. It was as though she had been dead for several days" (20/24). The epanorthosis, or correction, brings us down in a most unexpected way, by showing us that the rhetorical flight was true: "I was not mistaken. She *was* dead." Hedayat's gifts as a humorist perhaps never serve him so well as in this book, where they are unaccented, buried.

The task of a biographical psychoanalytic criticism would be to write a kind of part three of *The Blind Owl*, standing in the relation to the entirety of the text that part two has for part one, supplying a reality from which it is abstracted. We might speak of it as a structure with a false bottom. The places where we find biographical references are often taken as keys to the story; I suspect they are the opposite, the passages that make it difficult. Ideas from elsewhere crowd in on us once we know his life: his opposition to Islam; his fascination with India; his horror at the sight of the butcher across the street, which reminds us that Hedayat was at this time becoming a vegetarian; and the pervasive fear of sexuality, which reminds us that he remained a bachelor in a society that discouraged such reclusion. The links clearly exist, but it does not seem to me possible with the evidence at our disposal to discern the processes of artifice and convention by which private obsessions were transformed into consistent, sharable patterns of experience, or in Fredric Jameson's restatement (paraphrasing Freud's introduction to Rank's *Myth of the Birth of the Hero*), how he managed to overcome "that inherent repugnance of the reader to the wish fulfillment of others which . . . constituted for Freud the chief strategic problem of the creative writer."[38]

Fiction is not a repository of materials for psychoanalysis to reconstruct; it is an institution parallel to psychoanalysis with its own frameworks of negotiation and its own rules of closure. The biographical subject fills the text, but mysteriously altered; it ends up a mysterious weave of intended and unintended patterning. We may guess the rewards these strategies have for a writer such as Hedayat. They permit a kind of fictional confession that is, since projected as the confession of another, under more nearly conscious control (a consideration of particular importance for the writer aware that writing is never a disinterested or innocent activity). Between the experienced fantasies that threaten and the esthetically distanced ones that revolve within consciously determined limits is a freedom that we as readers can never perceive directly. Submission to the demands of patterning creates the possibility of free play. The remarkable experiment of projecting his own ideas on an insane narrator makes it possible for us to read *The Blind Owl* as a retraction of the author's opinions. But if we were to read in that way it would blind us to the way in which the provisionality of fiction transforms ideas, and to the sanity of a writer who is willing to test the limits of his own commitments, to distort and parody them, to flirt with darkness and make himself his own devil's advocate.

Chapter Four

GOTHIC I: A GENERIC BACKGROUND

I

BETWEEN the Westernized novel in a non-Western culture and the theme of the unconscious there is a logical affinity. Perhaps you could derive the theme of the unconscious from the experience of the non-Western novelist, since the analogy is so near at hand between the unconscious (a context that amplifies elements of experience otherwise passed over or denied) and the context of Western cultural history that, also invisibly, shapes the non-Western novel from abroad. A tradition that is molded from abroad does not, however, necessarily know itself as a mixed tradition.

To the extent that we conceive of modern Iranian writing as an isolated tradition, self-sufficient and fully present to itself, it is likely to greet us with the otherness that colors dream images. An imported, transplanted literature carries, in other words, an inevitable aura of the uncanny, no matter how familiar its themes and setting, simply because it moves according to unseen rules, following the grain of foreign tropes and character types.

A warning: the analogy between Western influence and the unconscious could become pernicious, putting the Western critic in the role of analyst—omniscient, uninvolved—and the Iranian reader in the role of patient. If I am locating an alien element in the middle of Iranian modern tradition, it does not mean that we who "belong" to that alien tradition necessarily understand Hedayat more profoundly or more spontaneously. There are nuances in Hedayat that I know I am deaf to, expressions whose resonance I shall never hear; but at the same time, as Western readers we see into the wings at the performance, and it is my position that this lateral angle of vision can be a source of critical insight, as Hedayat's characteristic outsider's viewpoint was essential to his esthetic vision. Nor is the theme of the unconscious unrecognized in Iranian letters: I even suspect that the receptivity of Iranian intellectuals to the concepts of psychoanalysis is linked with their common experience of a cultural and economic life whose moving forces are outside their field of vision. In the 1960s the avidity with which Iranians read information in the popular press about clandestine activities of the CIA was, I think, altogether different from the fascination with which Americans read them. In addition to their justified dismay at the nature and extent of those disclosures, it was for Iranian readers a glimpse into a tantalizingly concrete subconscious scene, a concealed history of their own national life.

There is in the popular reading of Persian literature in Iran, as there is in its political life, an enormous thirst for secret readings that identify suppressed truths about well known poems. The twentieth century has been, after all, a period in which conspiracy theories have been increasingly plausible. And secret readings of Hedayat's works are, predictably, not uncommon. Mostafa Farzaneh even records a series of "keys" to *The Blind Owl* entrusted to him by the author (*ASH* 347–50), though if I read that passage correctly most of them are personal associations (e.g., a visit from his uncle memorialized in the opening scene), which have minimal bearing on the coherence of the finished work. The once popular idea that *The Blind Owl* was sufficiently explained by Hedayat's opium experiences represents a more misleading category of interpretive keys. What follows is a third category, perhaps not entirely innocent.

In my conspiracy theory the primary key to Hedayat's writing is his familiarity with Western literary institutions (though if he had been more aware of them as institutions the nature of that influence might have been different). If I claim that my conspiracy theory has an advantage over the others, that claim will rest on its willingness to admit the complexities of form. The virtues of Hedayat's use of his Western reading are not in the amount he assimilated or how completely he absorbed it:

the very fact that he wrote from within a decentered tradition, a tradition not fully present to itself, can be a source of authority in his writing. What we trace when we examine Hedayat's Western reading, to the extent that it is visible to us, is the gradual discovery of a problematic center in Western narrative—a center whose source of power is similarly grounded in uncertainty. The place we find this problematic center is in our tradition of the Gothic romance, particularly as Hedayat found it in Poe; but he did not arrive there by a direct route.

A French secondary education, with its trust in a stable archive, is everywhere evident in the works written before Hedayat's studies in Europe. In his 1923 essay on Omar Khayyam (*NP* 189–201) and his two works on vegetarianism, the use of citation is widespread and precocious. The quotations are often perfunctory, put forth as representatives of a single entity (more or less identical with the West), which seems to represent reason, an outsider's view unobstructed by habit or superstition. As Hedayat transfers his energies to fiction we no longer have the evidence of footnotes to trace his Western reading. We do, however, have his translations. I do not know for sure that the European writers Hedayat translated in *Afsâne* magazine in 1932 and 1933 were his own selections, but they have a common interest in the theme of the outsider's point of view, which suggests that they were. In Arthur Schnitzler's "Der Blind Geronimo und sein Bruder" (Blind Geronimo and his brother, translated as "Kur va barâdar-ash," *NP* 33–67) two brothers who beg for a living on a highway in the Swiss Alps experience a crisis of trust when the blind brother suspects the other of having cheated him. In "The Peat Moor" ("Torvmyr") by the Norwegian naturalist writer Alexander Kielland (1849–1906), which Hedayat translated as "Kolâgh-e pir" (The old crow, *NP* 3–7), the outsider's view is that of an animal, a crow raised as a pet and now free, flying over a landscape once familiar to him. (Today it reads like a study for Hedayat's "Sag-e velgard" [The stray dog].) In "The Abyssinian Marsh" by Gaston Cherau (1874–1932), we have what looks like a fragment from a traveler's narrative (I have been unable to locate the original) in which a "dragon-like" snake kills a doe in the process of giving birth, a parable about the amoral cruelty of nature (and a tableau not unlike the concluding scene of Hedayat's story "S.G.L.L.," *SR* 9–43).

Perhaps the least characteristic choice is the Chekhov story "Gooseberries" ("Tameshk-e tighdâr," *NP* 9–23), a more nuanced, leisurely, reserved vision of society than anything in Hedayat. In Hedayat's translation (as with Kielland and Schnitzler through a French intermediary) Ivan Ivanych Chimsa Himalaisky's story of his brother Nikolay Ivanych unfolds in a setting so like that of an Iranian landowner's country estate that a reader familiar with Iran can visualize the action easily in an indigenous setting.[1] The events of the story—in which a government worker is so obsessed with the idea of owning land (and cultivating gooseberries) that when finally he is able to buy an estate he refuses to acknowledge its evident shortcomings and begins to refer to himself as gentry (Persian *nojabâ'*), though his grandfather was a *muzhikh* and his father a private in the army—might be a scenario of the Reza Shah years in Iran. Ivan's impassioned summation, where he describes the ephemeral nature of our moral conscience and the inevitability of a harsher reality, the "man with the hammer" at the door, is in its way, despite its understatement, a Hedayatian moral.

The impress of Hedayat's Western reading on his short stories takes the general form of a traditional naturalism. In *The Blind Owl* naturalism has moved to the periphery, and his Western reading is often visible in specifics, even in citations. The series of translations and paraphrases from Rilke's *Notebooks of Malte Laurids Brigge*, which are scattered in fragments, without acknowledgment, through the text of *The Blind Owl*, create their own curious category of influence. Nothing in *The Blind Owl* calls attention to them as translations; on the other hand they aren't much of a secret. Al-e Ahmad refers to them briefly in his article (*AA* 83; trans. in *FYA* 31), and Manoutchehr Mohandessi examines them in more detail in his article "Hedayat and Rilke." There are three major appropriations, first among them the description of the smells that emanate from the plaster below the horseshoe nail described in the inventory of effects and furnishings of the speaker's room that opens part two:

> Just below the nail there is a patch where the plaster has swelled and fallen away, and from that patch one can detect the odours from the things and the people which have been in the room in the past. No draught or breeze has ever been able to dispel these dense, clinging, stagnant odours: the smell of sweat, the smell of by-gone illnesses, the smell of people's mouths, the smell of feet, the acrid smell of urine, the smell of rancid oil, the smell of decayed straw matting, the smell of burnt omelettes, the smell of fried onions, the smell of medicines, the smell of mallow, the smell of dirty napkins, the smell which you find in the rooms of boys lately arrived at puberty, the vapours which have seeped in from the street and the smells of the dead and dying.
>
> (50–51/50–51)

This sends us back to the passage in the *Notebooks* in which Brigge observes a house being wrecked and imagines the intimate household smells now exposed to the outside world:

> And from these walls once blue and green and yellow, which were framed by the fracture-marks of the demolished partitions, the breath of these lives stood out—the clammy, sluggish, musty breath, which no wind had yet scattered. There stood the middays and the sicknesses and the exhaled breath and the smoke of years, and the sweat that breaks out under armpits and makes clothes heavy, and the stale breath of mouths, and the fusel odor of sweltering feet. There stood the tang of urine and the burn of soot and the grey reek of potatoes, and the heavy, smooth stench of ageing grease. The sweet lingering smell of neglected infants was there, and the sultriness out of the beds of nubile youths. To these was added much that had come from below, from the abyss of the street.[2]

Hedayat's adaptation of the list shapes it in such a way as to emphasize chronological development and mortality in its closing items, but no one would miss the relationship.

The second such borrowing is the list of childhood fears

that resurface in the introspective section near the end of part
two:

> Lying in this damp, sweaty bed, as my eyelids grew heavy and
> I longed to surrender myself to non-being and everlasting night,
> I felt that my lost memories and forgotten fears were all coming
> to life again: fear lest the feathers in my pillow should turn into
> dagger-blades or the buttons on my coat expand to the size of
> mill-stones; fear lest the breadcrumbs that fell to the floor should
> shatter into fragments like pieces of glass; apprehension lest the
> oil in the lamp should spill during my sleep and set fire to the
> whole city; anxiety lest the paws of the dog outside the butcher's
> shop should ring like horse's hoofs as they struck the ground;
> dread lest the old odds-and-ends man sitting behind his wares
> should burst into laughter and be unable to stop; fear lest the
> worms in the footbath by the tank in our court yard should turn
> into Indian serpents; fear lest my bedclothes should turn into a
> hinged gravestone above me and the marble teeth should lock,
> preventing me from ever escaping; panic fear lest I should sud-
> denly lose the faculty of speech and, however much I might try
> to call out, nobody should ever come to my aid . . .
>
> I used to try to recall the days of my childhood but when I
> succeeded in doing so and experienced that time again it was as
> grim and painful as the present.
>
> (101–2/92–93; ellipsis in the original)

Here the list is even more clearly founded on a Rilkean passage, though Rilke's list is subtler and more clearly interior, a
matter of anxieties rather than fears. (Costello's choice of
"anxiety" rather than "fear" for the repeated word *tars* in the
passage above seems in this respect misleading.)

> Here and there on my coverlet lie lost things out of my childhood
> and are as new. All forgotten fears are there again.
>
> The fear that a small, woollen thread that sticks out of the
> hem of my blanket may be hard, hard and sharp like a steel nee-
> dle; the fear that this little button on my nightshirt may be bigger
> than my head, big and heavy; the fear that this crumb of bread
> now falling from my bed may arrive glassy and shattered on the

floor, and the burdensome worry lest at that really everything
may be broken, broken for ever; the fear that the torn border of
an opened letter may be something forbidden that no one ought
to see, something indescribably precious for which no place in
the room is secure enough; the fear that if I fell asleep I might
swallow the piece of coal lying in front of the stove; the fear that
some number may begin to grow in my brain until there is no
more room for it inside me; the fear that it may be granite I am
lying on, grey granite; the fear that I may shout, and that people
may come running to my door and finally break it open; the fear
that I may betray myself and tell all that I dread; and the fear
that I might not be able to say anything, because everything is
beyond utterance,—and the other fears . . . the fears.

I asked for my childhood and it has come back, and I feel that
it has been useless to grow older.   (Norton trans., 60–61)

The third borrowing is the passage that begins, "It would
seem that everyone possesses several faces," shortly after the
soliloquy that lists the childhood fears (102/93). This repro-
duces one of the earliest items in Brigge's notebook, the horrifying moment when the woman in the park with her face in
her hands "pulled away too quickly out of herself, too violently, so that her face remained in her two hands. I could see
it lying in them, its hollow form" (Norton trans., 16). Mohandessi adduces an additional example, the image of the last flies
of autumn, which occurs twice in *The Blind Owl* (84/78, 92/
85–86) and fits into a series of death scenes that figure as leitmotifs in the *Notebooks* (Norton trans., 144).

It is not hard to imagine a context in which we would call
this a kind of plagiarism. These passages are not, after all, like
Virgilian echoes of Homeric scenes. Much rests on the novelty
of Brigge's observations, on their reversal or distortion of
commonplace, "doxical" wisdom. On the other hand, Hedayat puts at least two of them to uses that change their meaning. This list of smells, for instance, works in *The Blind Owl*
to emphasize the sense of solidity and persistence of the wall,
the imprisoning closeness of the household, an effect that alters and in a way reverses the haunting mixture of persistence

and fragility in the passage that lies behind it. The quotation in Rilke in which faces are seen as masks carries with it an unbearable, for some readers a self-indulgent, horror, which Hedayat (for some readers, surprisingly) declines to copy. The mask passage in *The Blind Owl* is (in its own words) cool, dispassionate (*bâ khunsardi va bi-e'tenâ'i*—102/93), as if presenting information that is common knowledge, the summary of thoughts developed in serenity.

The influence of Rilke's *Notebooks* on modern fiction has been considerable: Sartre's *Nausea* (1938) is probably the most conspicuous case. It came out within two years of *The Blind Owl* and builds on Rilkean ideas in a direction that is sufficiently different from Hedayat's use of them to illuminate Rilkean elements of *The Blind Owl* by comparison. There are in *Nausea* no direct paraphrases like those in *The Blind Owl* (though the passage in the concluding pages in which Roquentin imagines a series of grotesque fantasies, which in his state of mind seem likely to occur, may be modeled on the list of childhood fears in the *Notebooks*);[3] stylistic affinities and thematic borrowings have, however, been sufficiently conspicuous to attract critical notice.[4] Sartre, in his exploration of consciousness as a continuum to be followed to its available limits, carves out space for a narrator who is tougher and more resistant to affect, less intimidated than Hedayat's by the disappointments or horrors of mundane experience and heightened awareness. When he speaks of Rilke in *Being and Nothingness* five years later, it is the treatment of the otherness of death in the *Notebooks* that he singles out particularly. The treatment of the numerous individualized death scenes Brigge recalls in such detail (from the grandfather to Christian IV, the man in the crêmerie, and eventually the flies in autumn) function to particularize death, to see it "as the final term *belonging to a series*," rather than as a barrier between one world and another: "there is no longer any *other side* of life, and death is a human phenomenon; it is the final phenomenon of life and is still life."[5] In the death scenes of the *Notebooks* Rilke "attempts to show that the end of each man resembles his life because all individual life has been a preparation for this end" (Sartre, 652).

Hedayat eventually read *Nausea* with some enthusiasm,[6] but his use of Rilke's *Notebooks* is less rather than more cool and dispassionate. There are moments in Hedayat when he seems to insist on the demystification of death, making it natural and serene (a kind of ultimate signified of the natural realm), but there is also a reliance on the language of extremes, which makes it necessary to stress the inaccessibility to consciousness of death, to keep death in reserve as a source of horror (or to juggle two points of view, one detached and accepting, the other horrified by its sudden apparition). What Hedayat seems to notice in Rilke is not the fluidity of those death scenes that bring consciousness up to the limit of nonbeing, but Brigge's sudden transitions from familiar to unfamiliar realms of experience. Perhaps the scene in the *Notebooks* from which Hedayat learned the most is not one of those he borrowed, but the episode in which Brigge remembers going to an old closet as a child, finding there exotic costumes and masks, which he tries on, only to frighten himself into unconsciousness when he looks into a mirror (Norton trans., 90–95). That scene is like a miniaturization of *The Blind Owl*.

Whatever else the silent acts of homage in Hedayat's borrowings from Rilke mean, they suggest a reader's relation marked by affect. It is the most personal references we are likely to employ without citation. But personal styles exist in relation to collective styles, fashions, and movements; we might think of Rilke as a guide who shows Hedayat the boundaries of naturalism and how to cross them. (Another figure lurks in the shadows here: it would be logical for Hedayat to have been an admirer of another German translated by Maurice Betz, Thomas Mann. Mann's experimentation with the leitmotif as a formal device that displaces character development as an organizational principle, to create a musical form, or what Joseph Frank has called "spatial form,"[7] is particularly illuminating as an introduction to modernism, because Mann makes the transition by degrees, never really abandoning the traditional nineteenth-century narrating voice. Hedayat at some point read Mann: Monteil mentions a 1930 edition of "Tristan," presumably in the Betz translation, with excited marginal comments in Hedayat's hand.[8] It would be nice, however, to know when he wrote them.)

The Notebooks of Malte Laurids Brigge, like naturalism, takes in details of experience that evade anticipated standards of decorum: they zero in on moments when social personas are painfully dislocated from their accustomed place, failures of will that show human life as the vector of blind forces— disease, poverty, mortality. But the *Notebooks* also includes an explicit commentary on naturalism. Brigge's meditation on the career of Ibsen, the quintessentially naturalistic figure (Norton trans., 74–76), does indeed deal with his grasp of social realities, but the emphasis is on Ibsen's dialectical relationship with his audience. An audience will not necessarily recognize its own reality, and as the naturalist perceives less obvious, more subtle aspects of that reality, the dilemma arises how to portray it in such a way that it is recognizable as reality: "Then you set about that unexampled act of violence in your work, which ever more impatiently, ever more desperately, sought equivalents among the visible for the inwardly seen" (Norton trans., 72).

We might see the first step beyond naturalism, then, as the awareness that it is not just a project of seeing things as they are, but a burden of translating them into accessible terms. The blindness Zola finds in his critics in the preface to the second edition of *Thérèse Raquin* ("Il faut tout le parti pris d'aveuglement d'une certaine critique pour forcer un romancier à faire une préface")[9] is a perverse refusal to see what is obvious. For Rilke blindness is everywhere; the man with the hammer does not visit every door. Our perception is inevitably restricted, and thus the necessity of repeating the word "saw" (*gesehen*) in the description of the blind peddler with his vegetable cart:

> Have I already said that the man was blind? No? Well he was blind. He was blind and he shouted. I misrepresent when I say that, suppressing the barrow he was shoving, pretending I did

not notice he was shouting "cauliflower." But is that essential?
And even if it were essential, isn't the main thing what the whole
business was for me? I saw an old man who was blind and
shouted. That I saw. Saw.   (Norton trans., 46)

Geoffrey Hartman has dubbed this aspect of Rilke "the
temptation of the eye": he argues that there is a tradition
available to Rilke as a seer, not a distinct movement like naturalism, but a string of writers whose affinities have become
clearer in retrospect: "Rilke . . . is aware that in submitting to
sense experience he follows a long line of literary precursors
who sought a modern descent into hell. The myth of this descent may be said to start with Novalis, reaching its climax in
French symbolism—Nerval, Baudelaire, Rimbaud—and its
conclusion with Rilke, although Thomas Mann will still concern himself with it."[10] The names of Nerval, Baudelaire, and
Rimbaud are, like Dante, often used for conjuring with rather
than analyzing, but this is a case where Rilke agrees. *Notebooks*, a more transparent indicator of its own sources than
The Blind Owl, often simply a compendium of its precursors,
cites two particular lines of filiation as a kind of manifesto of
the esthetic a step "beyond" naturalism.

Do you remember Baudelaire's incredible poem, "Une Charogne"? Perhaps I understand it now. Except for the last verse
he was in the right. What should he have done after that happened to him? It was his task to see in this terrible thing, seeming
to be only repulsive, that existence which is valid among all that
exists. Choice or refusal there is none. Do you imagine it was by
chance that Flaubert wrote his Saint-Julien-l'Hospitalier? This,
it seems to me, is decisive: whether a man can bring himself to
lie beside a leper and warm him with the heart-warmth of nights
of love,—that could not end otherwise than well.
                                        (Norton trans., 67–68)

Both "Une charogne" and "La légende de Saint-Julien l'Hospitalier" can be read as manifestos. Notice that the Flaubert
cited is not Flaubert the realist, but a Flaubert whose analytic
detachment is put to parabolic use. It does seem that Hedayat

did his homework and there are scenes in "St.-Julien" that left an impress on *The Blind Owl*: after Julien has mistakenly killed his parents (in circumstances reminiscent of the murder in *The Blind Owl*), he looks at his reflection and momentarily thinks he sees his father, and we are reminded of the speaker's climactic revelation in *The Blind Owl* of his identity with the odds-and-ends man. In the scene in which the leper enters Julien's hut and immediately squats on the floor we are reminded of the opening scene in *The Blind Owl*, especially when we see the speaker (like Julien) unexpectedly find a bottle of wine to offer the guest.

Baudelaire's "Une charogne" is more visible as a manifesto, perhaps because it is organized so schematically. In a much-quoted letter to his wife (19 October 1907), which seems to be the model of the letter in the *Notebooks*, or a rewriting of it, he notes with satisfaction that Cézanne in his last year recited "Une charogne" from memory: "I could not help thinking that without this poem the whole development toward objective expression, which we now think we recognize in Cézanne, could not have started; it had to be there first in its inexorability" (cited in *Notebooks*, Norton trans., 222). The indefinite article of the title "Une charogne" is deceptive: the carcass by the roadside is emblematic, an obsessive center of focus. Nothing in the poem suggests that it is incidental, part of a natural scheme of things, and the reader's disgust is made an essential component of the effect. There are three centers of attention: the speaker's insistent, needling voice, the carcass of the title, and the woman with whom the speaker is walking. It is not an untraditional triangle. In its way it is a commonplace of baroque poetry, like Marvell's "To His Coy Mistress" with the cards reshuffled. The immediate effect is that of a simple polarity between the dead animal, a soulless, inanimate presence, and the woman apostrophized as *mon âme*. The woman falls out of the picture for eight of the poem's twelve stanzas, but we are reminded of her because of a rhetoric that refuses to keep categories of desire and disgust separate. In the second stanza the carcass is momentarily a sexual object (its legs in the air *comme une femme lubrique*). In the third it is bathing in the sunlight like a roast in the fire. The imagery of food is brought even closer in stanza 9 through the presence of a fourth participant:

> *Derrière les rochers une chienne inquiète*
> *Nous regardait d'un oeil fâché,*
> *Epiant le moment de reprendre au squelette*
> *Le morceau qu'elle avait lâché.*

> Behind the rocks an anxious bitch
> eyes us reproachfully,
> waiting for the chance to resume
> her interrupted feast.[11]

The dog, since it has presumably been eating the carcass and regards the human intruders as competition, is an ironic mirror for our bestial impulses, and the motif of dogs in *The Blind Owl* who scratch at the scrap heap (15/19–20) and beg at the butcher's shop (53/52, 91/90–91, 122/109–10), and are said to understand the butcher's pleasure in his work, is probably suggested by this stanza.

On one level "Une charogne" is unproblematic: the speaker is between ugliness and beauty and tries to mediate between them. But this level oversimplifies the role of the woman. The lesson of the loathsome *charogne* is evidently for her benefit, and rhetorically the energy of the lengthy description is absorbed in the stanzas of peroration:

> *Et pourtant vous serez semblable à cette ordure*
> *A cette horrible infection,*
> *Etoile de mes yeux, soleil de ma nature,*
> *Vous, mon ange et ma passion!*

> Yet you will come to this offence [i.e., will resemble it],
> this horrible decay,
> you, the light of my life, the sun
> and moon and stars of my love!

There is no particular indication that this is, like "To His Coy Mistress," the rhetoric of seduction, and without a rhetorical

explanation the juxtaposition of woman and rotten meat becomes more a premise in itself than a device: the sliding of the
camera to her, marked by the conspicuous word *semblable*
(which attracts the reader's attention because of its key position elsewhere, in the last line of "Au lecteur"), has more the
power of an age-old association, so much so that we hardly
believe the future tense of *serez*. The identity between the
woman and the rotten meat is established already; it is, as the
reader senses in stanza 2, her sexuality. This much Brigge
seems to accept; his complaint is against the mock courtliness
with which the vision is compromised in the concluding
stanza:

> *Alors, ô ma beauté! dites à la vermine*
> *Qui vous mangera de baisers,*
> *Que j'ai gardé la forme et l'essence divine*
> *De mes amours décomposés!*

> But as their kisses eat you up,
> my Beauty, tell the worms
> I've kept the sacred essence, saved
> the form of my rotted loves!

The conclusion does indeed function as a retraction: to insist
that he will remember her the way she is, or will preserve her
in his poems (which he has at any rate failed to do in this one)
is to back off from the implied project of objective, indifferent
vision. It is characteristic of Rilke to read Baudelaire's vision
as a process rather than an accomplished fact, but it is clear
that Rilke, in the process of reading, has missed the rhetorical
dynamics of the poem. Elsewhere, in the Orpheus sonnets and
the Duino Elegies, Rilke is interested in the role of the muse or
inspiring woman in the processes of writing; here he seems to
take for granted that a vision of decomposition and decay
should accompany an imaginary speech act to a woman.

   Is there a Hedayatian reading of "Une charogne"? Certainly
the vision of persisting forms in the concluding stanza is like a
number of scenes in Hedayat's writing—for example, the
scenes from his reading of Omar Khayyam, where lovers sit

on riverbanks composed of the dust of former couples, or the moment in *The Blind Owl* when the speaker imagines the ethereal woman in death as "a dainty meal [*khurâk-e lazizi*] for the worms and rats of the grave" (22/25). The narrative of part one could be read as an elaboration of the concluding stanza of "Une charogne" in which, again, an elevated romantic love object is opposed to a world of ugliness only to merge with it, and, again, a peculiar satisfaction results in which the speaker claims to have preserved her beauty through a work of art ("I had no further need of the body"—26/29). Part two, on the other hand, resembles an attempt to establish the kind of detached, unmoved contemplation Rilke admires in the first eleven stanzas. And yet there is a limit to the impassivity. For Rilke there is an absolute, apocalyptic turning point at which one lies down with the leper and everything changes, though it is clear that Brigge does not reach that moment.

Later in the 1907 letter quoted above, Rilke speaks of Brigge as an alter ego who can indicate the nature of vision without necessarily embodying it: "And all at once (and for the first time) I understand the destiny of Malte Laurids. Isn't it this, that the test surpassed him, that he did not stand it in the actual, though of the idea of its necessity he was convinced, so much so that he sought it out instinctively until it attached itself to him and did not leave him any more?" (Norton trans., 222). The letter continues with a tentative retraction ("Yet perhaps he *did* stand it"), but it is not a decision we have to make. What matters is the notion that vision is an experience subject to degree. In *The Blind Owl* the (perhaps less ambitious) equivalent of embracing the leper would be to acknowledge his own past and with it his own responsibility. This comes near enough to happening that we can perceive it as a possibility—otherwise there would be no narrative line on which to string the fragments together—but the moment is infinitely deferred. The continuum of degrees between blindness and vision is in *The Blind Owl* much extended, and the result is to intensify its fictionality. The transparency of the speaker that licenses us to read the *Notebooks* as philosophy gives way in *The Blind Owl* to something more opaque and more modern. But with that opacity comes a paradoxical sensitivity unavailable to Rilke: Hedayat is more concerned with rhetorical surfaces and narrative stylization. In him, patterns Rilke was blind to in his reading of Baudelaire gravitate toward the foreground. What comes into focus particularly is the sexual scenario traditionally taken for granted. Part two of *The Blind Owl* can be read as the hidden plot of "Une charogne," where the act of verbal aggression gradually materializes into physical violence.

II

In the *Notebooks*, as Manoutchehr Mohandessi points out, Brigge speaks of transcribing a prose poem of Baudelaire "so that it might be very near me, sprung from my hand like something of my own" (Norton trans., 52; cited in Mohandessi, *FYA* 118). This is of course very like what Hedayat did to Rilke. But something very similar comes to us in the career of Baudelaire, who found in Poe his own half-conceived poems. As he wrote to Armand Fraisse in 1860:

> In 1846 or 1847, I came across some fragments by Edgar Poe: they had an amazing effect on me. And as his collected works were not gathered together until after his death in a uniform edition, I took the trouble to establish connections with Americans living in Paris, in order to borrow their files of newspapers, edited by Poe. And then, believe it or not, I found stories and poems that had been in my mind, though vague and confused and weakly constructed, which Poe had known how to arrange and bring to perfection.[12]

Students of influence can hardly ask for a more symmetrical and tidy case of visible filiation: three generations of writers whose strategy it was to "mistake" the writing of a precursor for theirs. Among the four figures in the chain—Poe, Baudelaire, Rilke, Hedayat—what Hedayat has in common with Poe is perhaps the most striking. Both Poe and Hedayat are centrally concerned with an esthetic of intensity that maximizes the distance between a normal, decorous reality and an

ugly or horrifying one and operates through suspense and sudden transitions—moments when we jump multiple degrees of
vision all at once. Poe is also a basic reference for the links
between sexuality and rhetoric in *The Blind Owl*.

Hedayat's familiarity with Poe's writings is not limited to
third-hand exposure. We can even pinpoint when he was most
likely to have read him. Isma'il Jamshidi in his memoires of
Hedayat quotes Mohammad Ali Jamalzade describing a meeting with Hedayat after the publication of "Three Drops of
Blood": Jamalzade mentioned the resemblance between those
stories and Poe's (to me, a surprising observation) and asked
if he had read them (Jamshidi, *Khodkoshi*, 33–34). Hedayat
said no, and there the biographical evidence ends, but it is not
hard to imagine that Hedayat shortly afterward (if in fact he
was telling the truth to Jamalzade) read them. On the other
hand, we have Mostafa Farzaneh's evidence that Poe was
among the list of writers Hedayat studied privately under the
tutelage of a priest at his French secondary school (*ASH* 149);
we know he read Poe eventually, because he mentions him in
his 1948 essay on Kafka.[13]

The most striking and apparently deliberate reference to
Poe in *The Blind Owl* (almost like the appropriations from
Rilke) occurs in what is probably *The Blind Owl*'s most famous passage. This is the description of dawn in part one, a
moment of stillness that stands outside the narrative proper
like the scene by the river in part two. Again it is a reverie on
the elements, a focusing of attention on the air at the moment
night fades, after the narrator has spent the night painting the
ethereal woman's portrait while sketching next to the bed
where she has died. It is a central moment narratively because
it marks the filling of two absences: the unapproachability of
the ethereal woman (whom he has now captured as an image)
and the emptiness of his art (compared explicitly to death:
shive-ye naqâshi-ye morde-ye man—24/27), now reversed by
his one successful portrait. Henceforth the action of part one
is without tension, episodic.

Henry D. G. Law excerpts this passage in his selection from
Hedayat's writings in the Persian Writers issue of *Life and*

Letters (254). Vincent Monteil, excerpting it in his book on Hedayat, prints it in lines like a poem (Monteil, 73). I follow his example giving the Persian text below, adding numbers to facilitate a close reading:

1. *Shab pâvarchin pâvarchin mi-raft.*
2. *Guyâ be andâze-ye kâfi khastegi dar karde bud,*
3. *sedâ-hâ-ye dur-dast-e khafif be gush mi-resid,*
4. *shâyad morgh yâ parande-ye rahgozari khâb mi-did,*
5. *shâyad giâh-hâ mi-ru'idand—*
6. *dar in vaqt setâre-hâ-ye rang-paride posht-e tude-hâ-ye abr nâpedid mi-shodand.*
7. *Ru-ye surat-am nafas-e molâyem-e sobh-râ hess kardam*
8. *va dar hamin vaqt bâng-e khorus az dur boland shod.*

1. The night was departing on tip-toe.
2. One felt that it had shed sufficient of its weariness to enable it to go its way.
3. The ear detected faint, far-off sounds
5. such as the sprouting of grass might have made,
4. or some migratory bird as it dreamed upon the wing.
6. The pale stars were disappearing behind banks of cloud.
7. I felt the gentle breath of the morning on my face
8. and at the same moment a cock crowed somewhere in the distance.   (26–27/29)

This passage is, like the opening paragraph of the book, much memorized and recited. It stands alone as a lyric description, but its emphasis on continuity, on presence and plenitude, with its momentary suspension of the narrator's alienated temperament, expands a germinal perception that comes upon him at the moment of her death:

> Within me I felt a new and singular form of life. My being was somehow connected with that of all the creatures that existed about me. I was in intimate inviolable communion with the outside world and with all created things, and a complex system of invisible conductors transmitted a restless flow of impulses between me and all the elements of nature. . . . At that moment I

participated in the revolutions of earth and heaven, in the germination of plants and in the instinctive movements of animals.

(22/26)

The bird in flight and the growing plants in the dawn quotation (Costello's translation reverses the order) are examples of the last two items in the list and serve as concrete expressions of the mood. The opening sentence is a little too arch in English, since we can hardly read it without hearing Carl Sandburg's "The fog comes in on little cat feet," but in Persian what marks it is Hedayat's characteristic materialization of abstract ideas: night is personified first as a person sneaking away, and then as a person capable of sleep. With the third phrase the preoccupation with sight momentarily gives way to an acute awareness of sound. It is almost as if the absence of the woman has ended a noise in his head. (We are almost, momentarily, in the world of Rilke's second Orpheus sonnet, "Und fast ein Mädchen wars und ging hervor," where the creation of art figures as a female presence within the ear, again a female presence whose real existence is put into question, and whose nearness to nonbeing is a defining characteristic.) The catalogue of fanciful sounds in the fourth and fifth phrases give next to no information; bluntly explicated they are simply markers for faintness, but the sense of hallucinatory, degree-by-degree amplification is effective first because a bird in flight would make less sound even than someone on tiptoe, second because it is not the bird he imagines hearing, but the sound of its dreaming. The figure peels back successive layers until at the heart of the scene is a bird that, unlike night, is still asleep, thus reminding us of a darkness that persists after dawn.

The conceit in which growing grass produces a sound is the converse of the dreaming-bird image. There an animate being was asleep, plantlike; here an inanimate one is imagined producing a sound simply through the act of growing. Both "sounds" suggest that the previously dead ambience has come to life: the air that buoys up the sleeping bird and the life force that sounds in the plants are both denials of the condition of the rest of the book. Both probe into worlds of possibility, or rather of figurative reality that is not the "reality" of the book, and only barely the reality of the speaker's fantasy. Phrases 4 and 5 are the farthest point of that looping outward, and the crossing is marked by the anaphora of *shâyad*, "perhaps" (a bracket between portrayed reality and the figural reality that ornaments it, like the "fast" of Rilke's "Und fast ein Mädchen wars").

The ecstatic vision is not only fragile but brief. As we switch to visual perception in phrase 6 we encounter an additional instance of faintness, but this time a concrete image, the "banks" of cloud (*tude*—"heap, crowd, mass," the same word that the Iranian Marxist party took for its name), intrudes as a barrier, and in effect the clouds blot out the sounds the speaker has imagined hearing as they cover the stars. Night goes out; the clouds come in. A second concrete perception, the breeze, functions, similarly, to occupy the place of the departed night, and with it the narrator's physical self comes into the picture, further breaking the mood of absorption. It is as if self-consciousness itself marked the dissolution of the visionary contact with reality, and this process is repeated syntactically as well. A series of verbs in which the landscape is the agent of subtle and refined acts (night sheds its weariness, sounds reach his ears, birds dream, plants grow, stars disappear) gives way to a conclusion in which the observer ascribes action to himself. The (untranslated in English) *dar in vaqt* (at that moment) of phrase 6 and the *dar haminvaqt* (at that very moment) of phrase 8 emphasize the speed (literally, the simultaneity) with which the vision disappears. It is gone before it can be acknowledged almost, and the sound of the rooster crowing comes, like the sounds it replaces, from the distance (*dur-dast* and *az dur*).

We have said that the dawn passage is unique and detachable, a moment of stasis between the achievement of the portrait and the narrator's disposing of the model. Presumably it is a moment of clarity produced by an act of artistic creation (the portrait), as if for a moment that creative intensity were projected outward. If it has a counterpart in part two it might be the epilogue. The sound of the cock announcing dawn suggests that the speaker is waking to a new level of reality, but the clouds coming in with dawn suggest the opposite. The personification of night as a being waking from sleep, a being who exists somewhere else during the day, suggests another entity—a kind of emblem of subconscious life. His manner of leaving (*pâvarchin*, "on tiptoe") is, as Henry D. G. Law suggests in a note to his translation of this passage, "one which would naturally be associated with a thief creeping along in the night and picking each step with care" (Law, 254). (The speaker applies that adverb to himself when he carries the wine from his closet to the bed where the woman lies—18/23.) This suggests a shadowy parallel with the old man who, also at dawn, also in a landscape of approaching clouds, sneaks away with the Rhages vase.

The reference to Poe in this passage is, once seen, perhaps clearer than its indirect and tenuous links to its own surrounding context in *The Blind Owl*. The reference in Poe is from a relatively obscure early poem, "Al Aaraaf," the apocalyptic verse romance usually counted among Poe's juvenilia. In part two of that poem the fairy Nesace calls to her presence a fairy colleague named Ligeia (no visible connection with the Ligeia of the 1838 short story):

> "Ligeia! Ligeia!
>   My beautiful one!
> Whose harshest idea
>   Will to melody run,
> O! is it thy will
>   On the breezes to toss?
> Or, capriciously still,
>   Like the lone albatross,
> Incumbent on night
>   (As she on the air)
> To keep watch with delight
>   On the harmony there?"

(II, 100–111)[14]

As in the fourth phrase of the dawn passage, the image depicts a spirit buoyed up by air, as if to sleep on it: "The albatross," Poe adds in his note to line 107, "is said to sleep on the wing." The image of a bird sleeping in flight, juxtaposed with the idea of audible thoughts, may occur in any number of places, but Hedayat's accompanying image is here too:

> "Ligeia! wherever
>   Thy image may be,
> No magic shall sever
>   Thy music from thee.
> Thou hast bound many eyes
>   In a dreamy sleep—
> But the strains still arise
>   Which *thy* vigilance keep:
> The sound of the rain
>   Which leaps down to the flower,
> And dances again
>   In the rhythm of the shower—
> The murmur that springs
>   From the growing of grass
> Are the music of things—
>   But are modell'd alas!—"

(II, 112–27)

I would have to know more than I do about the statistics of probability to determine how close we are to proof that Hedayat read "Al Aaraaf," but both the sleeping bird and the growing grass are unusual images.[15] The two together seem reasonable, if circumstantial evidence.

It seems that Hedayat read "Al Aaraaf" in English. It is not among the poems Mallarmé translated into French, and I have not located a French version elsewhere. (We do know that Hedayat read English: see, for instance, Monteil, 18.) If the edition in which he studied it was Killis Campbell's of 1917, the standard edition of the time, he would have learned that Campbell traces the image of the sleeping bird to the third story in Thomas Moore's *Lalla Rookh*, "The Fire-Worshippers," in which a Zoroastrian citadel in the Persian Gulf is described in terms of the birds that skirt it:

A ruin'd Temple tower'd so high
That oft the sleeping Albatross
Struck the wild ruins with her wing,
And from her cloud-rock'd slumbering
Started—to find man's dwelling there
In her own silent fields of air!

(II, 202–7)[16]

Moore's note adds, like Poe's but less skeptically, "These birds sleep in the air." I have not been successful in tracing a diffusion pattern for this image, but it is clearly not common knowledge, since both Poe and Moore assign it to a footnote.[17] Both are in their way poems with Middle Eastern reference (the title "Al-Aaraaf" is the name of the seventh sura of the Koran), and the sleeping bird may be considered a Middle Eastern reference, since Maturin in *Melmoth the Wanderer* (1820) speaks of the Simorgh as a bird with that habit.[18] If Hedayat did read "Al-Aaraaf" in the Campbell edition and pursued the footnotes to "The Fire-Worshippers" (which was available in numerous French translations),[19] he will have found it a congenial story. In it Hafed, a hero of the Zoroastrians who holds out with armed resistance against the Arab domination of Sassanian Iran, loves Hinda, the daughter of the Arabic governor Al Hassan. Although the Romeo and Juliet theme might not have appealed to Hedayat, whose two historical dramas about doomed Sassanians holding out against the Arab invasion (*Parvin dokhtar-e Sâsân* and *Mâz-yâr*) put both lovers on the doomed side, the tragic ending is in his mode, and Moore's identification with the heroic Zoroastrians would have been to his taste. (If we seem to be portraying Hedayat as a naive reader projecting his own political anxieties on the romantic fantasies of others, we should add that Moore in the twentieth edition explains that he came to conceive of the Sassanians in "The Fire-Worshippers" as an analogy for the Irish under British rule.)

In "The Fire-Worshippers" the bird is awakened by the

presence of a remnant of Zoroastrian culture. Perhaps one point of the dawn passage is that in *The Blind Owl* there is no such structure to bump into,[20] only a landscape of wretchedness and poverty. But by the same token the bird can be understood as an image of possibility, a figure only partly immersed in the mad world of the narrative, a force untouched by the scene of violence. There is nothing within the world of the narrative to say that the bird is like the red king in *Through the Looking Glass* or Father Time in C. S. Lewis's *Silver Chair*, over whom the heroes stumble in their escape from the cannibal giants, the mythic figure of the apocalyptic sleeper in whose mind the action is taking place, but the suggestion is planted of an alternate world, another monad tangent to the one in which we are trapped. We imagine a beatific, archaic prelapserian smile on the face of that unidentified bird, an expression we glimpse nowhere else in *The Blind Owl*.

Once we know that Hedayat did in fact read Poe, the specific devices we recognize from Poe pop up everywhere and *The Blind Owl* begins to look like an anthology of situations and tropes from Poe's short stories. Like Egaeus, the narrator of "Berenice," the speaker of *The Blind Owl* has blocked out the knowledge of violence against his wife. Like the narrator of "The Black Cat," he writes a confession of killing his wife neither expecting nor soliciting belief (*CWP* 3.849). The circumstances surrounding the death of the ethereal woman are, again, like those of Lady Rowena in "Ligeia"—from the apparently poisoned wine he gives her to drink, and her mysterious waking from death, to her growing in length after dying (27/30). Various verbal echoes of terms common in Poe suggest a precedent for some of Hedayat's most characteristic phrases: Fortunato's laughter in "The Cask of Amontillado," when he is being sealed in the catacomb, is "a low laugh that erected the hairs upon my head" (*CWP* 3.1263), like the laughter of the old man in *The Blind Owl*. The description of the house in part one of *The Blind Owl* ("When I shut my eyes not only can I see every detail of [its] structure"—5/12) echoes vaguely the speaker's memories of his schoolhouse in "William Wilson": "At this moment, in fancy, I feel the refreshing

chilliness of its deeply-shadowed avenues, inhale the fragrance
of its thousand shrubberies, and thrill anew with undefinable
delight, at the deep hollow note of the church-bell" (*CWP*
2.428), or in "Ligeia," the narrator's memory of the room in
which Rowena dies: "There is no individual portion of the
architecture of the bridal chamber which is not now visibly
before me" (*CWP* 2.321). The old man in the pit in the story
in India in *The Blind Owl* turns gray at once, like the hair of
the narrator in Poe's "Descent into the Maelstrom." (Here we
have a likely case of overdetermination, since Freud recalls in
The Interpretation of Dreams that the same thing happened
to his father.)[21] The speaker's plans to dispose of the ethereal
woman's body in *The Blind Owl* ("At first I thought of bury-
ing it in my room, then of taking it away and throwing it down
some well"—27/29) echo similar plans in "The Black Cat"
and "The Tell-Tale Heart."

The meditation on consciousness after death in part two of
The Blind Owl ("May it not be that people have this same
sensation in the grave? Is anything definite known about the
sensations we may experience after death?"—98/89) has more
than one analogue in Poe, from the apocalyptic discussions
between recently released spirits ("The Colloquy of Monos
and Una," "The Conversation of Eiros and Charmion") to the
case history of Stapledon in "Premature Burial," who declared
"that at no period was he altogether insensible—that dully
and confusedly, he was aware of everything which happened
to him, from the moment he was pronounced *dead* by his phy-
sicians, to that in which he fell swooning to the floor of the
hospital" (*CWP* 3.960–61).

III

My conspiracy theory requires for a formal cause more than
the influence of an individual writer. The list of situations and
tropes from Poe's writing tells us something specific about Hedayat's reading, but it is also a catalogue of generic conventions. Poe is the most direct source from which Hedayat is
likely to have learned the set of rules that constitutes the

Gothic, though he may have known the Gothic secondhand as a style regarded highly by the surrealists and perhaps through German expressionist films.[22] Poe's peculiar relation to the Gothic, however, makes him a special kind of source. Poe is an idiosyncratic and eccentric presence in world literature, but there is in him a receptivity to his predecessors even when he protests utter originality, a transparency to convention that makes him an encyclopedia of Gothic themes. He would provide Hedayat with indirect access to a body of works in which discontinuity and sudden revelation, sudden shifts in the degree of vision, replace the detached vision of naturalism. Even without knowing the Gothic novel in its specific textuality he would see in Poe the consistent esthetic his short stories seem to search for.

As we begin to focus on the Gothic as a set of rules, a language that makes *The Blind Owl* possible, we should acknowledge that it is available to us in a different way than it was to Hedayat. There is no research that allows us to trace directly the path Hedayat may have taken between the roles of consumer and producer, from recognizing the Gothic language in his reading to entering the system, speaking that language in his own writing. For us, however, that language has become increasingly visible in recent criticism, and we can trace the nature of its generic constraints by focusing on its history.[23]

The problem of the Gothic is that it has always been so easy to talk about. What marks it as a genre, along with the traditional catalogues of stage machinery, is this recognizability, its clear-cut boundaries and its high level of predictability. (Ann Radcliffe's *Mysteries of Udolpho* is in fact one of Michel Foucault's examples of "initiators of discursive practices," in his essay "What Is an Author?" of writers who create not just a new text but a new set of textual rules.)[24] Wellek and Warren, in their chapter on genre in *Theory of Literature*, greet the Gothic with enthusiasm characteristic of the critical tradition, like a small business that has withstood the competition and produced a successful franchise:

This is a genre by all the criteria one can invoke for a prose-narrative genre: there is not only a limited and continuous subject matter or thematics, but there is a stock of devices (descriptive-accessory and narrative, e.g. ruined castles, Roman Catholic horrors, mysterious portraits, secret passageways reached through sliding panels, abductions, immurements, pursuits through lonely forests); there is, still further, a *Kunstwollen*, an aesthetic intent, an intent to give the reader a special sort of pleasurable horror and thrill ("pity and terror" some of the Gothicists may have murmured).[25]

What makes the Gothic rare among narrative genres is the ease with which we feel we can separate it from the non-Gothic. It has the most visible genesis of any major type on record, with its conception in Horace Walpole's famous dream of 1764, unusually recognizable descendants, and in a modern form, the drugstore romance, made possible by the popular success in 1938 of Daphne du Maurier's *Rebecca*. And so it survives in the form of fables, scenarios that prescribe how women attain power, adhering to a pattern much stricter and more formulaic than the nineteenth-century Gothic. It is this recognizability and circumscription that tempts us to feel we can look into the workshop and hear the collective writers' intention. It is our ability to distance it, to see it as secondary, tangential, and therefore not completely part of history (in a process not unlike that we often apply to Middle Eastern literatures), that gives it its symmetry and esthetic wholeness as a class.

The process of abstracting generic patterns from individual works does not necessarily require an appeal to human universals manifested through ahistorical frameworks, but that appeal is the temptation. An appeal to historical specificity may work to ward that temptation off: it may be that our familiarity with the Gothic in its contemporary, unadventurous form restricts our understanding of its variety from *The Castle of Otranto* to Maturin, Charlotte Brontë, and Poe. If it is more various than our classifying instincts would like, it is also nearer the center of Western writing and consequently harder to distance and isolate. George Steiner's *Tolstoi or Dostoevsky* demonstrates eloquently how the Gothic conventions not only inform popular culture of every kind but press insistently into high literature, where it is as central to the classic curriculum as Dostoevsky.[26] An affinity between Gothic conventions and film became evident early in the history of the medium. And there has been in France, at least since Huysman's *A rebours*, a more or less respectable offshoot of Gothic in which a pictorial, discursive narrative unfolding with minimal plot lingers sensually over a Gothic setting: Rodenbach's *Bruges-la-morte* (1892) is an influential early example that may have left an imprint on Hedayat, and Julien Gracq's *Au chateau d'Argol* (1938) updates the tradition.

The particular set of ideas around which the stylization of the Gothic is formed, that sinister, sexualized setting where the tenuous seen environment threatens to give way to a mysterious unseen world behind it, constitutes a privileged world view in the political sphere as well, perhaps most visibly in the first three decades after the French Revolution.[27] We may even, with the popular dissemination of psychoanalytic thinking, speak of Gothic science. (Geoffrey Hartman has seen the importance of a Lacanian approach to Freud in just this, that it evades the Gothic shudder we are used to in a naive application of Freudian categories, in which "love is also shown to be hate, or a concealed motive is disclosed, or the echoing of 'faeces' in 'faces.' ")[28]

The Gothic is not so much a genre that passes its charter on to selected descendants as a set of patterns that explodes, leaving its traces in the far reaches of Western thought. Among the possible ways to simplify the potential chaos of a generic history there are are two that should be acknowledged here, neither of which are quite appropriate to our purposes. One answer to the potential chaos of genre history is the clarity of a theory that totalizes. The problem it presents to us as students of the Gothic is that we have two uses of the word "genre," sufficiently distant from each other that it may be misleading to use the same word for both. Tzvetan Todorov's *The Fantastic* distinguishes between theoretical genres, those wide

subdivisions such as Aristotle's epic and drama, which begin
with the sum of literary experience and work inward, and historical genres, which move from the individual work outward.[29] On the face of things the two seem to divide the field
between them, but in fact they are incommensurate groups.
There is no collection of finite sets—historical novel, detective
story, *nouveau roman*—that will add up to or coincide with
"narrative" as a genre, and there is no possibility that working
outward from the small sets we will meet the totalizing categories going the other way.

Todorov's *Fantastic* has, however, given us a taste for a high
degree of theoretical order by implying the contrary. His examples include many of the same works that mold the tradition of *The Blind Owl*, and his readings of them do not suggest that the term "Gothic" will help us much. He begins with
a considerable challenge to our faith in historical genre: quoting Lévi-Strauss—"The notion of social structure is not related to empirical reality but to the model constructed according to that reality" (17)—he argues that the fundamental
underpinning of literary texts (i.e., their structure) is not manifested on the level of subject matter. This puts structuralism
in opposition to the French schools informed by phenomenology, represented by Georges Poulet, Gaston Bachelard, and
Jean-Pierre Richard, and to, in Anglo-American criticism, the
influence of Northrop Frye (and in an earlier generation
W. Jackson Knight), all of whom participate in what Gérard
Genette calls, in an essay on Richard that Todorov cites, the
"sensualist postulate, according to which the fundamental
and hence the authentic, coincides with sensuous experience"
(Genette, *Figures I* [Paris: Seuil, 1966], 94; Todorov, 96).[30]
Words such as "fundamental" and "authentic" prejudice the
argument, but in either case the readings circle around a stable
point, whether a structural or a sensualist point.

Todorov's attempt to ground the concept of genre in linguistic universals, in fundamental qualities of the speech act,
produces a construct of great esthetic beauty. The act of defining the fantastic as an act of uncertain perception and locating
it between two modes of certain vision, first supernatural acts

whose validity within the world of the story is unquestioned (the marvelous) and then the explained supernatural (the uncanny/*étrange*), makes of the fantastic a narrow seam across the middle of world literature, a set of texts whose common qualities are unfolded with such luminous authority that the reader is likely to be blinded to a fundamental logical problem: it is not so much that, as Christine Brooke-Rose and Theodore Ziolkowski have both pointed out, [31] his theoretical category turns out in the concluding chapter to be a historical category (a moment in the history of realism), but that behind the unfolding of that class of texts is a silence in which are hidden unanswered questions. Is the genre of the fantastic a catalogue of works or of moments within works? Are there other genres that exist at the same level of abstraction? Where would we go to look for them? The Gothic as a category does not seem available to reformulation of comparable theoretical elegance. It at any rate comprises indifferently Todorov's uncanny (the explained Gothic in the manner of Ann Radcliffe), marvelous (Lewis's *Monk*), and fantastic (Poe's "Ligeia"), all of which are traditionally admitted to the Gothic canon. In order to make audible the background of *The Blind Owl*, the landscape against which it echoes, we require a greater tolerance for chaos.

Another alternative, for many readers a discredited alternative, is to refer the problem outward to the wider generic framework of historically accepted classifications. When Northrop Frye speaks in *The Secular Scripture* of Gothic narrative as the vehicle by which romance reentered the mainstream of English literature after an absence of nearly two centuries (Frye, 4), he risks making romance an ahistorical category, but it is no less a real insight. ("Even a false window," Gerard Genette has said of Frye in another context, "can give real light.")[32] When we allude to romance as an explanation for features of an individual text we are indicating a vast unsolved problem: Frye is undeniably our ranking expert on the subject, and taking the coherence of the romance tradition as a given, while the tradition remains in some fundamental way undefined, is for him a strategy that sheds light (though he is ex-

plicit on this point only briefly, 60–61); a critical analysis that
is concerned with historical cause and effect will have a different set of much less satisfying problems.[33]

Nonetheless it explains something to say that readers of the
Gothic have felt that it taps archaic sources of narrative authority. Perhaps this is a way of saying that romance forms
tend to function, especially in the Gothic, as literary reference,
as conscious artifice that leads our attention outside the texts,
an effect contrary to that of the novel (which denies its artificiality). We might speak of the Gothic conventions as synonymous with conscious stylization in the nineteenth century
rather than as one among other stylized options. It is the high-
profile genre of the epoch, the stylized alternative of the novel
as the Renaissance pastoral is the high-profile genre, the stylized alternative, of the epic. (In fact the two have much in
common. We might not be far off in calling them inversions of
each other: pastoral a vision of a limited world in which desire
is based on the acceptance of limitation, Gothic a scene of
striving and confinement in which limits are a source of suffering.) The realm in which the coherence of the Gothic manifests itself is located in the writer's will, in the shared desire
to stylize. The Gothic is not often a dramatic form, but it is a
theatrical one. (If we call it a world of masks we are already
in the realm of privileged Hedayatian images.)

Definitions of the Gothic ordinarily begin with the Gothic
setting, and here we will not quarrel with tradition. It has been
traced from the eighteenth-century cult of ruins: Gothic in our
sense begins when the ruins have an inside, which can be penetrated, perceived as an enclosure.[34] This allows the ruin, previously the site of natural life (the lion and the lizard in the
Omar Khayyam quatrain), to be occupied by humans. The careers of Walpole with his Strawberry Hill and Beckford with
his Fonthill Abbey suggest that it is a traceable progression
from visiting ruins to living in them. After 1789 the image of
the antique enclosure accumulates new, paradoxical associations, the Bastilles and feudal enclosures exposed to light by
the French Revolution—about which public opinion outside
France is ambiguous, horrified both at the brutality of the an-

cien régime and the powers that had overthrown them. (As Sedgewick points out, the violence produced by the overturning of the monastery walls traditionally matches or outdoes the violence inside—*Coherence of Gothic Conventions*, 24–26.) It is doubtful that many Gothic writers used this ambiguous, latent political significance purposely; what the Gothic offers technically for a writer's conscious use is a set of devices that provide emotional intensity at an exotic distance, both geographical distance and the distance of purposeful artificiality.

The Gothic edifice stems from a more visible act of imagination than most dwellings in literature, and once established is more aware of itself as stage setting, as a literary construct with a literary past. Julien Gracq, in the preface to *Au chateau d'Argol*, explains his modern use of Gothic machinery in such terms: "The always alluring repertory of crumbling castles, noises, lights, spectres in the night, and dreams, enchants us particularly by its utter familiarity, giving as it does to the feeling of uneasiness its indispensible violence by warning one in advance that one is going to shudder ["que l'on *va* trembler"—Gracq's emphasis], and could not possibly, it seemed, be neglected."[35]

Sometimes the awareness of Gothic predecessors becomes nearly tangible, as in the caves beneath the monastery in the Spaniard's story of Maturin's *Melmoth the Wanderer* (1820). The Piranesian dizziness of the underground cells and corridors that accordion out beneath the monastery are not only more meaningful to us but more effective seen as extensions of the underground world in which the climax of *The Monk* takes place. The story that the parricide tells Moncada of the couple, the monk and his lover disguised as a monk, who starve in confinement together (*Melmoth*, 158–65), takes its reference from an attempt to top *The Monk* by splicing together the scenes of Ambrosio's affair with Matilda and the death of Agnes. The most marvelous extension in this process is the discovery of another series of caves outside the monastery, which lead to the underground chamber of Adonijah. It not only provides a last-minute escape of the Saturday-morn-

ing serial kind, but since it is the scene in which Moncada transcribes the story of Imalee on her island in the Indian Ocean,
it in a sense provides (like Melmoth's telescope, from which
she sees the temples of the major religions on the mainland)
another lateral extension to the other side of the earth.

I suggest that what is constitutive of the genre is not the
setting itself or the particular recognizable character types
who live there, but a relationship between them, a metonymy
whereby setting is used to reflect character. (In this it resembles pastoral again, since the echoing of innocent society in its
natural setting is the fundamental stylization of that form.)[36]
Both setting and character are sites of mystery or duplicity,
typically the mystery of subverted authority. In *Otranto*
Manfred's role as hereditary monarch combines themes of domestic and political authority, powers of father and king. (The
abuse of authority is commonly a revelation of sexuality
where we do not traditionally expect it, as when Manfred
breaks the barriers between generations by claiming the fiancée of his dead son and offers his daughter Matilda to the fiancée's father.) The other scene of medieval barbarism, the monastery (conventional particularly in Protestant England),
becomes central to the Gothic with Lewis's *Monk*; and of
course the Gothic site that persists most importantly into the
twentieth century is the laboratory, where a sublime confusion of wires and test tubes, apparatus whose function it is not
to be understood, has an effect not unlike that of the caverns
and passageways beneath the Gothic castle or monastery. The
relation of character and place is often visible in the title: it is
The Castle of Otranto rather than "Manfred," "The Tragedy
of Matilda," or "Theodore's Revenge." Manfred's ancestors
have usurped the castle, and retaining possession of it is the
goal of his ambition, and therefore its defining limit. The central source of horror in *The Mysteries of Udolpho*, the niche
behind which is the wax figure of a decaying corpse, turns out
to be a memorial of a family crime, a place where family history and family dwelling overlap.

Two qualifications complicate the equation. First, setting is
not uncommonly a function of character even in the strictest

realism, where character is conceived as a product of environment (Taine's *milieu*): there is more than one form of character/setting metonymy.[37] What distinguishes the Gothic use of the device is that the information conveyed by the setting is its mystery. Second, the mimetic notion of character never completely disappears. We speak of the novel as the locus of mimetic character, the romance as the locus of projections, segments of "real" character expanded to fit seemingly complete bodies, in Kellogg and Scholes's terms, "fragments of the human psyche masquerading as whole human beings,"[38] sometimes implying that the two are mutually exclusive categories. Often the generic challenge is to mix or parody, to write one in terms of the other.

An influential article by Francis Russell Hart, "The Experience of Character in the English Gothic Novel" (in *Experience in the Novel*, ed. Roy Harvey Pearce),[39] emphasizes one category of mixing, arguing that a novelistic conception of character penetrates frequently into the class of narratives we consider romance. Hart takes as central to the Gothic the dictum of Walpole in the preface to the second edition of *The Castle of Otranto* that his purpose was "to conduct the mortal agents in his drama according to the rules of probability; in short, to make them think, speak, and act, as it might be supposed mere men and women would do in extraordinary positions" (105). He argues that manifestations of the demonic or supernatural are often, even typically, not attributable to sensationalist effects but, like the scene in *Jane Eyre* in which Jane meets Rochester in the forest and each fantasizes the other a supernatural being, to the irony that novelistic characters, realistically conceived, are forced to deal with what seem antirealistic, demonic phenomena.

Lewis's *Monk* (1796) is at the center of the Gothic both formally and historically. It is also a book in which readers have intuited a subtle affinity with *The Blind Owl*. (In fact a 1982 appreciation of Hedayat by Ermanno Krumm opens with quotations from Antonin Artaud's praise of Lewis, altering the quotations by substituting the title of *The Blind Owl* for *The Monk*.)[40] Hart's essay cites *The Monk* as an example of

detailed, psychological, novelistic depiction of character in the
middle of a romance. For Hart, Ambrosio's successive stages
of degradation into sin, his metamorphosis from a decision-
making being into a passive participant in the mechanisms of
his fall, are fundamentally novelistic. "Any interpreter of him
as a nightmare monster, a dark symbol of sexual violation,
must overlook many pages of character exposition. The
reader may not want them; he may reject them as bad psychology or bad fictional method; but they are there nonetheless, and they establish a norm of character" (100). This is, up
to the final phrase, a point well taken, but it is not the experience of the novel that norms of character emerge from those
particular pages.

Ambrosio's character is also predicated on the conventional
equation of personality and setting. Ambrosio has a conventional romance mystery surrounding his birth; he has been
raised as a foundling by Capuchin monks, so that when his
affair with Matilda begins it is the opportunity for the conventional sermon on reclusion. It has the feel of a novelistic exposition, as do passages of exposition in part two of *The Blind
Owl*, but it cleaves very closely to what we already know before we have opened the book:

> It was by no means his nature to be timid: but his education
> had impressed his mind with fear so strongly, that apprehension
> was now become part of his character. . . . His instructors care-
> fully repressed those virtues, whose grandeur and disinterested-
> ness were ill suited to the cloister. . . . Add to this, that his long
> absence from the great world, and total unacquaintance with the
> common dangers of life, made him form of them an idea far
> more dismal than the reality.[41]

It would be difficult to say whether the character tells us more
about the setting or vice versa. (In a way it tells us as much
about the contemporary reader, since Ambrosio's dark view
of the outside world is so much a mirror image of the English
Protestant's ignorance and overestimation of the terrors behind monastery walls.) The character/setting trope is as recognizable in this developmental, mimetic form as in the mys-

terious sympathy between Roderick Usher and his house. Hart is correct, following John Berryman's introduction to the Grove edition, in considering the particular virtue of *The Monk* to be the intrusion of Ambrosio's keenly discerned fall in the midst of otherwise melodramatic and conventional narrative; but this does not make it novelistic in its essence. Its force is relational.

The reader's experience of Ambrosio's interior self is not in itself remarkable, but it is in relation to the romance plot that surrounds it, in which it is a kind of hole bored into an otherwise conventional surface, that it takes on its enormous power. Not the least powerful of its effects is the intensity with which *The Monk* causes the reader's attention to bifurcate: the normal signals of romance patterning tell us we are to sympathize with the cardboard figures, the Raymonds and Alphonsos whose names we have to look up again when we re-tell the story, but when we encounter the novelistic hole that runs through the action we identify momentarily with Ambrosio. That confusion of sympathies echoes other doublenesses that mark *The Monk*, its satirical eye for manners and class behavior as a background for episodes of the demonic and supernatural, a deepening of traditional Gothic motifs, which intensifies them in the same gesture that questions their validity.

This ambivalence is crucial. The Gothic setting amplifies character, but in the process simplifies it, diffuses it; it is a projection that enlarges, but in the process distorts, like the sight of the speaker's shadow on the wall in *The Blind Owl*. There is always a space between the dwelling and the occupant who is represented in it. The dwelling is often enough a means of representing the occupant's dark other self, but often it simply figures the public self, a representation of the inhabitant as authority figure. It is in Lacanian terms a way of concretizing the name of the father, the identity whose detachable nature is the source of anxieties attending the transition from imaginary to symbolic, or from mirror state to the realm of language.

It would not be accurate to call the edifice a stable signifier that might allow us to say Gothic means this or that consistently, or that some single scenario will predictably occur. The mansion can collapse with the death of its proprietor, as in "The Fall of the House of Usher," or it can lose a single wall as at the conclusion of *Otranto*. (There would be a kind of justice in the castle's going down altogether as a punishment for Manfred's crimes and those of his ancestors, but the narrative requires that there is something left for Theodore to inherit.) The destruction of the edifice by fire is a common method of delivering the Gothic hero from an oppressive former self, as in *Jane Eyre*, where it kills Rochester's former wife and even visits him with a temporary punishing blindness in the process. The conclusion of Daphne du Maurier's *Rebecca* is a variation. The fire in Poe's "Metzengerstein"—appropriately for the animistic world, which frequently governs the relation of setting and character in Poe's works—is a means of transforming the owner into his new form, the horse through which his opposition to his rival persists. ("Metzengerstein" adds the additional Poeian theme of the work of art that comes alive, and in the scene in which the pictured horse emerges from Metzengerstein's tapestry it is clear that the agent of vivification is the light of the fire from the neighboring castle—*CWP* 2.22–23.) In *The Blind Owl*, as we saw in the previous chapter, the persistence of the setting colors everything else with its brooding solidity.

Chapter Five

GOTHIC II: POE AS GENERIC BACKGROUND

I

THE themes of aggression that are the focal point of *The Blind Owl* have their formal cause in the Gothic tradition. Poe's "Berenice" offers us a way to examine this tradition directly, since its violence is linked to the relation of self and dwelling. It is, in addition, the Poe text with the clearest analogies in *The Blind Owl*. Like *The Blind Owl*, it focuses on aggression against the speaker's wife, an act of aggression erased from memory and called forth at the climax. In *The Blind Owl* the narrator finds his wife's eye in his hand; in "Berenice" it is another detachable, easily fetishized object, or objects, her teeth. It is, like *The Blind Owl*, a story in which the consciousness of the narrator is a central issue. Egaeus, the speaker of "Berenice," performs no acts that we see: the bulk of the narrative is his description of himself, which fades to a scene of him in his study, where he remains. Here, as in *The Blind Owl*, the gap in consciousness is accompanied by a concern for an ungraspable preexistence ("a remembrance of aerial forms—of spiritual and meaning eyes—of sounds, musical yet sad; a remembrance which will not be excluded; a memory like a shadow—vague, variable, indefinite, unsteady"—*CWP* 2.209–10). As in the coda of *The Blind Owl*, the act of aggression is revealed to the reader by his soiled clothes. In both cases the turgidity of the ending presses the limits of decorum or, for a modern reader, our ability to read it seriously, which amounts to much the same thing. Poe admitted this in a letter to T. W. White, the editor of the *Southern Literary Messenger* ("The subject is far too horrible. . . . The tale originated in a bet"—*CWP* 2.207), which suggests with ambiguous disparagement that the object of horror was more or less arbitrary, like what Hitchcock called a McGuffin, what Egaeus calls the *incitamentum* of his reveries (*CWP* 2.212).

The problem of determining the straightforwardness or irony of the relationship between an individual work and its predecessors is as important to Poe as it is to Hedayat. We may, I think, take Poe at his word that the premise around which the story was molded was chosen arbitrarily or whimsically (there was indeed a scandal in Baltimore in 1833 that involved grave robbing in order to obtain human teeth for dentists—*CWP* 2.207); this does not preclude the possibility that the story is carefully written and the characterization sufficiently precise to guide Hedayat's hand in the age of psychoanalysis.

David Halliburton, whose phenomenological study of Poe has probably done more than any other work of criticism to translate the European enthusiasm for Poe into terms accessible to American readers, has shown that the discontinuity of Egaeus's perception is visible in the syntactic texture of his monologue. Halliburton demonstrates how we can see attention lapse in the opening sentences:

> Misery is manifold. The wretchedness of the earth is multiform. Overreaching the wide horizon as the rainbow, its hues are as various as the hues of that arch—as distinct too, yet as intimately blended. Overreaching the wide horizon as the rainbow! How is it that from beauty I have derived a type of unloveliness?—from the covenant of peace, a simile of sorrow? But, as in ethics, evil is a consequence of good, so, in fact, out of joy is sorrow born. Either the memory of past bliss is the anguish of to-day, or the agonies which are, have their origin in the ecstasies which might have been. (*CWP* 2.209)

Halliburton demonstrates in Egaeus's opening words an identification between referentiality and self-consciousness: "The thing consciousness is aware of here is not the external world but its own operations. Indeed, so long as it remains reflexive there can be no room in it for the external world."[1] Such a consciousness, he continues, cannot differentiate between reflexive perceptions and those of outside phenomena; it can perceive both, but not at the same time, and this condition creates the time lag of sentences 4 and 5,

> when the narrator . . . repeats with surprise his own statement about the rainbow and when he asks how he could have arrived at it. He wants to know what has been happening inside his own head. At the same time he wants to know what has been happening in the world. But in both cases something surrounds him like a wall, shutting him away from the object of his curiosity. That something, that impenetrable medium, is his own consciousness.   (Halliburton, 200)

Halliburton confines himself to states of consciousness latent in the texts; if we trace them to their formal sources we can isolate the texts' rhetorical focus, the intensity of Ciceronian coordination that directs our attention not so much to the logical order of the scene described, but around its own syntactic contours. There are analogies between this characteristic focus and the hermetic sense of enclosure that informs Poe's settings, which in turn is linked with the esthetic of hermetic closure he argues for in his criticism.

This rhetorical self-consciousness works to a different effect in the opening lines of "Ligeia," which unfold without a specific setting (indeed, where the absence of specific setting is the point of the paragraph): "I cannot, for my soul, remember how, when, or even precisely where, I first became acquainted with the lady Ligeia" (*CWP* 2.310). In the elocution that introduces her the absence of memory is itself the controlling information, so that the speaker's perception occludes his subject. When some thirty lines later the second paragraph begins, the absence is still in the foreground: "There is one dear topic, however, on which my memory fails me not" (*CWP* 2.310–11). The characteristic identification of the act of narration with its object is analogous to the identification of Gothic edifice with its inhabitant: the text becomes another curlicued facade difficult to distinguish from the figures within it. This is what makes Poe the link between Gothic tradition and the tradition of Mallarmé. The fetishism of place merges with fetishism of language.

It is of some importance for Hedayat's reading of "Berenice" that the particular image that stops Egaeus in his opening reverie is that of a rainbow. The appropriateness of a rainbow is its "overreaching" shape, which he imagines cutting off his vision into the sky beyond in much the same way that (as he explains, describing his monomania) it is inconsequential, trivial objects that cut him off from outside reality. The origin of the image seems to be his own syntax—the symmetrical, copular form of the opening sentence, which expands over the following two like an algebraic equation. Later, Berenice's teeth are described in terms appropriate to a rainbow ("the white and ghastly *spectrum* of the teeth"—*CWP* 2.215), so that the closing lines of the story, where Egaeus discovers that he has extracted them, are reflected in the opening and the overreaching shape of the narrative is manifested on the level of imagery.

Another way of stating the contradiction in the image of the rainbow is that a rainbow is made of light, but it keeps Egaeus from seeing. Hedayat's narrator, like Egaeus given to the device of stopping to examine what he has just said (the trope of *correctio*), opens his story on a similar anomaly in the second beginning of *The Blind Owl*, the passage in which he introduces the ethereal woman as an angel: "In this mean world of wretchedness and misery [*faqr va maskanat*] I thought that for once a ray of sunlight had broken upon my life. Alas, it was not sunlight, but a passing gleam, a falling star, which flashed upon me, in the form of a woman—or of an angel" (4/10–11). Costello's translation interprets visibly, substituting Poe's words from the opening of "Berenice," I assume purposely. (*Faqr* and *maskanat* both convey denotatively the idea of economic poverty; compare Lescot's French translation, which says "en ce monde vil et misérable," whereas Baudelaire's French equivalents were *malheur* and *misère*.) As in "Berenice" sorrow is the result of joy, and the specific incident is introduced as a universal manifesto of misery.

The image of light is also ambiguous: "In its light, in the course of a second, of a single moment, I beheld all the wretchedness [*badbakhti-hâ*] of my existence and apprehended the glory and splendour" (4/11).[2] The light is presented as a mixed blessing because it is beautiful in itself, synonymous with the ethereal woman, but also the agent that has revealed to him the relative ugliness of his own environment. The ethereal woman is in a larger sense a paradox because she is at once a source of vision and an obstruction, the channel through which the speaker acknowledges the existence of his wife but at the same time a device he substitutes for her.

Costello's choice of "wretchedness" and "misery" suggests that he noticed the resemblance of *The Blind Owl* to "Berenice." "Berenice" itself looks consciously back at a tradition too; the chain of ancestors and the mansion that is a concretion of their eccentricity and a way of immersing the speaker in the generalized identity of convention:

> My baptismal name is Egaeus; that of my family I will not mention. Yet there are no towers in the land more time-honored than my gloomy, gray, hereditary halls. Our line has been called a race of visionaries; and in many striking particulars—in the character of the family mansion—in the chiselling of some buttresses in the armory—but more especially in the gallery of antique paintings—in the fashion of the library chamber—and, lastly, in the very peculiar nature of the library's contents—there is more than sufficient evidence to warrant the belief.
>
> (*CWP* 2.209)

Egaeus seems for a moment to introduce himself straightforwardly, but the emphasis turns out to be on "baptismal" and not "Egaeus," so that the rest of the paragraph turns on a negation, the concealment of the family name. The tactic of concealment has two sides: on the one hand it suggests a realistic dimension to the story, as if we should surely recognize that family name if we heard it. (The notion of a family name concealed on account of its familiarity is varied nine years later in the observation about the geographical guessing game in "The Purloined Letter" [*CWP* 3.989–90], that it is the obvious place-names written in enormous letters that are the hardest to find. This is in small the gesture of romance, which makes the action seem distant and exotic in order to say truths intended to appear utterly familiar and universal.) The familiarity of Egaeus's last name paradoxically takes him out of the known world, into a literary frame of reference that loops out first into a medieval past and then anchors itself in the physical mansion.

Finally, what most epitomizes the family is not so much the edifice as a whole but a particular room, or rather the books in it. Appropriately for a narrative that hearkens insistently to its own conventionality, its hero seems to have been born in the library: "The recollections of my earliest years are connected with that chamber, and with its volumes—of which latter I will say no more. Here died my mother. Herein was I born" (*CWP* 2.209). The parenthetical observation that he will say nothing of the books is not true (he will list them in some detail in the second section), a significant error not only because it shows an example of Egaeus's limited self-awareness, but also because it is a phrase from one of his books (the epigraph of the story, the Latin quotation translated from the obscure ninth-century poet Ibn Zayyat, which suggests that visiting the grave of a deceased beloved will alleviate the lover's pain) that turns out to be the final impetus (*incitamentum*) for Egaeus's act of aggression against Berenice. Halliburton's comment on the chamber links the association of hero and room with the act: "the objective correlative of [Egaeus's] . . . consciousness is the chamber . . . so far as he is aware, he has never left it; he *cannot* leave it, consciously, because its boundaries are identical with consciousness" (Halliburton, 200–201). For Egaeus's act of violence to take place offstage means that it takes place outside his knowledge, without his conscious volition. (The scene in which Egaeus visits Berenice's seemingly lifeless body, laid out before her burial, was deleted from the 1845 reprint in the *Broadway Journal*, an act of censorship that becomes clearer in light of Halliburton's reading.)

Eve Kosofsky Sedgewick's redefinition of Gothic conventions proposes that the source of horror is not contained in the Gothic space at all, but in the relation between the inside and outside. The relation between worlds outside and inside the Gothic barrier (inside and outside the monastery walls, or inside and outside the barriers of subjective experience, as in the relation of the dream world to the waking one) is typically one of identity. Thus the real Gothic horror is the crossing of the barrier, or waking to find the nightmare was true. Her proposal allows a stunning structural linkage of the theme of enclosure and that of the double; settings become, like selves, enclosures that we escape only to find the same thing awaiting us outside. It also puts limits around the concept of the setting that can be applied to "Berenice." It is as if in "Berenice" Poe attempted to take the technique of spatial compression farther than it would go effectively. If the house is a concretion of a character's sinister or eccentric nature, we expect to penetrate to its core spatially; the center or depths of the house we expect to be the locus of its most intense vision of evil. But in "Berenice" the horror takes place outside, and the walls of the house work as a barrier between us and Egaeus's crime.

The nature of the crime also complicates our response. Egaeus realizes at the end that he has dug up Berenice and extracted her teeth; presumably our horror stems from the enormity of that aggression. But then there is the additional detail that Berenice was actually in a cataleptic trance and (in another minor romance theme well known from *Romeo and Juliet*) buried alive. This means that digging her up has saved her life (unless the shock of having her teeth removed has dispatched her again). The agents of horror work against one another.

The schematic nature of "Berenice" allows us to see more clearly than elsewhere in Gothic writing the transition from the Gothic trope to the Freudian image of the mind as an incompletely knowable construct. Egaeus's edifice and mind are an uncanny foreshadowing of popular Freudianism, and it takes next to no imagination for us to see the outside world as the land of the unconscious and the chamber as Egaeus's conscious self. (A more traditional spatialization might make the outside world the conscious realm, the repressed an inner world to which one penetrates.)

Hedayat, working out a similar use of the chamber image, has the advantage and greater burden of being on the other

side of Freud, so that an equation that remains a tour de force
in Poe can be at once more schematic and less rigorous. The
house in part one of *The Blind Owl* is introduced to us as one
of the few concordant elements of the speaker's life: "I am
fortunate in that [*be hosn-e ettefâq*] the house where I live is
situated beyond the edge of the city in a quiet district far from
the noise and bustle of life" (5/12). The seemingly gratuitous
detail that the house by "chance" (*ettefâq*) fits the speaker's
personality is one of our primary signals that we are in a realm
of convention in part one. (Explicit reference to chance in fiction is always a place to look for authorial fingerprints.) Hedayat's first move is to reduce the Gothic setting in scale: instead of the convention of antiquity and exotic geography, we
have simply the house outside of town, separate from other
dwellings, "built by some fool or madman heaven knows how
long ago" (5/12).[3]

It is not an edifice with depths; there is no library, though
its counterpart in part two is the scene of a manuscript in
progress, and there is only minimal reference (in part two) to
the house as a link with the past of the speaker's family, but
the identification of house with self is made in more than one
way. The term translated in English as "ventilation hole," *sur-
âkh-e havâ-khowr* (hole that sucks air), makes the edifice figuratively a being that breathes, a body. As the scene of writing
that we discussed at length in Chapter Three, where speaker,
lamp, wall, and shadow combine to form an allegorical tableau, the room becomes a representation of consciousness
rather than the bodily self. And Hedayat pushes that connection to the point of redundancy (the closet with its wine, for
instance, might be, like the shadow on the wall, an image of
the unconscious). In part two, where the emphasis is on the
lack of difference between his house and those of his neighbors ("My room, like all rooms, is built of baked and sun-
dried bricks and stands upon the ruins of thousands of ancient
houses"—50/50), both equations persist. As a family inheritance the house is less a patrimony than a reminder of an
anonymous sequence of mundane daily events and bodily
functions, the stifling history of the smells emitted by the flak-

ing plaster of the wall (50–51/50–51). Meanwhile the emphasis on the speaker's two windows (51/51) suggests the analogy of room and head we know in Beckett's *Endgame* or *Malone Dies*.

We spoke of Poe as an encyclopedist of romance themes. It is as if he stripped the conventions down and redistributed the components to see with how few parts the machine will still run. If we see the romance patterns as a template located in a noumenal realm, repeatedly incarnated in narratives more or less responsive to the demands of realistic cause and effect (I am summarizing a little abruptly Frye's vision of romance), we may speak of Poe's gift as an ability to take the conventional narrative, the one we already knew before we begin to read, and position us in such a way that a new system of cause and effect flows through it. In "Berenice" the drastic removal of background contexts (economic and class relations, the "outside" world) calls our attention to consciousness, and the tangible thickening of the syntactic medium brings the linkage of setting and personality as far into the foreground as it will go. And thus the experience of the narration makes us share Egaeus's consciousness, with its inordinate attention to contingent detail. The romance conventions, too, are embodied in rhetorical figures:

> Berenice and I were cousins, and we grew up together, in my paternal halls. Yet differently we grew—I, ill of health, and buried in gloom—she, agile, graceful, and overflowing with energy; hers, the ramble on the hill-side—mine, the studies of the cloister; I, living within my own heart, and addicted, body and soul, to the most intense and painful meditation—she, roaming carelessly through life, with no thought of the shadows in her path, or the silent flight of the raven-winged hours. Berenice!—I call upon her name—Berenice!—and from the gray ruins of memory a thousand tumultuous recollections are startled at the sound!
>
> (*CWP* 2.210)

Here at the heart of the most conventional romance passage of "Berenice" the syntactic level seems bent on annexing the level of narrative. In fact, the syntactic thickening is the medium in which conventionality is established. The antithesis Egaeus is at such pains to elaborate can be made the act upon which the entire story is structured. The antithesis, Barthes has argued,[4] is the most stable of figures, because the identification of opposites is seemingly the most innocent, the least disruptive of operations, and here the opposites in question are the least problematic of pairs, male and female. And as they exfoliate into other equally unremarkable pairs—inside and outside, premeditated and spontaneous, pensive and thoughtless—we seem almost to be in the world of Milton's "Il Penseroso" and "L'Allegro." The apostrophe that breaks the antithesis, the name "Berenice," which goes flying forth from Egaeus's imagined reclusion, is like the *correctio* of the opening passage ("How is it that from beauty I have derived a type of unloveliness?"). He catches himself trapped by his own elocution, as if a pane of glass had gone up between the two terms of the opposition. (Hedayat's prose is of course radically unlike Poe's in its insistently "plain" Persian, its simplified lexicon, and its resistance to the ornaments of antithesis and elegant variation. It may be, however, that this innovative simplicity ends up calling attention to the syntactic level, much as Ciceronian complexity does in Poe.)

The antithesis is not unknown to romance: the trope of the couple separated by opposed environments is venerable. (*Romeo and Juliet* is one form of it. Hawthorne's "Rappaccini's Daughter," possibly influenced by "Berenice," carries that symmetry to its most schematic form, where the character and setting are identified so insistently that to remove character from setting is to end her life.) The image generated by the apostrophe we quoted above, where Egaeus interrupts himself to call out Berenice's name, is one of the most subtle and efficient images in Poe's oeuvre. The link Halliburton observes between consciousness and dwelling becomes momentarily explicit, except that the paternal halls are projected forward in time as a ruin; in 1835 it is already commonplace for a Gothic hero's mind to be a fine ruin, but for the heroine to be present in the ruin, unobserved, and not as a unitary being but multiplied—and not as an object of contemplation but as a multiplicity of potential objects that dissolve into a cloud of recollections—is to carry the possibilities of allusive language to their limits. (It is no wonder that Lacan was able to read Poe as a progenitor of psychoanalysis.) The flight of the tumultuous recollections, as if they were nesting birds (or bats) startled by the sound of Berenice's name, leaves us with the antithesis restabilized and the split between the knower and what he knows again intact.

After this passage the transition to the present begins with an account of their twin illnesses: Berenice's physical disease, the source of her deathlike trances, which threatens "even the identity of her person" (*CWP* 2.211), and Egaeus's mental one, the monomania that we have been looking at in his prose, which disturbs the identity of his conscious self. Physical health thus becomes immobility and mental acuity becomes instead an absence of consciousness.

What "Berenice," and in fact all of Poe's romances, creates might be called segmented romance, romance without the forward motion. If we shut down the romance cycle at a given point and retain the plot conventions without the marriage at the end, thus without the teleological expectation of a much postponed curtain, the romance conventions cease to have their seemingly necessary connection with marriage, or love, or passion—though it may be that romance is always about desire. Poe's violent endings, that imposed closure that seems to require a QED rather than a "finis," are a response to his withdrawal from the conventional ideology; the same may be true of the endings of Hedayat's short stories. Segmented romance retains the focus on interiority that is traditional in romance, but without the will that shuttles it forward so that the traditional relation of desire to its object is loosened; vision enters the system at a new angle. "Berenice" alludes to the marriage convention just enough to remind us where the framework is, distantly, located. We are told only that "bitterly lamenting her fallen and desolate condition, I called to mind that she had loved me long, and, in an evil moment, I spoke to her of marriage" (*CWP* 2.214). The next episode is the sight of her teeth, which initiates his obsession.

In "Ligeia" we have two love stories (the theme of the light and dark maidens, which Frye has identified as one of the most readily visible forms of unconscious convention—see *Secular Scripture*, 83–85; *Anatomy of Criticism*, 101, 196), but love stories that impinge on each other. The opening is perhaps more like the anticipated romance world than we are used to in Poe; we glimpse a courtship at a distance, in an ill-defined exotic setting whose physicality is attenuated by the controlling framework that he cannot remember where he met her first. (Again the trope of endlessness, or should we say beginninglessness.) There follows an expanded *occultatio* in which he confesses with great eloquence that he is unable to describe her physically and hints at the extent of her occult learning. The first event of the narrative is her death, and it is only in the aftermath of that event that we have a story susceptible of synopsis. If we were to flatten out the arabesques, in fact, we would have a rather traditional Gothic account narrated from inside the victimizing Gothic character.

The Gothic setting that occupies the middle of "Ligeia" is one of the models of the type, but with the difference that it is not a family inheritance, not a given already embedded in the landscape: we watch him buy it and outfit it, more like a writer than a character in his fiction:

> I had no lack of what the world calls wealth. Ligeia had brought me far more, very far more than ordinarily falls to the lot of mortals. After a few months, therefore, of weary and aimless wandering, I purchased, and put in some repair, an abbey, which I shall not name, in one of the wildest and least frequented portions of fair England. The gloomy and dreary grandeur of the building, the almost savage aspect of the domain, the many melancholy and time-honored memories connected with both, had much in unison with the feelings of utter abandonment which had driven me into that remote and unsocial region of the country. Yet although the external abbey, with its verdant decay hanging about it, suffered but little alteration, I gave way, with a child-like perversity, and perchance with a faint hope of alleviating my sorrows, to a display of more than regal magnificence within. (*CWP* 2.320)

The old harmony between inhabitant and dwelling is in place again, but the cause and effect have been reversed: instead of an ancient mansion that has stamped its gloomy impress on the latest scion, in the manner of Egaeus or Roderick Usher, or the accidental coincidence of them (*hosn-e ettefâq*) as in *The Blind Owl*, the environment is molded by the fancy of the speaker. Consequently, the position ordinarily occupied by family history is occupied by an individual. One effect of that substitution is to put Ligeia subliminally in a position of unusually sinister power. It also makes the character of the speaker open-ended in a way that is new to the conventions. The sinister inhabitant of the Gothic setting can be seen from inside: we get such glimpses of Ambrosio in *The Monk* or Medardus in Hoffmann's *Die Elixiere des Teufels*, and at times we are invited to sympathize with the Gothic figure as a site of suffering consciousness. Here we have not only a kind of interiority, but an explanation (rather than the usual undefined angst) of the origin of his mood. And so the exotic setting becomes an effect of the narrator's grief, a concretion made possible by Ligeia's wealth. Ligeia's wealth is also made to account for his second marriage: "Where were the souls of the haughty family of the bride, when, through thirst of gold, they permitted to pass the threshold of an apartment so bedecked, a maiden and a daughter so beloved?" (*CWP* 2.321).

It is hard to imagine a more completely passive role than that occupied by Rowena. First she is a commodity exchanged for wealth, another piece of stage setting, and of course from Ligeia's point of view she is raw material to be restamped in her own form, a receptacle for Ligeianess. Nor is she part of a network of emotional relations, unless we count this passage:

> In halls such as these—in a bridal chamber such as this—I passed, with the Lady of Tremaine, the unhallowed hours of the first month of our marriage—passed them with but little disquietude. That my wife dreaded the fierce moodiness of my temper—that she shunned me and loved me but little—I could not help perceiving; but it gave me rather pleasure than otherwise. I loathed her with a hatred belonging more to demon than to

man. My memory flew back, (oh, with what intensity of regret!)
to Ligeia, the beloved, the august, the beautiful, the entombed.

                                                        (*CWP* 2.323)

It is a scene of bondage in which we are hardly given time to
see from Rowena's point of view. The theme of the second
wife confronting the shade of the first was to become a standard theme of Gothic writing: again we can adduce Daphne
du Maurier's *Rebecca* and, closer to Poe's time, *Jane Eyre*.
Rochester's first wife comes to us (until Jean Rhys's *Wide Sar-
gasso Sea*) as stage setting—the source of uncanny laughter
from her hidden room and an explanation for the mystery surrounding Rochester's character. Jane Eyre is a Rowena figure
seen from inside. She is consequently more nearly a character,
less schematic, easier to identify with. Rowena is more a point
on a circuit than a character in the narrative: the space
through which Ligeia attempts to move in order to regain
physical life, and presumably to visit the narrator. Rowena
will come back to us shortly, but here I emphasize the schematic nature of the story in order to ask what unspoken contexts come to take the place of the relatively explicit social
contexts of novelistic treatments.

It is not hard to see *Jane Eyre* and *Rebecca* as statements
about the powerlessness of women;[5] the social vacuum of
"Ligeia" forces us to supply the rest. Marie Bonaparte discusses it in a group of analyses titled "The Live-in-Death
Mother"; Daniel Hoffman classifies it as one of the category
of tales he titles, in an inspired borrowing from Chaucer criticism, "The Marriage Group."[6] The difference is one of emphasis. Bonaparte wishes understandably to get back to first
principles (mothers are always a safe bet) and sees Ligeia's return as a memory of Poe's mother's death from tuberculosis;
Hoffman's treatment is more interesting because it takes the
story on its own terms and allows us to watch the deductions
on which a Bonaparteian reading rests. The nodal point of the
interpretation is of course the famous conclusion, the deathbed scene in which the dying Rowena repeatedly comes to life
and relapses, finally transformed into the figure of Ligeia.

But why shall I pause to relate how, time after time, until near the period of the gray dawn, this hideous drama of revivification was repeated; how each terrific relapse was only into a sterner and apparently more irredeemable death; how each agony wore the aspect of a struggle with some invisible foe; and how each struggle was succeeded by I know not what of wild change in the personal appearance of the corpse?   (*CWP* 2.328–29)

I suspect that generations of readers have felt there was something more going on in this passage than was immediately apparent, a residue of emotion beyond the horror of Rowena's compromised identity. Hoffman, citing an earlier observation that the narrator made in passing, that "the outwardly calm, the ever-placid Ligeia, was the most violently a prey to the tumultuous vultures of stern passion" (*CWP* 2.315), makes the deathbed scene equivocal:

> Are these the throes of the dying body struggling to live, or of the living body struggling to die? What other experience does this description suggest than the repeated, excited violation of the body in successive, spasmodic orgasm? Death is usually a metaphor of sexual experience, all the more so because his own nature did not permit him to know,[7] nor did the prurient mores of his class and time allow him to describe, sexual union in a normal way.   (Hoffman, 256)

There are questionable assumptions in Hoffman's reading (What are the normal ways of describing sexual union? Is sexuality really so much less a mystery from our historical vantage point?), but they do not invalidate the connection he establishes between the hysterical tone of that passage and the fear of women that we sense throughout Poe's work. When later he deals with the lovingly detailed eyes in "Ligeia" (counterpart of the dental obsession in "Berenice"), he does so in a masterful tour de force, making the psychoanalytic connections without recourse to psychoanalytic language—making them in fact in a kind of parody of the language of Poe:

> Consider in what ways mouth and eye resemble each other. Each is an orifice in the body, surrounded by lips or lids which seem

to open and close by a will of their own. Each is lubricated with
a fluid of its own origin, and each leads inward—toward the
stomach, toward the brain, toward the mysterious interior of the
living creature. The thought may occur which other orifice of the
body—of the female body—these two, in the respects just mentioned, might be conceived to resemble. And let us propose, for
the purposes of this investigation, a male ratiocinator who is
rendered incapable of referring to, of dealing with, of describing,
of touching, that female part.   (Hoffman, 234–35)

If that sliding of meanings from visible, public sites to private
parts—i.e., to psychoanalytic bedrock—is more rhetorically
effective in Hoffman's appropriation of nineteenth-century ra-
tiocination than in the clinical discourse readers have grown
to resent in Bonaparte, it may be that we should rethink the
limitations of the prurient mores of Poe's class and time. We
read Hedayat in a generation that distrusts the claim of psychoanalysis to penetrate to origins, and yet our reading of him
is drawn by the psychoanalytic gravitational tug; we will keep
this caution in mind as we make the next connection.

The deathbed scene in "Ligeia" looms behind *The Blind
Owl* in the scene in which the ethereal woman visits his house
in book one, lies upon his bed, and dies. Again we have an
episode in which he offers her a glass of wine, and the three or
four drops that fall mysteriously into Rowena's glass, which
precede her initial decline, suggest the poisoned wine in *The
Blind Owl*. The climax of part one is the woman's momentary
revival, which allows him to paint the portrait:

> All at once as I looked at her a flush began to appear upon her
> cheeks. They gradually were suffused with a crimson colour like
> that of the meat that hangs in front of butcher's shops. She re-
> turned to life. Her feverish, reproachful eyes, shining with a hec-
> tic brilliance, slowly opened and gazed fixedly at my face. It was
> the first time she had been conscious of my presence, the first
> time she had looked at me. Then the eyes closed again.
>
> The thing probably lasted no more than a moment but this
> was enough for me to remember the expression of her eyes.
>   (25/28)

It is perhaps necessary to consider how the two narratives are shaped to see how nearly the placement of this passage copies the effect of the end of "Ligeia," or how the same fetishism develops the same effects. If we are still skeptical that Daniel Hoffman's equation is operating in *The Blind Owl*, consider that in the eye's most vivid and morbid manifestation he finds it by lifting her dress: "I took the key from my pocket and opened the lid. I drew aside a corner of her black dress and saw, amid a mass of coagulated blood and swarming maggots, two great black eyes gazing fixedly at me with no trace of expression in them" (34/35). We have returned to the theme we made central in the previous chapter in the scene by the river Suran, the icon of the poet gazing at the lip of a vase, contemplating it as if it were the point of his own origin. If we suggest that all the passageways beneath the surface in *The Blind Owl* lead to the same place, we risk being as reductive as psychoanalytic interpretation can be; Gothic criticism would plunge into the cavern for a denouement, but we want a mode of vision that acknowledges that centerpoint without erasing the space between.

If what Hedayat told Mohammad Ali Jamalzade is true, that he had not yet read Poe when he wrote *Se qatre khun* (Three drops of blood), the Gothic story of that collection, "Gojaste Dezh," will allow us to observe Hedayat's sense of the Gothic before Poe. It certainly reads like an experiment in traditional Gothic minus Poe, Gothic that is gleaned from the usual sources in film and popular culture. The sinister setting is a deserted castle outside of town where the alchemist Khashtun practices his arts. This is the concluding story of the collection, the one in which the sinister protagonist, Khashtun, ends up killing a virgin because the formula for creating gold requires it, and discovers at the moment after the murder that the victim is his daughter. There is a germinal interest in history: the pre-Islamic names of the characters suggest a vague antiquity, already a vista of ruins:

> The castle of Makan was enormous and formidable, with three fences and seven ramparts, made of straw and lime, and it

sat atop the mountain near the village of Asi-Vishe boldly facing
the azure sky. Two hundred years before there had been a flour-
ishing community here, full of buildings and homes . . . [and
now] the destructive forces of nature and mankind had combined to ruin them: vegetable gardens grew at the feet of damp
walls and cracked foundation stones, and little by little they en-
croached on the scene [*mikhord va feshâr midâd*]. A stony silence reigned over this kingdom and the fields which surrounded
it.   (*SQKh* 245–46)

The narrative divides into five parts, which can be seen as
schematic treatments of Gothic conventions. The first is the
description of the castle. The second is the dialogue between
Khashtun and Rowshanak, a confrontation of opposites that
establishes Rowshanak's innocent sensuality (he has run into
her swimming in the stream in front of the castle and she tells
him that she lives only to swim) and allows Khashtun to make
philosophical observations of a kind we associate with Hedayat (e.g., "We shouldn't fool ourselves: life is a prison. . . .
Some people paint figures on the prison walls . . . some try to
escape and scrape their fingers to no avail. Some just cry, but
in the final analysis we're forced to fool ourselves, just fool
ourselves"—*SQKh* 251–52). A third section focuses on the
perspectives of the villagers and their rumors about Khashtun.
In a pair of closing scenes we see Khashtun in the environment
that reflects him (an alchemist's laboratory full of alembics
and flasks), where we hear a soliloquy that negates the philosophical dialogue in terms so caricatured that they look forward to the cartoon miser of *Hâjji Aqâ*: "All those people who
are disgusted by me now will fall to the ground at my feet.
They'll beg me just to swear at them; they'll kiss the hem of
my robe . . . money . . . money (he cackles to himself) . . .
money will be as common to me as ashes" (*SQKh* 259).

There is a fundamental ambiguity of character that readers
of *The Blind Owl* will recognize: just as in *The Blind Owl* a
conflict of identification provokes us to agree with the speaker
when he criticizes his society but to see him as insane in the
same critical act, so here Khashtun, who is the Hedayatian

philosopher in the dialogue with Rowshanak, becomes at the conclusion not just the mad scientist but a mad scientist whose sole motivation is wealth. (We have discussed a similar pattern in "Suratak-hâ" [Masks] from the same collection.) If we find "Gojaste Dezh" naive, it is not for this discrepancy in itself; the split between outside and inside is a venerable one, especially in Gothic, where revelations of benevolent characters who turn sinister are accepted. We can see how Khashtun's overpowering greed creates a link between the power of Gothic conventions and the demand for a thematics of social concern. The incidental Gothic details of Khashtun's physical presence and surroundings (the dark, cavelike underground room with its five dewy steps leading down to it, his long Nosferatian fingers) create the impression of a cold-blooded narrator, taking in the horrifying scenes he describes with a dispassionate eye, and this impression is at its height during the scene that details the sacrifice:

> He quickly pulled away the white cloth in which she had been wrapped and Rowshanak's face appeared, with its dishevelled hair and long eye lashes, eyes shut and breathing gently. . . . From a page of his book he began to chant a spell by the light of his oil lamp. When he was through he bound her hands and feet tightly to the bench, picked up the sword and with a single stroke lowered it into Rowshanak's throat. Blood erupted and spattered Khashtun's face and head. He wiped his face with the sleeve of his robe. Again he began to chant his secret spell. In the light of the furnace, with his bloody face and staring eyes, his beard working up and down beneath his chin, he took on a mysterious appearance [be-shekl-e marmuzi dar âmade bud]. Rowshanak gave a massive shudder and her head drooped from the edge of the board. Khashtun picked up an instrument like a funnel, with one end open and a narrow spout on the other, and held it beneath her throat. She gave another more violent shudder and her head jerked to one side. Khashtun took her bloody head and twisted it, and as the blood began to drip in single drops Khashtun collected it as carefully as possible in little glasses. He picked up still another glass, began to press against

her throat, brought the oil-burning lamp closer and three drops from the final drops of her body's blood dripped into the jar. But through the trembling light of the oil-burning lamp a patch of moonlight fell across her forehead; he saw Rowshanak and recognized his daughter. (*SQKh* 262–63)

There is a half page that follows in which Khashtun repents his violence, but the damage is done both within the narrative and in a wider sense. The narrator's dispassionate eye is also a kind of complicity. The climactic passage we have quoted is sinister for many reasons, but we will put the formal ones in the foreground.

We might speak of the narrative as an act of creation on two levels: the creation of the characters unwinding their fates and the creation of the imaginary law of nature according to which the death of a young woman is necessary for the fulfillment of fantasies of wealth. Khashtun's horrified repudiation of the act is not a terribly effective device for establishing the moral perspective, since nothing in the narrative denies the validity of the equation. It may reinforce it. In other words, the equation may seem a compliment to the ladies on the surface of things, but once scrutinized a little, it simply makes the equivocal claim in the abstract and denies it in a particular case.

Another way to reestablish the moral perspective is to read allegorically, making Khashtun the representative of a society governed by greed and the story a moral critique of that greed. But since his greed is unmotivated within the story, its validity depends on the assumption that we will recognize greed as an overriding problem in Iranian society. (As social evils go, greed is among the safest scapegoats.) If we set it momentarily aside, as an imposed explanation (something like secondary elaboration in Freudian analysis), Khashtun's greed may seem a kind of alibi holding a series of fragments together. Without it the individual parts of the narrative come into relief: the sensuality of the initial dialogue, where after all Rowshanak is naked, holding a shirt against her front, and the overtones of rape in the account of the murder we have just read. The issue of Khashtun's greed, like the device of the narrator's seemingly detached and dispassionate voice, may seem simply a way to distract us from what would otherwise be obvious, that sensuality is very near the center of the story. The theme of the lecherous old man (such as Manfred in *The Castle of Otranto*) is common in Hedayat's writing, but we hardly need the wider context to tell us that the power that drives the narrative is its flirtation with the incest prohibition. Nothing suggests that Khashtun regrets the violation of Rowshanak except that she has turned out to be his daughter, a distinction that suggests incest (or loss of property) more than murder. (His regret is prepared for partly by an earlier remark he makes in the initial dialogue with Rowshanak—that we survive only in our children—but the effect of the story is not to suggest that Khashtun is horrified at being without an heir.)

Khashtun is insufficiently distinct as a character because he is insufficiently stylized, and here we can imagine what Hedayat would learn from Poe about efficiency of effect. Khashtun, for instance, is on the one hand defined as a wanderer who has abandoned his family, on the other as a presence defined by the laboratory setting; between the two his potential resonance as a Gothic character never materializes, though the component parts that would later make Hedayat one of the most formidable twentieth-century experimenters in the Gothic genre are visible. The narrating voice is a similar issue: Hedayat's naturalist detachment in "Gojaste Dezh" is obtrusive, discordant with the narrative's unmistakable sensual interest. It is a clinical voice that seems to insist on its innocence, and this voice too would be brought into the circuit of Gothic guilt in *The Blind Owl* (where the clinical voice is equally suspect with the romantic, emotional one).

We have delayed a discussion of victimization as a Gothic trope, though it is one of the basic mandatory features of the Gothic scenario, eminently present in every narrative we have discussed. In postponing it we have imitated the Gothic scenario; a Gothic convention perhaps latent from the beginning, certainly fully fledged in Poe, is the deemphasis of the victimized female character. Egaeus admires Berenice "not as an object of love, but as the theme of the most abstruse although desultory speculation" (*CWP* 2.214). The women's names in Gothic narrative, as Eve Sedgewick has suggested in a brilliant aside in an innovative article on Gothic, "suggest the blank, the white, the innocent and the pristine: Blanche (who lives in Chateau-le-Blanc), Virginia, Agnes, Ellena Ros*alba*, Emily St. *Aube*rt, even Signora Bianchi."[8] And here we must acknowledge a moral dilemma similar to that which we experience as members of a society whose "defense" is predicated on nuclear weapons: the position that is traditionally considered realistic, hard-headed, and neutral is posited on forgetting the irrationality of actually using them. Here similarly, we are putting ourselves in a rhetorical position that discusses fantasies of dismemberment, for the most part against women, as if it were necessary as a first step to forget the possibility that such fantasies, even when not acted out, make more thinkable all the petty violences that go on as a matter of course. And so I adopt a clinical voice as we enter that realm of violence and victimization (as if we were not there already), but not without misgivings.

We can see where the victimization comes from historically, the sequence in traditional romance where the woman is kidnapped by pirates and pursued by the pirate captain; here it is prolonged and segmented in such a way as to take on its own narrative logic. What has happened in the meantime is that the victimizer has become more a character seen from inside, so much so that his properties color the environment in which he acts. The boat is fixed in place; the storms that are acts of deliverance in the traditional romance are now another adjunct of the stage setting—another projection of mood. The thematics of the Gothic derive largely from the project of an ever more intense setting—a greater feeling of substantiality and a world defined by sensation and sensationalism. And however "tortured" the Gothic hero is, there is the paradoxical complicity between him and the setting that echoes him. The victimized woman exists in a tenuous manner somewhere between the two. There is no single way to motivate the mandatory episodes of victimization. To say that the Gothic is defined by a woman on foreign territory is to leave infinite means of getting her there.

It has been acknowledged in recent criticism that the Gothic scenario can be used in different ways: to acknowledge the truth of woman's powerlessness can affirm it or subvert it, or of course it can hedge in infinite combinations. Ellen Moers's brilliant observation about Ann Radcliffe shows subversion at work very early in the tradition:

> For Mrs. Radcliffe, the Gothic novel was a device to send maidens on distant and exciting journeys without offending the proprieties. In the power of villains, her heroines are forced to do what they could never do alone, whatever their ambitions: scurry up the top of pasteboard Alps, spy out exotic vistas, penetrate bandit-infested forests. And indoors, inside Mrs. Radcliffe's castles, her heroines can scuttle miles along corridors, descend into dungeons, and explore secret chambers without a chaperone, because the Gothic castle, however much in ruins, is still an indoor and therefore freely female space. In Mrs. Radcliffe's hands, the Gothic novel became a feminine substitute for the picaresque, where heroines could enjoy all the adventures and alarms that masculine heroes had long experienced, far from home, in fiction.[9]

What Ann Radcliffe saw in the underground corridors of *Otranto* was paradoxically a site of escape. Its paradoxical nature is important, because those otherwise forbidden ambulations are possible only within that forbidden fantasy space. It is as if one buys the icon of a walking woman only at the price of a sinister, threatening backdrop for her to walk in. Moers's observation has the contradictory dream-image quality that translations from fiction to social reality ought to have. This is a useful qualification to Leslie Fiedler's famous characterization of Radcliffean Gothic:

> Through a dream landscape, usually called by the name of some actual Italian place, a girl flees in terror and alone amid crumbling castles, antique dungeons, and ghosts who are never really ghosts. She nearly escapes her terrible persecutors, who

seek her out of lust and greed, but is caught; escapes again and
is caught; escapes once more and is caught (the middle of Mrs.
Radcliffe's books seem in their compulsive repetitiveness a self-
duplicating nightmare from which it is impossible to wake); finally breaks free altogether and is married to the virtuous lover
who has all along worked (and suffered equally with her) to save
her.[10]

The Gothic scenario, in other words, is a crossing point for
competing interests and ideologies. (It is, in the term Frye uses
of romance, repeatedly kidnapped.) But even this image may
mislead us because it is so difficult to determine whether anyone knows on which side they are skirmishing. The meanings
of the violent confrontations are always subject to reinterpretation. The Marquis de Sade admired Ann Radcliffe's novels;
imitators beginning with Matthew Lewis, whose *Monk* dis-
mayed her, portrayed the new Emilys and Ellenas as "quintessentially a defenseless victim, a weakling, a whimpering, trembling, cowering little piece of propriety whose sufferings are
the source of her erotic fascination" (Moers, 137). Fredric
Jameson has distinguished (in *The Political Unconscious*,
107–8) between what he calls semantic and syntactic approaches to genre.[11] A semantic approach takes the genre as a
mode and looks for a "Gothic spirit," the "message" of
Gothic. A syntactic approach would ask, like Propp, how
Gothic operates, what its rules permit the Gothic writer to say.
For Jameson the two are fundamentally incommensurate: it is
clear that I have been attempting to construct a syntactic understanding of Gothic as a genre, but nonetheless I am
tempted to feel that there may in fact be something like a
Gothic vision, in spite of the multiple purposes to which it is
put.

The schema that the Gothic emphasis on setting revolves
around, or shuttles through, is in its way a blueprint of relations between the sexes. It would be misleading to say that a
particular message, feminist or antifeminist, is coded into the
Gothic system, but the asymmetry of sexual relations is unmistakably written into the foundations of Gothic style, if

only because the gentleman is represented at two places in the equation, the maiden only in one. The subversions of, say, Radcliffean Gothic exist for us only when we acknowledge that a scenario of women engaging actively and positively in the realm of power goes against the grain (which requires us, of course, to acknowledge that there is a grain). A clearly didactic and committed treatment of Gothic themes such as *Jane Eyre*, where the subject of woman's powerlessness makes available even to the slow-witted the rage of a talented, powerless woman, does so by its charming accommodations to the given structures of power. *Jane Eyre* is as much about the obstacles that keep Rochester from pursuing his desire, the prices he must pay, the punishments he must undergo, as it is about the person from whose point of view the story is told. (Appropriately, Rochester's blindness is effected by a falling beam of his house; the edifice has become an intermediary between the first wife, who set the fire, and Rochester, as the exotic edifice in "Ligeia" becomes an intermediary between Ligeia and the speaker.) To the extent that the personality of the Gothic character ensconced in the Gothic setting is the subject of the narrative, we are in the realm of male apologetics, an account of the mysterious barriers that prevent our talking sense across the gaps that separate the genders. If we continue to speak of a Gothic "vision," to some extent with irony, it is an intensification of what we have all experienced—the structure of families, the power we feel flowing through them, the conflicts that lie latent in them projected into the narrative as potential violence.

The two settings of *The Blind Owl* can be read as a commentary on this definition of the Gothic vision: they are scenes first of romantic solitude, in which domestic drama is simply not an issue, and then of domestic claustrophobia, in which the closeness of the family (the nurse's intimacy, the reminder of dying generations who have lived in the house before him) gradually takes the place of the unexplained existential anxiety of the opening. What Hedayat seems to have perceived, or intuited, about the Gothic traditions is exactly this domestic context; much of the beauty of the dreamlike, unexplained mi-

metic spareness of the first part of *The Blind Owl* is the resonance we hear within that silence, the psychoanalytic dimensions to which the narrator is deaf, and the stock of Gothic
narratives with their roots in generations of previous Gothic
writers. What is the difference between the ethereal woman's
unmotivated, mysterious arrival at his door and the arrival of,
say, a new governess at the Gothic castle in *Jane Eyre* or *The
Turn of the Screw* or the arrival in state of Isabella in *The
Castle of Otranto* or Emily in *The Mysteries of Udolpho*? One
difference is that it follows those narratives and in a sense de-
natures them, comments on them by draining them of their
context. Drained of context, the opening scenes are like an
encyclopedia of excerpts, Gothic motifs against a blank backdrop; part two allows context and with it affect to flow back
in, and the positioning of the murder makes us feel it is there
to explain something—perhaps about romantic love, perhaps
about the Gothic conventions, perhaps about families.

To say that the Gothic is on the one hand male apologetics
but on the other hand a space in which both men and women
try out provisional scenarios is of course to neutralize the eth-
ical question I raised a moment before. Thus we remind ourselves again: with Hedayat it is necessary to deal with ugly
misogynist fantasies. The death of the ethereal woman in part
one is seemly and seemingly gentle; the counterpart scene in
part two is not only violent but underlined with all the emphasis that narrative closure makes possible: its place in the narrative validates it, makes it seem summational, profound, the
logical outcome of what has preceded.

So many threads converge in the closing pages of *The Blind
Owl* that the ballistics of the narrative make murder and enu-
cleation of the eyeball seem narratively satisfying, appropriate, natural. There is the suspenseful postponement of the
deed: the narrator goes to perform it once, but is put off by
the sounds of a sneeze. There is the recurring theme of the
reappearing bone-handled knife: he throws it away, but the
nurse brings him another (presumably with the hint that he
will use it to commit suicide—120/107–8). There is the gath-
ering power of themes of a dwindling selfhood, culminating in

the image of a self absorbed magically into the walls of the house: "In the light of the smoky oil-lamp my shadow, in the sheep-skin jacket, cloak and scarf that I was wearing, was stretched motionless across the wall. The shadow that I cast upon the wall was much denser and more distinct than my real body" (123/110)—followed by the dizzying concept of his shadow reading the manuscript he is writing, the concept we made central to our reading in Chapter Three. There is even an economic motivation suggested by the visit of the wife's brother, who admits ingenuously that she had hoped to have an heir to displace him ("If I hadn't had a miscarriage the whole house would have belonged to us"—122/109). We have said that the economic motivation is unnecessary, something like the imposed theme of greed in "Gojaste Dezh," but set against the background of the Gothic equation between self and dwelling, or self and patrimony, we can see at least this appropriateness to that episode: to the extent that the house, and the narrator's role as its perverse owner, defines his identity, the economic threat is a threat to his grasp of self.

The murder itself is of course not solely a murder, but the solution to a puzzle (another version of the death of the ethereal woman in part one) and an act of physical union. As an act of union it provides something like the traditional conclusion of romance, a kind of parody that we have been prepared for by the use of romance themes throughout the narrative; as an act of violence it satisfies the generic expectations of the Gothic. But of course it is both things simultaneously, and the result is of some importance. The violence is portrayed as an accident ("For some reason [*nemidânam cherâ*] I kept the bone-handled knife in my hand"—125/112), and it materializes only gradually, beginning with a threat to individuality that is experienced as pleasure. Even if we didn't know that such a description of sexuality was unprintable in Iran in 1936 (surely it would have been as unprintable in the United States), we should point out simply on its own mimetic vividness what an extraordinary passage this is:

> Her legs somehow locked behind mine like those of a mandrake and her arms held me firmly by the neck. I felt the pleasant

warmth of that young flesh. Every atom in my burning body drank in that warmth. I felt that I was her prey and she was drawing me into herself. I was filled with mingled terror and delight. Her mouth was bitter to the taste, like the stub-end of a cucumber. Under the pleasant pressure of her embrace, I streamed with sweat. I was beside myself with passion [*az khowd bi-khowd shode budam*]. (126/113)

We might notice first that the technique is not a description of bodies and body parts, as we might expect from a writer of Hedayat's naturalistic interests. Hedayat understood very thoroughly the eroticism of repetition and of judicious transition from specific to figurative language, but his understanding is never so clear as in this passage. It is of some importance that he is (from his point of view) visiting her in disguise (leave aside our interpretation that the disguise is his actual self), since the force of each figure is a draining away of selfhood, an imagery of being possessed rather than possessing. The experience of giving way to it is temporary, however:

Her hair, redolent of champac, clung about my face, and a cry of anguish [*ezterâb*] and joy burst forth from the depths of our beings. Suddenly I felt that she was biting my lip savagely, so savagely that she bit it through. Used she to bite her nail in this way or had she realised that I was not the hare-lipped old man? I tried to break free from her but was unable to make the slightest movement. My efforts were useless. The flesh of our bodies had been soldered into one. (126/113)

Iraj Bashiri has quite rightly identified that bite as figuratively like the cobra's bite that transforms the uncle into an old man in the story of Bugam Dasi,[12] and of course since among the old man's features is a harelip, her bite is an appropriate mark to accompany the "transformation" that follows. The split occasioned by her bite is also a split of consciousness, as the spontaneous activity of what preceded gives way to reflection in narrated monologue. (The questions the narrator asks himself are characteristic: first that the bite might be habitual, spontaneous, second that it may be premeditated, a conscious act of punishment—and notice how the second possibility reaffirms his insistence that he is someone other than the odds-and-ends man.)

An intense foreshortening accompanies the aftermath of this fall into consciousness. Everything speeds up, and speed functions as a way to deemphasize conscious agency.

> I thought to myself that she had gone mad. As we struggled, I involuntarily [*bi ekhtiâr*] jerked my hand. I felt the knife, which I was still holding, sink somewhere into her flesh [*be yek jâ-ye tan-e u foru raft*]. A warm liquid spurted into my face. She uttered a shriek and released me. Keeping my fist clenched on the warm liquid in my hand, I tossed the knife away. I ran my other hand over her body. It was utterly cold. She was dead. And then I burst into a fit of coughing—but no, it was not coughing, it was a hollow grating laugh, of a quality to make the hairs on one's body stand on end. In terror I threw my cloak over my shoulders and hurried back to my own room. I opened my hand in the light of the oil-lamp: in the palm of my hand lay her eye, and I was drenched in blood.   (126–27/113–14)

In a text that is like a lexicon of fetishized objects we would be wrong not to notice the way the knife acts out the erotic scenario on another level. But a greater narrative jump is the sudden (and if we were to hold Hedayat too closely to the demands of likelihood, unreasonable) addition that he has not only killed her but taken out her eye, thus enacting a fantasy of sexual union in which the man possesses the partner's sexuality as a presence.

We might see the conclusion as a series of substitutions or concretions, products of what has ensued previously in the narrative. The much-postponed scene of union releases the coiled intensity, the increasing pressure of desire that occupies the bulk of the story; the eyeball, besides being a device to produce a sudden escalation of horror, in some sense sums up that scene and, in turn, leads us back to "Berenice" and "Ligeia." (We should add to the catalogue the cat's eye that the narrator perversely and without apparent motivation cuts out with his penknife in "The Black Cat" and the old man's "vulture" eye in "The Tell-Tale Heart.") This puts the eyeball in a very central position indeed, so central that narratively speaking it may be forced to signify more than the available circuits will carry. There have been in the text frequent references to the woman's eyes, their liquidity and their reproachful expression; those serve to make the eye an appropriate node where meanings may converge. (On the other hand, we should acknowledge that in a sense the eye is an arbitrary object; at the risk of being cold-blooded, we can imagine heart, hand, ear, or teeth in its place.) We cannot help wanting to make the eye a specific representation of something with a clear outline, but we should begin by acknowledging its contradictory function: it is on the one hand a talisman of power, a physical concretion of her essence (like the portrait in part one in which he captured her mysterious expression); on the other hand it is obviously a reminder of his failure too, a symbol he takes on the wrong level by possessing physically.

We could say much the same of Egaeus in "Berenice," that he has made the teeth an intermediary between himself and her. The teeth were, remember, linked with the image of the rainbow in the opening paragraph of "Berenice," and when in fact his fatal obsession is born it is "their white and ghastly *spectrum*" that catches his eye (*CWP* 2.215). And since a spectrum can mean either an optical after-image or the band of colors in the rainbow, we are back at the image of Egaeus's opening paragraph, that of a brilliance that hides what lies beneath it. What the imagery underlines is the impossibility of his obsession being resolved, since it is as a reflector of light from elsewhere that the teeth take their power as a source of desire. Similarly in "Ligeia" the famous passage in which Ligeia's eyes are compared to subtle sources of esthetic beauty (a vine, a butterfly, a stream, a meteor, a double star in the constellation Lyra) is an effective *occultatio* but hardly a definition of their power; we are perhaps closer to a definition at the end of the narrative, when Rowena's eyes become the passageway through which Ligeia first makes her entry. Teeth and eyes function as intermediaries, as reflective surfaces, as mirrors, and the project we observe is the speaker's attempt to grasp the mirror instead of the object reflected. Lacanian lan-

guage, which makes desire by definition incapable of resolution, an infinite series of slidings from the ungraspable object
of power, works very well in dealing with this process. The
image of the narrator with the physical object, the lifeless eye
in his hand, is perhaps a cautionary message for the reader not
to settle for the lifeless object of a single unitary reading.

And yet we do have a privileged meaning as a starting point:
Daniel Hoffman's equation is as valid as anything that has
been said about Poe. But what does it tell us to know that eye
is a kind of code word for vagina? With Poe we feel secure,
perhaps wrongly, in assuming that he said with it more than
he intended. With Hedayat we feel the equation is deliberate,
but this does not tell us its function in the narrative. To portray the eye removed from its socket is to tamper with the
equation: is it an act that makes the site of the eye more like
what it is felt to resemble, to "castrate" it, or is it an attempt
to reduce that resemblance and thus to lessen its power over
him? Or is the eye, more straightforwardly, simply an object
of power that is by definition desirable? Psychoanalytically,
the equation of eye and vagina produces an image that embodies contradictions from the start, since it represents the threat
of castration but does so tangibly, offering us an object that
denies the threatening absence.[13] Like the figure zero, or the
word *absence*, it belies its own signified, tames it.

Lest we forget the obvious, the eye is also an organ of vision,
so much so that we are often tempted to think of it as capable
of taking in the scene unassisted by the anatomical network in
which it is embedded. "It is never eyes which look at us," Sartre cautions in *Being and Nothingness*; "it is the Other-as-sub-
ject" (Sartre, 339). A narrative such as "Ligeia" or *The Blind
Owl*, which promotes the eye to something like a character in
the story, creates thereby an animistic universe where intersubjectivity is called into question, diffused, mystified: there is
always the suspicion of an invisible consciousness present only
in traces. Not only is the narrator of *The Blind Owl* constantly
looking at things—judging and misjudging—but he is constantly under threat of being observed through the windows,
mirrors, and shadows that surround him. The world of *The
Blind Owl* is an animistic space and a kind of panopticon.

We have not drifted as far from the psychoanalytic dimension as it may seem: the novelistic realm of intersubjectivity is also a world defined by its absences—enigmatic expressions, unresolved relationships, and invisible intentions. There are touchstones in our monuments of Western narrative where the phenomenon of intersubjectivity is presented in its greatest detail and enigmatic irresolution: the question of when Penelope recognizes Odysseus in *The Odyssey*, what exactly is going through Eve's mind in book nine of *Paradise Lost*, the history of Molly Bloom's infidelities in *Ulysses*; we may suspect that the device we have been examining functions to superimpose the absences that run through such encounters with the more clearly defined absences that are the subject of castration anxiety. The presence of the fetishized eye makes the absence tangible and allows us to deal with it in the abstract.

II

I have been speaking as if "Ligeia" and *The Blind Owl* were the only narratives of their kind, but in doing so I have been avoiding a prominent one, Georges Bataille's 1928 pornographic novel, *L'histoire de l'oeil*, where eyes occupy the foreground and exchange places with private parts so regularly and with such minimal regard for naturalistic plausibility that we know we are in the realm of allegory. In its notorious ending a violent orgy, in a church in Seville, concludes with the priest's eye being removed. Michael Wood has called this scene "impossible to describe but a liberation to read" (*New York Review of Books*, 31 May 1979, 10), and in fact one feels a little ridiculous just summarizing it. The heroine Simone slips the eye into herself. The narrator sees it as the eye of the innocent girl Marcelle, who has committed suicide in a previous chapter, and the result is an inversion of the fantasy we experienced in the conclusion of "Ligeia" and *The Blind Owl*:

> She was lying prostrate, on her side, and as I separated Simone's thighs I found myself face to face with what I suppose I had been waiting for all along, as a guillotine awaits its victim's head. My very eyes seemed to have become erect in their sockets with hor-

ror. I saw clearly, in the furry recess of *Simone*'s vagina, the pale
blue eye of *Marcelle* looking out at me, weeping urine tears. . . .
I held Simone's thighs open as the urinary spasm contracted
them and rivulets of burning urine streamed beneath the eye
across the lower limb.[14]

At the end of *The Blind Owl* the unstated equation of vagina
and eye makes the otherwise predictable, traditional penetration of the knife into her body a violent reduplication of intercourse, a reading of intercourse as aggression.[15] At the end of
L'histoire de l'oeil the equation is stated the other way
around, instead of an eroticized eye a vagina that seems to see.
The effect of the climax of *The Blind Owl* is a scene with an
unspoken meaning, an implication or allegory, whereas the
effect of the conclusion of *L'histoire de l'oeil* is that of a meaning on the surface (perhaps more like the bold letters on the
maps, the Europes and Asias that Poe's Dupin says are harder
to find). Bataille's hero is, like Hedayat's, contemplating the
mystery of sexual difference, but Bataille creates in the process
a more transparent philosophy. This means that the thematic
aspect of *L'histoire de l'oeil* is more visible, more distinct,
more clearly separate from the doxa of common wisdom. It
would stretch things to call *L'histoire de l'oeil* a feminist manifesto, but Bataille's enterprise of confrontation with the realm
of impropriety valorizes the feminine by making it an image
of excess and the anarchic. He uses the formulas of escalating
transgression, which are traditional in pornography, in much
the same way various hands use the formulas of the Gothic; in
fact the escalating transgressions of horror that inform the
Gothic remind us of the pornographic formulas, and there are
even Gothic moments in *L'histoire de l'oeil*, such as the sequence in the madhouse where Marcelle is incarcerated.

The conclusion of *L'histoire de l'oeil* is still another variation on the victimization that concludes "Ligeia." Simone is,
like Ligeia, an instructor in dark mysteries; Marcelle, her vir-
ginal counterpart, the light-haired, blue-eyed innocent who
has been a partner in their orgies, gone insane, and finally
committed suicide at the midpoint of the narrative, is in a

sense her Rowena, except of course that their functions are reversed at the climactic moment, and it is the innocent whose eye returns to haunt the dark, mysterious heroine. The perverse ingenuity of this concluding tableau is not without its moral. We learn from it that impropriety is not a self-sufficient universe, that a philosophy of darkness requires its complement, that at the core of the realm of excess is a weeping priest's eye to remind them of Marcelle. There is a serenity in the expression of that curiously framed eye that works against the hysteria of the ending. The perfect symmetry between Simone's uncontrolled urination (a repeated leitmotif accompanying scenes of her orgasms) and Marcelle's seeming tears suggests a mechanical relationship between the realm of excess and the realm of propriety. In a passing phrase the scene of the eye is a "lunar apparition" (vol. 1, p. 69), a scene of sadness, melancholy and distant, unworldly, like the face of the moon, and the unexpected reserve that that image introduces into a scene of sensationalism is typical of Bataille: it focuses on the issue and reminds us again of the allegorical dimension that is less explicit in *The Blind Owl*.

The eye in the narrator's hand at the climactic moment of *The Blind Owl* is, narratively speaking, a device to intensify the effect of horror and hysteria. Nothing slows down our reading to call attention to the moral of the story. In the case of *The Blind Owl* the moral (if that is the word) emerges from the set of equations we have been examining: first the eye as a code word for vagina, second the equivalence that emerges from the conclusion, between sexuality and violence, orgasm and murder. (There is much violence in *L'histoire de l'oeil* but no such equation.) Neither is a new equation, but they take on specificity from the narrative in which they are set, and which they structure. Once located in a particular domestic situation, the seemingly abstract equation becomes a commentary on society, and the "philosophy" of *The Blind Owl* another version of the male apologetics ingrained in the conventions of Gothic writing. If *L'histoire de l'oeil* is a critique of domesticity from the standpoint of a vaguely conceived excess and erotic plenitude, *The Blind Owl* grounds its critique from inside: it gives us the spectacle of a participant in the domestic world whose horror at the rules of daily life raises his perception of the mundane to a kind of mythical intensity.

It is not a myth, but it is clearly interested in the thematics of myth, and like myth it articulates a social disjunction. If we start with Lévi-Strauss's proposal that "mythical thought always works from the awareness of oppositions towards their progressive mediation"[16]—that is, toward a scene that embodies in an image some irreconcilable contradiction in the community's view of itself—*The Blind Owl* becomes a kind of myth in reverse, acknowledging potential mediators and rejecting them. The mediation in question is marriage: the speaker is in a position where he is torn between his sexual desires and his loathing for them in his role as the old man, who is his sexual self. To put it in psychoanalytic terms is perhaps too easy; it is the conflict between one's own and one's parents' sexuality. The sacrament of marriage transforms what the child saw as frightening in his parents into something that is permitted for himself, but of course the speaker's dilemma is that he is able to reduce the sacrament to the words in a book: "The preacher [*âkhund*] by the process of reciting a few words in Arabic over us, had placed her under my authority" (63/60).

A secondary theme amplifies this doubt through a channel of imagery appropriate to Hedayat's biography: the ritual of marriage has a parallel in the ritual by which raw flesh is pronounced permissible food. Hedayat's vegetarianism is not explicitly a part of *The Blind Owl*, but the horror with which the butcher and his two sheep are described makes it hard, as we have said, not to remember it. Again, his refusal to accept a distinction basic to society produces a vision of horror: instead of a tradesman performing a ritually correct act, he sees the dismemberment of a body take place across from his window every morning, and at crucial moments this becomes very conscious indeed: "His movements . . . struck me as helpless, even comical. I felt that this man had no business to be a butcher at all and was only acting a part" (95/87). The analogy is not perfect between preacher and butcher; the possibility is left open here that another butcher who knew the proper anatomy might play the part properly.

If I am reading the text correctly for its "moral," the place where the rising tide of ironies finally fails to reach, it grows out of the central image of the climax, the identification of intercourse with aggression, and says that the relations of the sexes are just like violence. The terms of the narrative make this a tragic if melodramatic discovery; it argues that the world seen rightly is full of odds-and-ends men—that is, fathers—people who have taken the violence of sexuality as a normal state of affairs. There grows out of this equation a whole ideology of horror directed at the world of generation that Yeats in a serener text sums up as "whatever is begotten, born and dies."

To glance a second time at parallels with Faulkner, much the same ideology seems centrally present in his fuller fictional world. Bayard Sartoris's flight from domesticity in *Sartoris*, again a work informed by Gothic patterns, takes the form of risks, ending with his flying the test plane that kills him. The additional detail that his son Johnny is born the day of the crash is a nice Hedayatian duplication, which demonstrates what he is fleeing from. Faulkner's growing, sentimental attraction to the character of Ratliff (the vacuum cleaner salesman), who is so conspicuously free from the world of desire and family politics, is a fantasy solution to the same problem. Such characters are notably absent from Hedayat's world, where escape is not only absent as a possibility, but where it isn't much of an issue. I can imagine a revisionist reading that says since the speaker is insane this is a portrait of an insane definition of sexuality, that we all know sexuality is not violence, that the ending warns where such madness leads. That objection would have to be tested against the rhetorical force of the ending, which invites us to welcome the sexual union and the violence in the same act. The climax is a real climax; to read the book is to experience it.

The revisionist reading would be a worse reading than mine. I can also imagine a better reading than mine, which would trace a relationship I can intuit but not specify in its detail, between the statement that sexuality is violence and the fear of women that underlies that statement. The equation is like the alchemical formula in "Gojaste Dezh": as long as we accept it as plausible the denial of Khashtun's greed is a moral statement. Similarly, as long as we accept the implication of the climax, that we have witnessed a profound truth about the laws of nature, we can accept the pessimistic, Schopenhauerian conclusions of the rest of the book. There is a moral dilemma here that does not stop with Hedayat, since to read the book is to share the fantasies. How do we differentiate between a fiction that explains fantasies of violence against women and a fiction that simply expresses them, acts them out, rationalizes them? (An educated and in no way unsophisticated reader remarked to me that the book was frustrating to read, but the ending at least was satisfying because the villain—i.e., the wife—was so completely punished.)

The Gothic conventions are, we have said, a vehicle for making visible the circuits of power that account for the equivocal position of women in society; since Poe the tradition has offered very particular fantasies that explain the fear of women. What makes the brutal fantasies of *The Blind Owl* appropriate subjects for a feminist inquiry is not the story's implication that its narrator is wrong. The text isn't clear enough in its rejection of his madness, and in any event generations of readers delighted by the ending have demonstrated that the readers' experience works toward identification with the speaker. The act of violence is a source of narrative power whether it is rejected or not. The question appropriate for our feminist inquiry is whether or not those fantasies explain their source in the process of expressing them, whether they make visible the systems in which they are immersed. It is not our job to decide whether we like or dislike the narrator.

0

Chapter Six

SALOME: THE PARABLE OF THE ARTIST

I

In CHAPTER THREE we argued for a realistic reading of the narrating character on the grounds that a psychoanalytic decoding would naturalize or recuperate *The Blind Owl*'s antirealistic elements. This project was a partial one, even on its own terms, and in Chapters Four and Five we emphasized the generic limits that dissolve the speaker's individuality again. Hedayat's fascination with the archetypal and parabolic seems to stand in the way of any understanding of the narrative that places it in history. We are faced with the dilemma that on the one hand we read to come closer to the represented world and to identify emotionally with the characters who inhabit it, while on the other hand looking closely at the characters resolves the phenomenon of character into narrative elements of a more fundamental, microscopic order. In the case of *The Blind Owl* character is defined as much through contingent artifacts and stage setting as by social relations or intersubjectivity. Here what swim into focus are the artworks of part one, the paintings that define the narrator's obsessions. We are hovering in an uncertain area where the most equivocal form of communication is going on between Hedayat and ourselves: his imaginary artist has painted a picture that we pretend to be looking at, but that in fact we can come no closer to than the words on the page.

It is not particularly innovative to make these tentative moments claim our attention above more "direct" forms of representation. Works of art within works of art have always provided our anthology pieces, from the shield of Achilles to Keats's Grecian urn and Yeats's "Lapis Lazuli." Books nine to twelve of the *Odyssey*, generally accepted as a founding text for Western culture, are of course also stories within a story. The way that lies between us and a social context is to focus on the grain of the narrative, which is most tangibly visible where Hedayat shows us works of art within his writing. To pursue them is to postpone the goal of looking through *The Blind Owl* as if it were transparent to the society behind its walls. The detour runs westward again and focuses on a specific Western pattern, the story of Salome, behind which opens out a series of parables of the artist in European literature. They are parables that will return us to a theme *The Blind Owl* understands profoundly, a recurring Western fantasy that victimization and the artistic act are inevitably connected.

The Blind Owl is full of works of art. First, it purports to be a found manuscript. A found manuscript is not in itself necessarily a work of art, but part one of *The Blind Owl* at least is the notebook of an artist. We should perhaps remind ourselves that there are, in part one, two specific works, both of them reproduced more than once: one the painting designed on pen cases, the old man and young girl in a Persian-miniature setting, the other a portrait of the ethereal woman's face. In its repetitions this scene takes on the consistency that the stable reference points of characteristic behavior might take in a text dedicated to the novelistic portrayal of character. The second work manifests itself twice, once in the sketch the narrator makes by the ethereal visitor's deathbed, the other on the surface of the vase that turns up where the woman is buried. It is probably worth repeating this, since it is a common misreading to see the painting on the vase as another repetition of the pen-case tableau. In *Hedayat's Blind Owl Forty Years After* three writers make this error, including Al-e Ahmad (*FYA* 31, 149, and 165). But there is, of course, considerable emphasis in the text on the difference between the two. Indeed, the climax of part one is the narrator's belief that he has for once created something of a higher order than his pen cases. And if there were any doubt in the text, Hedayat executed a stylized sketch of the vase with its portrait in a frontispiece to the mimeographed Bombay edition of *The Blind Owl*. It is regularly reproduced in Persian editions of the book.

Its stylization is unmistakable. The semicircular lines that define the two sides of the vase are asymmetrical; the left edge is discontinued halfway down and both upper and lower rims are left unfinished, creating a vase that feels more open, less defined than our sense of equilibrium requires. The woman's face is a narrow oval (reminiscent for some observers of Hedayat's face) with eyes of exaggerated size (looking away from the apparent source of light on the surface of the vase) and with other features only hinted at by dots. The sense of effacement could be considered elegant or deathlike. The angle at which the bangs fall suggests a high forehead: a physiognomy of delicacy, perhaps ill health. A pair of curves to suggest breasts in fact produce the appearance of a male chest. The asymmetry of the vase edge is repeated in the unnatural roundness of her shoulders and a motif of flowers that frames the face.

The contrast between the portrait and the pen-case tableau can be summed up simply by describing the surfaces on which they are drawn: the first on a rectangular object (the papier-mâché pen case), the second an object of greater antiquity, whose roundness functions to repeat in small the circling motion of the narrative with its obsessive repetitions. The one is angular and distanced and holds the tools of a writer; the other is sensual, curved, and functions to hold flowers. It is easy to see which is the more positive of the two poles within the world of *The Blind Owl*. The identity of jar (or vase) and woman that Hedayat admired in Khayyam, and the identification of flesh with clay in the scene by the river Suran, suggest that in painting the sketch of her face he has penetrated into her world.

The portrayal of works of art in fiction is always a potentially paradoxical enterprise, a kind of parabasis in which the writer seems to be giving us a glimpse behind the narrative surface into the processes of creation; but readers have long experience in containing that potentially disruptive moment. When the characters of the pen-case drawing appear as characters in the narrative, they seem to broach their boundaries, to have shifted mimetic levels. We have the option of making this a Pygmalion story or making those characters into the models on which the pictures were based. The act of naturalizing the text is largely a decision of how much supernatural we are willing to leave in.

But the pen-case tableau is also a link with the world outside the novel, because the grotesque man with a young woman is the icon repeated so frequently throughout Hedayat's fiction that it becomes a kind of signature. In his short stories "Dâsh Akol" and "Mohallel" (*SQKh* 61–87, 221–41) we even have the detail of the doubling of the old man into a protagonist whose emotions are sincere and another who mocks him. The old man Khodadad in "Lâle" (*SQKh* 129–44) is a lover only in imagination, but there is no doubt of the erotic nature of his love for the young girl he adopts. The final scene of "Gojasteh Dezh" (*SQKh* 245–64) repeats that scenario in a Gothic atmosphere closer still to the world of *The Blind Owl*. In "Dâvud-e guzhposht" (Davud the hunchback, *ZG* 75–84) there is not only a grotesque figure who contemplates proposing marriage to a girl who is normal, but also an explanation for Davud's deformity in the incontinence of a syphilitic father, thus foreshadowing the sense of horror at the process of generation that characterizes *The Blind Owl*. Felicia in the story "Lunatique" (written in French, 1945)[1] reverses the pattern with her infatuation for the old Hindu cobbler, a reversal foreshadowed in *The Blind Owl* by the scenes in part two that show the wife as a willing participant in the relationship with the old man.

We seem to be sketching a very personal signification for the central motif of *The Blind Owl*, an obsession peculiar to Hedayat; but we should keep in mind that in the opening pages of *The Blind Owl*, the pen cases are represented momentarily as something more than a private image: "Strangest of all," the narrator observes, "I found customers for these paintings of mine. I even despatched some of my pen-case covers to India through the intermediary of my paternal uncle" (6/13). The story is never tested against another measure of reality, but it does remind us that the pen-case theme is not confined to Hedayat: that sketch becomes a subterranean passage to popular iconography in both Persian and European literature. Popular illustrations of Persian classical poetry in contemporary editions, inheritors of the Persian-miniature tradition, often show an old man, the poet, confronted by a young woman, the beauty of imagination, frequently in paradisiacal settings that include a cypress and a stream. The allegory is probably not indigenous. (It goes back as far as the figures of Plato and Diotima in the *Symposium*.) Taken in its broadest context it might be linked with the Beauty-and-the-Beast motif, which has its most powerful expression in contemporary Western popular culture in the film *King Kong* (1933), a film that made an unmistakable impression on Hedayat when it played in Tehran. The first *qaziye* (case) of the ephemeral satires of *Vaq vaq Sâhâb* (1933) is "Qaziye-ye King Kong" (10–15), in which a grotesque young man in the balcony of the theater where that film is playing seduces the girl sitting next to him, presumably because of her sympathy for the beast on the screen.

It would be possible to pursue the likelihood that the tableau is for Hedayat, as for his narrator in *The Blind Owl*, an obsessively repeated motif; it seems better to consider it a popular icon to which he was unusually attuned. It is clear, however, that it is in *The Blind Owl* that Hedayat dealt with it most thoroughly, reproducing the same icon in multiple narrative situations, in effect running the tableau through a full cycle of transformations, the old man moving from other to self, the woman from ethereal virgin to whore. It does not seem likely that we will reduce the figures in the tableau to fixed meanings. Perhaps the point is that the figures in the paintings occupy unstable roles, that the position of old man can be that of the victim (the spectator rendered helpless by the woman's beauty) or that of the oppressor (the master who has chained her), as in the embroidered curtain in the childhood memory of part two (82–83/77). In its popular form the role of the woman is ambiguous (Fay Wray in *King Kong* or Marlene Dietrich in *The Blue Angel*), and for that reason the most ambiguous incarnation may be the most interesting, the figure of Bugam Dasi in the fantasy of the narrator's parents at the beginning of part two. In the curiously buoyant, fairy-tale atmosphere of that narrative within the story, the figure we know from part one as the mysterious, ethereal visitor and whom we will recognize later in part two as the speaker's wife is in the role of his mother. The identification of wife and mother make this a nodal point in the text, a still center where themes converge and Bugam Dasi is appropriately the only character in the text who is given a name.

And a mysterious name at that. To my knowledge the only writer who has discussed it is W. W. Malandra in his preface to Iraj Bashiri's *Hedayat's Ivory Tower*: "Dasi is, of course, a well-known word meaning 'female servant, slave' and espe-cially in the compound devadasi denotes a 'temple prostitute,' precisely the occupation of the lady in question. Bugam, on the other hand, is no Sanskrit word, nor, as far as I know, does it belong to any vernacular."[2] Malandra goes on to suggest two possible Sanskrit origins for *Bugam*, both of which would require a considerable knowledge of Sanskrit on Hedayat's part. It seems more likely to me, however, that Bugam is not, strictly speaking, a name at all, but a transcription in Arabic script of an archaic title, the Urdu word *begam*, from an east-ern Turkish feminine of *beg* or *bey*, usually anglicized as *be-gum*. (The Oxford English Dictionary lists also *Beggoon, bee-gum*, and *begaum*.) Hedayat is likely to have known the word through French, where it is better known than *begum* in En-glish (e.g., from Jules Verne's title *Les cinq cents millions de la Bégum*). The vowels are, of course, altered, but the word is I think recognizable.[3] If Bugam Dasi is in fact Begum Dasi, the oxymoron of its two parts, echoing the oxymoron of the book's title, emphasizes the woman's ambiguous role as a fig-ure of authority and a victim of seduction, mother and femme fatale. I am not sure the text supports Malandra's suggestion that she is a temple prostitute, but it is clear that her function is to worship the lingam, which makes it ironic that she is dis-missed for becoming pregnant.

Bugam Dasi also suggests another art because she is by pro-fession a dancer. In this she could be said to characterize an-other world. Painting, the art of part one, and writing, the art prominent in part two, are solitary enterprises, responses to the narrator's fragmented experience. Writing is for the narrator a way of piecing together his illusions, in his words a way of introducing himself to his shadow. Painting is a passive reproduction of those obsessions, though it is represented to us as an art with degrees of validity. Music and dancing, on the other hand, are social arts, ceremonial communion with natural forces (e.g., the lingam) and with the past of the community. The music to which the narrator imagines Bugam Dasi dancing is "a music of mysterious significance, concentrating in itself all the secrets of wizardry, the legends, the passion and the sorrow of the men of India [*ke hame-ye esrâr-e jâdu-gari va khorâfât va shahvat-hâ va dard-hâ-ye mardom-e Hend dar ân mokhtasar va jam' shode bude—56/55*]."[4] This dance is perhaps the most important fact about the India of the story. It is not a realistic setting in which more mundane concerns are likely to compete with it.

Although *The Blind Owl* was published (if that is the term for the mode of its first appearance) and perhaps completed in India, its Indian scenes have none of the realism of Hedayat's Indian settings in his French story "Lunatique," or even the germinal, undeveloped realism of the speaker's own neighborhood in the segment of *The Blind Owl* that follows the story of Bugam Dasi. We see India only through the environment of the lingam temple, which is presumably its center. We know there are two merchants there, the speaker's uncle and father, but other than this no hint of a recognizable economy: we see characters with occupations like priest and temple attendant, and at the center of this India is the ritual music and Bugam Dasi's dance. Even the speaker's obsessive narrative repetition temporarily gives way in the process of narrating her story to a lyrical, musical repetition that centers on the second description of the dance (57–58/56). If we were to follow the implications of this polarity between a music-centered India and a decadent, artificial Iranian setting, the fallen counterpart of that music would be the Koran recitation of the odds-and-ends man, which is described immediately before the Bugam Dasi story (53/53).

The idea of the dancer as an embodiment of social values is not part of the Islamic world, except perhaps in the Mevlevi darvish order—a significant exception, though it is not one that would have appealed to Hedayat. It is central to Hinduism in Siva's role as Nataraja, or Master of the Dance,[5] or in the countless folkloric accounts of Krishna as an irrepressible dancer. It is difficult to tell how much Hedayat may have known about that tradition; it is clear, however, that through the image of the dancer he constructs a sexualized geography that combines his anti-Islamic reading of history, his reading of the Arab invasions as an undermining of Aryan purity, with the sense of horror that we find directed toward the world of generation on a domestic level elsewhere in *The Blind Owl*. The father and uncle, merchants, representatives of an Islamicized Iran, transgress the rules of an archaic maternal world, a virgin Mother India.

The image of the dance as a high art, even a theological art, is not deeply embedded in Western thought. We have the image of the music of the spheres, as least as far back as Psalm 19 ("The heavens declare the glory of God"). But an image of the dancer as central to Western esthetics is a relatively recent phenomenon, a development of the late nineteenth century that finds its clearest manifestation in French *symbolisme* and its offshoots.[6] Ironically, Hedayat's portrayal of India in the Bugam Dasi story is one of his clearest links with European esthetics. Frank Kermode's seminal discussion of the dancer in *The Romantic Image* (1964) approaches that complex of ideas through the poetry of Yeats. The central analogy sees beauty in poetry as physical beauty, poems as women. The spontaneous grace of unpremeditated gesture, unspoiled by education, is the virtue of Yeats's idealized women. "In women, as in poems," Kermode paraphrases, "the body as a whole must be expressive; there should be no question of the mind operating independently of the whole body."[7] The equivalent in poetry is an esthetic that avoids direct statement. Kermode sketches a polarity between "discourse," which is referential, direct, awkward, and the "image," which is not subject to paraphrase, which is indirect and elegant (Archibald MacLeish's "A poem should not mean but be"). But Yeats, through the parable of the dancer, exploits implications of that esthetic that are not immediately obvious: if the ideal of beauty is spontaneous in the dancer, it is achieved at great cost of rewriting and effort by the poet ("blear-eyed wisdom out of midnight oil" in "Among School Children"), and it is in this connection that in Yeats the figure of the dancer is seen as an image of destruction as well as beauty. "The Image," Kermode adds, "is never for long dissociated from the consideration of its cost; and to see how the dancer contrives to emblematize this also we must turn to the figure of Salome" (Kermode, 73), which Yeats does continually, throughout his career—Salome whose dance is bought at the considerable price of John the Baptist's head. "It is hardly too much to say," Kermode argues, "that whenever Yeats refers back to the historical concept of unity of being, or to the aesthetic one of beauty as a perfectly proportioned human body, the image of Salome is likely to occur to him" (Kermode, 76). He traces the theme of the dancer as a fatal woman to its clearest expression in the later plays, "A Full Moon in March" (1935) and "The King of the Great Clock Tower" (1935), where the dancer is a fatal woman who dances before the decapitated head of a poet.

It is of course very unlikely that Hedayat read Yeats, but this complex of ideas is by no means confined to him. It is again simply a question of Yeats being singularly attuned to a popular obsession. As Kermode demonstrates, it is everywhere: in the poetry of French *symbolisme*, in the criticism of T. S. Eliot, and in us through the effects of American New Criticism. The paradigm of the artist who attempts to re-create with great effort, consciously, ponderously, the results of a spontaneous mode of production is also formative in the Wagnerian and Nietzschean vision, which sees myth and folklore as patterns for high art, an esthetic that Hedayat was instrumental in establishing in Iranian letters. We are then speaking not so much of influences as of common modes of perception that are in the air. Nonetheless, particular chains of influence that link the dancer and the modernist are visible. We can even

point at particular individuals whose physical presence inspired artists, such as Toulouse-Lautrec's model Jane Avril or
the American dancer Loïe Fuller, who fascinated Mallarmé; a
sketch of Fuller is on the cover of the Vintage edition of *The
Romantic Image*. Gustave Moreau's painting of Salome is a
pivotal artifact, which enters literature through Huysmans's *A
rebours* (1884), whose protagonist, Des Esseintes, buys it. The
description of the painting is lingering and static: Huysmans
begins by describing the Tetrarch Herod, a kind of surrogate
observer in whom the spectator sees himself, a role the old
man figure frequently plays in the tableaus of *The Blind Owl*.
Herod is seated like a statue "frozen like some Hindu god in a
hieratic pose"[8] amid the vapors of perfumes and incense,
while Salome, holding a lotus in her hand, is described frozen
in the postures of the dance:

> With a withdrawn, solemn, almost august expression on her
> face, she begins the lascivious dance which is to rouse the aged
> Herod's dormant senses; her breasts rise and fall, the nipples
> hardening at the touch of her whirling necklaces; the strings of
> diamonds glitter against her moist flesh; her bracelets, her belts,
> her rings all spit out fiery sparks; and across her triumphal robe,
> sewn with pearls, patterned with silver, spangled with gold, the
> jewelled cuirass, of which every chain is a precious stone, seems
> to be ablaze with little snakes of fire, swarming over the mat
> flesh, over the tea-rose skin, like gorgeous insects with dazzling
> shards, mottled with carmine, spotted with pale yellow, speckled
> with steel blue, striped with peacock green. Her eyes fixed in the
> concentrated gaze of a sleepwalker, she sees neither the Tetrarch,
> who sits there quivering, nor her mother.   (64)

Hedayat's lingam temple is a lower-budget production, but he
has an eye for the same details:

> At this moment I can picture Bugam Dasi, my mother, wearing
> a gold-embroidered sari of coloured silk and around her head a
> fillet of brocade, her bosom bare, her heavy tresses, black as the
> dark night of eternity, gathered in a knot behind her head, brace-
> lets on her wrists and ankles and a gold ring in her nostril, with

great, dark, languid slanting eyes and brilliantly white teeth, dancing with slow, measured movements to the music of a setar, the drum, the lute, the cymbal and the horn, a soft monotonous music . . . and, as she performs her rhythmic evolutions, her voluptuous gestures, the consecrated movements [*harakât-e moqaddas*] of the temple dance, Bugam Dasi unfolds like the petals of a flower. A tremor passes across her shoulders and arms, she bends forward and again shrinks back. Each movement has its own precise meaning and speaks a language that is not of words. . . . Above all, the voluptuous significance of the spectacle was intensified by the acrid, peppery smell of her sweat mingling with the perfume of champac and sandalwood oil.

(55–56/54–55)

The resemblances extend beyond the obvious details. Even Hedayat's insistence that Bugam Dasi's erotic intensity is impersonal, consecrated, public, enters into Huysmans's description of Moreau's Salome. ("She had become . . . the symbolic incarnation of undying lust" [Huysmans, 66].) The expression, or lack of it, in the eyes of Moreau's Salome as Huysmans describes her is significantly like the expression of the ethereal woman when she first appears in *The Blind Owl*, who "appeared to be quite oblivious of her surroundings" (8–9/14). The lotus in her hand is also of some interest: Des Esseintes ponders its meaning at length, wondering if it is meant as a phallic emblem, a talisman of fertility, or a reminiscence of the ancient Egyptian funeral custom by which the sexual organs of female corpses were ceremonially "purified" by the insertion of that flower. The analogous flower, the *nilufar-e kabud* (D. P. Costello's "blue morning glory," Roger Lescot's *capucines violettes*), which the ethereal woman holds in *The Blind Owl*, has a fuller independent life as a leitmotif, but both provide a talismanic connection with another world.[9] It seems of some importance that Des Esseintes's thoughts travel so readily from the lotus to the image of a female corpse, first because it brings us back to the relation between the vision of the exotic female and the violence that has been our primary leitmotif in this discussion, but more parochially because the *nil-*

ufar in *The Blind Owl* also grows in the spot where the ethereal woman is buried (31/33).

We may be dealing here with conscious borrowing, but it is a complex process. As Mario Praz has shown, the Salome passages in *A rebours* lead us back to Flaubert's *Tentation de St.-Antoine*, and indeed to a whole network of nineteenth-century Salomes.[10] Flaubert's Herodias, too, dances "in the manner of Indian priestesses" in "Hérodias."[11] The Salome story is adopted by Western writers with varying effect, but the constant element seems to be a fascination with the idea of anomalous beauty: in Flaubert's "Herodias" it is the anomaly between beauty and naiveté, the young Herodias's ignorance of the power her beauty has over the spectators (in a famous lapse she forgets the name of the man whose head she has been instructed to ask for); in Mallarmé's *Hérodiade*, it is the opposite anomaly of absolute beauty and absolute, tragic self-awareness in the same body. The Salome story, since it deals with the power of beauty over the tetrarch's temporal power, lends itself inevitably to movements that emphasize the power of art. It was popular not solely for its violence, but also because it says that beauty is a significant force in history, a force with no necessary connection to morality. In the dynamics of the narrative, the head of Saint John functions as a way of translating Salome's beauty into quantifiable terms, as the thousand ships are a way of defining Helen's beauty tangibly in Marlowe's famous line. Thus Wilde's *Salomé* (1892) multiplies the device by having the Syrian officer Narraboth commit suicide over her, so that we are guided by more than Herod's taste alone.

Wilde's *Salomé* explores dimensions of the parable that open out in many of the same directions as the Bugam Dasi interlude, in variations that allow us to hear echoes between them. The obstacle to a parabolic reading is that Salome, unlike Bugam Dasi, shows evidence of a psychologically complex "inner" self. Her obsession with Iokanaan can be harmonized with a revenge theme, since Herod has killed her father, Herodias's previous husband. (The further parallel that Iokanaan is imprisoned in the same enclosure where her father was kept intensifies the identification.) This does not necessarily mean that the motivations are self-evident. It is after all Iokanaan whose death she brings about, not Herod's. But to make Salome a Hamlet figure, with Herod and Herodias as Claudius and Gertrude, does not clarify our experience of the play. As Jane Marcus has pointed out, Hedwig Lachmann's libretto for Strauss's *Salomé* is for the most part an exact translation of Wilde: "The only notable omission is the early conversation among the soldiers which describes the twelve-year imprisonment of Salome's father in the cistern which holds John the Baptist, and his subsequent murder on the order of Herod and Herodias."[12] One wonders if he omitted it in order to minimize the potential inwardness of Salome's character, which complicates our reactions beyond the demands of the play.

Jane Marcus's suggestion that *Salomé* can be read as "a parable of the woman artist's struggle to break free of being the stereotype of sex object" (Marcus, 102) does not require Wilde's intention to be useful to us: it is unmistakably a play about an individual's freedom and about affect experienced by someone in whom it is not expected, a woman artist for instance, though it is a misleading suggestion if we take it to understand that her art is somehow revolutionary or innovative. The question here, as in *The Blind Owl*, is how much realism the parable will absorb, and what kind.

The realistic contexts in *Salomé* take two major forms, political and domestic, both contexts relevant to the parable. Wilde perhaps more than any other reworkers of the Salome tradition presses its relation to history.[13] Wilde's Herod is the tetrarch, the figure of authority, but he is terrified of the other forms of authority that surround him, and of course it is his own desire—the wish to see Salome dance—that most compromises his power. We as readers who inhabit Herod's future see that the power of Iokanaan is beyond Herod's temporal reach. The power of Salome's beauty seems in this connection particularly ambiguous: does it mean that the pagan energy of her dance is supremely important because it is a necessary agent of the fulfillment of prophecy, or is it that her beauty is meaningless in the face of the coming order, which Iokanaan ushers in? In either case it seems to argue that art has an intermediary status: it is a phenomenon between the limited powers of the Herods of the world and the vast historical forces that dwarf them. Salome's art is not a distinct third power that comes between the other two so much as a device that rechannels the direction of preexisting powers: she intervenes between two aspects of Herod's character—the impersonal, official power that occupies him in his office as tetrarch, and his personal desire. We might find an analogy for Herod's two roles in Salome's doubleness, the beauty that is her impersonal possession, like Herod's power, and the inwardness that we may assume motivates her. We might see *Salomé* thus as a parable that locates art, defines it as a place where personal and impersonal realms cross over.

The other major context, that of domestic conflict, suggests clearer counterparts with *The Blind Owl*. In *Salomé* the father figures are multiplied with abandon almost as great as Hedayat's. There is Salome's father, Herodias's previous husband, Philippos (unnamed in *Salomé*), about whom we know less even than we know about Hamlet's father. There is Herod the stepfather, who occupies Philippos's position in relation to Herodias, and there is Iokanaan, who can be seen as a father figure by virtue of his occupying the same cistern as Philippos (and of his opposition to Herodias's marriage, so that we have a lecherous father substitute and a stern, chaste one). The image of Salome between two father figures could suggest any number of parabolic meanings, among them the question of the genesis of beauty (pagan sensuality versus Christian asceticism, both of which she rejects, or rather uses against each other).[14]

In the Bugam Dasi story the conflict is between the power of romance (the affair between the father and Bugam Dasi) and the invisible offstage powers who are in charge of the lingam temple. But it is not, strictly speaking, a conflict between biology and the law. The punishment by which the uncle and the father are put together in a room with the cobra in a way reduplicates the consequences of a fall into sexuality. Expo-

sure to the snake in effect alters the father's identity, projecting on the parents the doubling we have discussed in the narrator.

Bugam Dasi is also between two father figures, though of
course they are father figures only from the perspective given
us by the narrator. The father and uncle are interlopers rather
than authority figures, and because they are identical the focus
is on the act of doubling rather than on what they represent.
And since authority in the Bugam Dasi story is represented
only offstage, authority is seen as a formal system rather than
the initiative of an individual. The reader feels it flow through
the father figures rather than originating in them. The dance
that attracts them is part of the same scheme that leads to their
punishment. Instead of deflecting or rechanneling power, it
simply participates in it. The two powers, in other words,
amount to conflicting currents in the same order of things. In
other words, Hedayat's parable is an attempt to define the nature of things as if human choice were not an issue.

Parables that track the themes of art and creation down to
the politics of the family romance should not surprise us. The
genetic metaphors of creation are so common in popular esthetics that they constitute part of the field a writer inherits
and must explore. Mallarmé is perhaps the poet who examines this field furthest, and his early speculations examining
the separations between signifier and signified (in Foucault's
terms, "the Mallarmean discovery of the word in its impotent
power")[15] are the subject of Derrida's account of Mallarmé in
"La double séance" in *La dissémination*. Derrida takes for a
starting point an ephemeral piece titled "Mimique," one of the
commentaries on contemporary theater from *Crayonné au
théâtre*, and traces Mallarmé's commentaries on the problematic ontological status of writing, closing in on a network of
images that we might call the brushstrokes of the parable we
have been looking at from the middle distance.[16] Instead of a
family romance we have a depersonalized (one might even say
clinically represented) act of generation that never quite takes
place, a vision of spilling seed at a site dubbed the "hymen,"
whose ambiguity (like the anomaly of Bugam Dasi's role as

lingam priestess and the expulsion that follows her pregnancy) signifies, paradoxically, both marriage and the membrane associated with virginity. In other words, it presents the imagery of generation but denatured (a little like Xeno's paradox).

The subject of "Mimique" is a pantomime in which a Pierrot figure acts out the murder of his wife. Derrida focuses on his role as a mime, an art like writing in its status as a blunted (deferred, attenuated) form of communication, and the text's ability to refer simultaneously within and without its own boundaries: "A writing that refers back only to itself carries us *at the same time*, indefinitely and systematically, to some other writing" (*Dissemination*, 202). The mime is like writing because of the indirection that makes a referent problematic: "one can never know what the allusion alludes to, unless it is to itself in the process of alluding" (*Dissemination*, 219). The dancer here, as in Kermode's "image," is a privileged figure, but not as a vision of spontaneous esthetic grace; instead the dancer represents the sliding, slippery nature of writing. "The hesitations of the 'veil' [*voile*] the 'flight' [*vol*], the 'leap' [*voltige*], as they condense down toward the point of an idea or of a dancer's toe . . . are always, *in addition*, descriptions/inscriptions of the structure and movement of the literary textile, a 'hesitation' turning into writing" (*Dissemination*, 239).

There may be little difference, practically speaking, between a system in which dancing is a rare condition for writing to aspire to and a system in which dancing is imbued everywhere in the writing process, but unperceived except by the trained eye. It may be that one way to think through the differences between French and Anglo-American criticism is to think of the absence of a Mallarmé in English; it is hard for someone trained in Anglo-American New Criticism to imagine what it might mean to have for a major poet someone whose writing invites such close, meditative attention, which teases us out of thought so efficiently.

But there is also Pierrot's wife to consider. We cannot help but come back to the question of Chapter Five: why the piece from which radiated all of Mallarmé's esthetics, the piece that described nothing at all except itself, which was ultimately

about its own production, should have for its only content—
a content evidently so colorless, nay transparent, that it passed
by without comment—the murder of Pierrot's wife. It is not
enough to say that in *The Blind Owl*, as in the late nineteenth
century in Europe, the image of the dancer comes to represent
the problematic edges of the artistic process. The act of violence that keeps popping up does not seem an accident. The
mime dances, his wife dies; Salome dances, Iokanaan dies.

II

Wilde's Salome has a distant predecessor in Olympia, the mechanical woman of Hoffmann's "The Sandman" (1816), not
herself a dancer, but a singer whose art helps to lead the hero,
Nathanael, to his fate. There is a case to be made for an extensive affinity between Hoffmann and Hedayat: their common
interest in folklore, the occult, and the mechanics of hallucination, the state between sleep and waking (Costello's "between death and resurrection," *bayn-e khâb va bidâri*—1/9).[17]
Mostafa Farzaneh has Hedayat list Hoffmann among the authors he read in secondary school (*ASH* 149), so if we needed
to we could argue for direct influence.

"The Sandman" is not part of the same stream of images
from the second half of the nineteenth century that we have
been discussing. It stands outside the parable of the artist, behind it so to speak, using the same thematic material we are
familiar with at the other end of the century. In fact, what has
given "The Sandman" such a central place in recent criticism
has been its problematic generic status. "The Sandman" is not
a Gothic work, though Gothic themes abound in it (the mad
scientist, the double, the ingenious repetitions). Hoffmann is
never interested primarily in setting (his specialty is a narrative
speed that is impatient with setting). He is, however, an exper-
imenter in genre. Having inherited a romance form recently
widened by the popularity of the Grimm brothers' literary versions of *Märchen* (the folkloric equivalent of romance), he developed a particular talent of skirting the rules, of alluding to
romance without quite fulfilling the usual expectations. We

expect the marriage to Clara with which the story concludes, but over the course of the action the stakes have risen in such a way as to make that marriage a weak solution.

One writes about "The Sandman" only with apologies, though: the usual critical necessity of retelling the plot, since it must be told again each time, becomes embarrassing. (It is after all a story about repetition.) The number of intimidating essays dealing with "The Sandman" is by now considerable.[18] At the risk of considerable repetition, but perhaps less than there should be, "The Sandman" is the story of the student Nathanael encountering a crisis of his own past. It opens with a letter to his adopted brother, Lothar, recounting a moment of repetition from his childhood. A friend of Nathanael's father, the lawyer Coppelius, a grotesque figure despised by the children, has seemed to reappear to Nathanael in his student quarters in the form of an itinerant Italian optician, Coppola. In the focal scene of the letter Nathanael recounts a childhood incident in which he spied on alchemical experiments carried out by Coppelius and his father. The sinister nature of that scene is intensified by its sequel, in which Nathanael's father is killed by an explosion that accompanies their experiments. The character of Clara, Lothar's sister, Nathanael's fiancée, is the love interest. We are clearly in a realm where, as in *The Blind Owl*, light is an image charged with value: Clara's eyes are described as a lake by Ruisdael, reflecting a cloudless sky. Later, Nathanael calls her an angel of light (*ein Engel auf den lichten Pfad*). Her name (from Latin *clarus*, "bright," "shining") fits the same set of images.

The fate that Nathanael feels has overcome him in the person of Coppola is not the part of the narrative that has entered popular memory: this privilege belongs to the mechanical woman Olympia, since made famous in Delibes's ballet *Coppélia* (1870) and Offenbach's *Contes d'Hoffmann* (1880). Nathanael falls in love with Olympia (after a glimpse of her through a spyglass he has bought from Coppola); in the scene made famous in Offenbach's version he courts her at a ball where she is being presented as the daughter of her creator, the science professor Spalanzani. When, later, he spies her being violently dismantled in an argument between Spalanzani and Coppola, the shock drives him insane. Seemingly recovered, he returns to Clara, and what looks like a standard romance ending is averted abruptly when the lovers for no discernible reason decide to climb a tower. Nathanael takes out the spyglass he bought from Coppola, looks through it, and promptly relapses into insanity. He attempts to strangle Clara, who is saved by Lothar, and ends by jumping off the tower.

The overlap with romance is obvious. Nathanael's initial vision of Olympia through a crack in the curtains of Professor Spalanzani's house is enough like the first glimpse of the ethereal woman in *The Blind Owl* to suggest that the same kind of furtive love is at issue, and his despairing walks outside of town after the curtains have been pulled has its counterpart there too. The scene in which Coppola's laugh breaks into Nathanael's reverie as he watches Olympia through the telescope is of course a recurring theme in *The Blind Owl*, where the old man figure plays the same function repeatedly.

The device of the light and dark heroines, which we mentioned in passing in connection with "Ligeia," has in the Gothic the variation of the two wives. Hoffmann experimented with it constantly, often in the form of the apprenticeship choice, where the hero wavers between two women who represent different careers. Traces of the "professor's daughter" theme, which would become common again in science fiction in the twentieth century,[19] seem about to surface in "The Sandman" too, but of course when Olympia's nonidentity is revealed we are left only with Clara. This is also a traditional variation; we have seen it already in Jensen's *Gradiva*, not to mention *The Blind Owl*.

The isomorphism between *The Blind Owl* and "The Sandman" becomes clearer still in the light of a third text, a short story in which Hedayat rehearses the identical theme around the motif of the inanimate love object. " 'Arusak-e posht-e parde" (The mannikin behind the curtain, *SR* 79–96)[20] is probably the short story that, of many owllike texts, most thoroughly foreshadows *The Blind Owl*. In it, Mehrdad, an Iranian student in Le Havre, falls in love with a mannikin in a dress-store window. It is in part a satire on the limitations of a traditional, conservative Iranian upbringing. We are told repeatedly that Mehrdad is an exemplary student and a perfect conscientious son, "one of those boys who have become proverbial in Iranian households. Still [after nine months in France] he would no sooner hear a woman's name than a blush would spread all over his face" (*SR* 81). He has never spoken to a woman outside of his immediate family (a *zan-e nâ-mahram*, a woman beyond the degree of family relationship within which marriage is forbidden), and "at the age of twenty-four he had the social awareness and poise of a French fourteen-year-old" (*SR* 82). The assumption is that if anyone were ever raised to observe the puritan traditions of Iranian traditional morality this is how he would turn out, and as a satire the story focuses on the comic elements of his eccentricity. He falls in love with the doll immediately after graduating from his nine-month French course and immediately after that (representing himself as a foreign dressmaker) buys it. Hedayat pulls the narratorial curtain at this point so that we never learn what exactly Mehrdad's relationship with the doll is, Platonic or carnal, but we learn that it is a stable one. "Five years later," the story continues, "Mehrdad arrived in Tehran. He had three suitcases with him, one much larger than the others which looked like a coffin" (*SR* 92). At home he keeps the dummy in his bedroom, behind a curtain (that ubiquitous Hedayatian motif), and spends his evenings sitting in front of it with a drink, playing romantic music on the phonograph.

" 'Arusak-e posht-e parde" is founded on a pun. *'Arusak* means a child's doll as well as a dressing dummy; the root of the word is *'arus* (bride), presumably because children's dolls traditionally portray women in wedding array. Mehrdad's use of the *'arusak* is (as with so many cases where the process of embodiment and materialization of linguistic phenomena generate narratives in Hedayat) a physical demonstration of the root meaning. In the scenes that follow Mehrdad's return to Iran, where the intended *'arus* behind the *'arusak* comes into the picture, the tone begins to vacillate (very much in the manner of "The Sandman") between the comic distancing of the first pages and something more somber. Mehrdad's fiancée, Derakhshande (the name means "shining," "luminous," something like Clara), comes into the picture: she has been living in his household waiting for him over the six years he has been abroad (no doubt growing very old for a bride according to the standards of her society). It becomes clear that Mehrdad has stayed five years after his graduation because of his fear of marriage and that the doll is a substitute for Derakhshande. Once he is home, Derakhshande attempts to lure him away from the doll by dressing like it and wearing her hair in the same style. Finally she installs herself in its place behind the curtain. Mehrdad, meanwhile, has bought a revolver (presumably to "kill" the dummy; *SR 95*), and in one of those seemingly gratuitous violent endings we are used to in Hedayat, his horror at seeing the dummy begin to move causes him to shoot it and kill Derakhshande.

In Freud's opposition to Jentsch, his predecessor in the study of the uncanny, a central issue is the importance of Olympia to the uncanny effect, which Freud questions. We have perhaps already voted here, having put the ethereal woman of part one at the center of *The Blind Owl*. All these women who have been capturing our attention ironically dominate the narratives they occupy. We have been watching male figures whose obsessions are defined by the object of their love, and even when the being of the woman is attenuated, marked somehow by nonbeing, that nonbeing is the gap around which everything else is shaped. When we discover a woman whose definitive feature is that she is a machine, we may feel that we have come to the heart of the process, or the limit the process was tending toward, as if with a woman who was clearly imaginary we could see more clearly the nature of obsessed love. Olympia in her fundamental absence tells us a great deal about the rules by which women enter literature. (Clara, by contrast, introduces herself in her letter to Nathanael as a woman who thinks like a man—a negative definition with the opposite effect.) "Who in this story," Hélène Cixous asks, "would say or want to say, 'this doll isn't a woman?' Such a denial would amount to no more nor less than its contrary: 'This woman is not a doll' " (*Prénoms de personne*, 47). To have a female character absolutely without interiority is to see in intensified form processes we knew existed already.

Olympia as a doll is a nonwoman; in this the joke is on Nathanael. But of course to the extent that women occupy a system (most visible when they are portrayed in fiction) that makes them dolls or mannikins, the joke is on all of us. There are times when the reader of Hoffmann cannot help suspecting that he is perfectly aware of these things. It does not take training in the social sciences to see that dolls and women are peculiarly, uncannily aligned from childhood. It is considered natural that little girls are encouraged to play with lifeless models of humans, to invest affection in them as if they could return it. This is considered training for motherhood (perhaps it is). Hoffmann's story "Nutcracker and the King of Mice,"[21] since made famous in Tchaikovsky's ballet, is about exactly this: gender-linked reactions of Fritz and Marie to their Christmas presents are what generate the narrative. Marie alters with her imagination the grotesque nutcracker (in a sense this is how she makes it come to life), whereas Fritz's reactions are marked by his refusal to be satisfied. When the benevolent grotesque old man, their godfather Drosselmeier, makes them a doll house with moving figures, Fritz's reaction is to demand that the figures move in other ways, that the man at the window come down and walk with the others, that the image (self-portrait) of Drosselmeier come out the other door. When he is told that they move only according to the mechanism he returns to his toy soldiers, who may fit the category of "doll," but who are mobile and will obey his commands. (Does this mean that the Fritzes of the world will be immune to Nathanael's problem?)

Dolls are associated with women: they are what women are encouraged to become (as in the binary opposition "guys" and "dolls"), and they are instruments women are expected to use in order to become what they become. And so we might conclude that Nathanael's encounter with Olympia is a confrontation that feminizes him. There are two ways to read this, however: metaphorically dolls might be dangerous items that reduplicate themselves, fascinating the beholder in the manner of doubles or mirrors, until in Blake's phrase "they become what they behold"; or dolls might be, metonymically, extensions of self through which one overcomes such specularity. Through playing with dolls the little girl learns to extend her will, to control imagination in such a way as to prevent being overcome by such apparitions as Olympia.

Freud's stand on Olympia is well known: he opts for the former reading, deemphasizing her role in the creation of the uncanny and giving Nathanael a realistic biography that eradicates Olympia still further as an agent. Olympia, it concludes,

> can be nothing else than a materialization of Nathanael's feminine attitude towards his father in his infancy. . . . [She] is, as it were, a dissociated complex of Nathanael's which confronts him as a person, and Nathanael's enslavement to this complex is expressed in his senseless obsessive love for Olympia. We may with justice call love of this kind narcissistic, and we can understand why someone who has fallen victim to it should relinquish the real, external object of his love.
>
> (*Complete Psychological Works* 17.232)

We are faced with one of the fundamental problems of the vocabulary we have for talking about fiction: to attach the verb "to be" to fictional characters is already to use figurative language. To say that Olympia "exists" to a lesser degree than another character is to forget something important: that none of them exist, except in the figurative sense in which we grant "existence" to fictions. This is why "The Sandman" fits a category with works such as *The Blind Owl*, which have multiple levels of narration, stories within stories and plays within plays—because its cast "exists" on two distinct orders of being: characters whose being we accept throughout, and Olympia, who is a character only until we learn better. (And yet even when we reread, the residue of belief remains to the extent that we see her through Nathanael's eyes.) Freud's commentary, as Cixous demonstrates with subversive, sly authority, gets derailed because it does to Nathanael what Nathanael does to Olympia: it confers an unestablished interiority on its subject/object. (This in turn enables him to verify his interpretation at the end of the paragraph by citing all the patients he has had who share Nathanael's problem.)

We should not let Cixous's corrective reading blind us to the perspicuity of the argument with which Freud derives his conclusion about Nathanael. The long footnote interpreting "The Sandman" begins with a remarkably astute identification of a pivot in the narrative, the point at which repetition folds the story back on itself. The two scenes are first the episode in which Nathanael spies on Coppelius and his father in their late-night alchemical experiments and then the scene in which he walks in on Coppola and Spalanzani fighting over their mechanical creation:

> In the story of Nathanael's childhood, the figures of his father and Coppelius represent the two opposites into which the father-imago is split by his ambivalence; whereas the one threatens to blind him—that is, to castrate him—, the other, the "good" father, intercedes for his sight. The part of the complex which is most strongly repressed, the death-wish against the "bad" father, finds expression in the death of the "good" father, and Coppelius is made answerable for it. This pair of fathers is represented later, in his student days, by Professor Spalanzani and Coppola the optician. The Professor is in himself a member of the father series, and Coppola is recognized as identical with Coppelius the lawyer.[22]
>
> Just as they used before to work together over the secret brazier, so now they have jointly created the doll Olympia; the Professor is even called the father of Olympia.
>
> (*Complete Psychological Works*, 17.232)

This does indeed redistribute the action of the story in a way that shows us why Nathanael's horror in the second scene is so intense: as a return of the original crisis it fits the classic definition of the uncanny as the return of the familiar in disguised form. (It is also close to the definition of the double. Had Freud wanted to write a still longer footnote, he might have cited Otto Rank's *Double*, which is probably the source of his insight.) His redistribution of narrative elements is observant: the problem is the status of "identity." What is the force of the equal sign that goes between Coppelius and Coppola, or for that matter between both of them and Nathanael's father? It is (to risk another problematic copula) the same question we ask reading *The Blind Owl*, where narrative repetition is hidden on the surface and at least one episode reduplicates the alchemy scene of "The Sandman" closely enough to be a willed allusion or a tribute. Perhaps it will be so clear that it is redundant of me to say it, but the scene in which the uncle and father are tested in the room with the snake in the Bugam Dasi story is as good a structural fit for the alchemy scene as the scene Freud suggests for its counterpart.

It is the sexuality of parents that divides the father into those two figures. In the world of *The Blind Owl* the parents' furtive sexuality is emblematized by the image of the snake, which persists into the generation of the narrator as a bottle of wine poisoned with its venom.[23] Our closest view of the cobra comes at the end of the Bugam Dasi story, in another of the reprises that marks the lyrical narration of that episode:

> Is my mother still alive? Perhaps at this moment as I write she is bending and twisting like a serpent, as though it were she whom the cobra had bitten, dancing by torchlight in an open space in some far-off city of India, while women and children and intent, bare-bodied men stand around her and my father (or my uncle), white-haired and bent, sits somewhere on the edge of the circle watching her and remembers the dungeon and the hissing of the angry cobra as it glided forward, its head raised high, its neck swelling like a scoop [*kafche*] and the spectacle-shaped lines on the back of its hood steadily expanding and deepening its color. (59/57–58)

It is one of the most self-consciously artful moments in the book; the word *kafche* (scoop) catches the eye because in the previous description of the snake it was shaped like a spoon (*qâshoq*), so that the swelling hood has been absorbed without explicit comment into the contours of his prose. This is also the first allusion to the spectacle-shaped lines on the hood. Hedayat's use of a coinage, *mâr-e nâg* (evidently from *nâg*, the

Hindi word for "snake," source of the new Latin *naja*, the genus name for the Indian cobra),[24] instead of the normal Persian term *mâr-e 'aynak-dâr* (literally "bespectacled snake"), allows him to postpone and therefore to emphasize the image of the glasses until the closing scene we quoted above. Emphasized in this way, those markings not only defamiliarize the snake but tempt us into a reading even more directly biographical than Freud's commentary on Nathanael. In Iran, where Hedayat's face is familiar through a photograph in which he stares owlishly at the camera through prominent spectacles, it is easy to feel that this snake gives us a distorted, perhaps mocking self-portrait, as if the author had left his signature on the most equivocal spot available. (If so, the book's equivocal disgust 'and fascination with sexuality takes on a biographical, personal coloring.)

Their counterpart in "The Sandman" is the imagery of fire. Bachelard has commented on Hoffmann's fascination with that element,[25] and there is an emphasis in the alchemy scene on the mysterious source of the fire, which becomes the source of a sinister alteration of the father:

> My father opened the folding door of a wall cupboard, but what I had always believed was a cupboard was not. It was rather a black recess which housed a little hearth. Coppelius went to the hearth, and a blue flame crackled up from it. All kinds of strange utensils were about. God! As my old father now bent over the fire, he looked completely different. His mild and honest features seemed to have been distorted into a repulsive and diabolical mask by some horrible convulsive pain. He looked like Coppelius, who was drawing sparkling lumps out of the heavy smoke with the red-hot tongs he wielded and then hammering the coals furiously. It seemed as if I saw human faces on all sides—but eyeless faces, with horrible deep black cavities instead.[26]

We are spying on a place that seemed familiar but whose secret recesses were in fact unknown. The scientists seem altered in their rhythmic exertions, and the empty, unformed faces in the background function as an emblem to remind us that the act we are observing has to do with human generation. Fire

here is what makes reality malleable; it is a source of deceptive, distorting light and it makes substances melt in order to
be reformed. Molten metal in this world is like the moist sand
the narrator caresses in the scene by the river Suran in *The
Blind Owl*. (Bachelard's comparison of Hoffmann and Poe as
poets of fire and water in *The Psychoanalysis of Fire*, 90–92,
could be extended to include Hedayat as a poet of earth.)
Once it is established that fire and the parents' fearful sexuality are linked, it is logical that the father should be killed in an
explosion, and the power of fire persists into the next generation in the form of the pharmacy located beneath Nathanael's
student lodgings, which has exploded during his first trip back
home and which is the occasion of his changing his lodgings
to a place across the street from Professor Spalanzani, from
which he begins to spy on Olympia.

The motif of the sealed chamber where fathers are distinguished from (or confused with) one another (a motif
glimpsed in the cistern of Wilde's *Salomé*) is not new in "The
Sandman." Hoffmann came closer still to the *The Blind Owl*
version in *The Devil's Elixirs* (a book Hedayat mentions to
Farzaneh; *ASH* 143), in the story the hero Medardus hears at
court: two friends who resemble each other (Francesco, who
turns out to be Medardus's father, and the duke) fall in love
with the Italian princess Giacinta. She marries the duke, but
he is killed in the marriage chamber on the night after the cer-
emonies under mysterious circumstances. Giacinta, like Bugam Dasi, is found to be pregnant, and it is assumed that Francesco (like the uncle in *The Blind Owl*) has "taken advantage
of his resemblance to her consort," thus furnishing a prototype for the crimes of Medardus and his double in the next
generation.[27]

There is more at stake in the sealed chamber motif of "The
Sandman" than in *The Devil's Elixirs* or in *The Blind Owl*,
because Nathanael is brought into the scene when he is heard
from behind the curtain where he is hiding. Again and again
in "The Sandman" vision becomes a kind of action and repeatedly the screen between observer and observed breaks
down. This is particularly clear in the sequence of events that

generates the title: Nathanael identifies Coppelius with the Sandman on the evidence that the Sandman is said to come when the children go to sleep. It is not an illogical assumption, but like Freud's it draws equal signs prematurely. A psychoanalytically minded reader might say with as much validity that the Sandman is a euphemism for what happens when the children go to sleep, that their parents have their private life, on which children are expected not to spy, and that the Sandman is an image employed to enforce compliance. On the level of Nathanael's perception, however, the concept of the Sandman is an emblem of his own ignorance, that which is on the other side of sleep. (We have it on Nathanael's mother's evidence that the Sandman is in fact a figurative expression: " 'My dear child, there is no Sandman,' my mother answered. 'When I tell you that the Sandman is coming, it only means that you are sleepy and can't keep your eyes open any longer, as though someone had sprinkled sand into them' "—Kent and Knight trans., 94.) The definition that validates the title of the story (Coppelius equals Sandman) is then a project consonant with psychoanalysis, an attempt to cover the unimaginable with a tangible image, to represent prematurely what is not available to perception.

The technical challenge of writing a narrative in which the cardinal acts are acts of vision requires more than rapid unfolding of events: the narrator's point of view is itself in constant motion, a series of turns. The epistolary opening, where Nathanael describes his childhood encounter with Coppelius to his adopted brother, Lothar, is (as often in Poe) a common device to establish a sense of immediacy; but the next letter, in which Clara reveals that he has misdirected his letter to her, not only allows us to see Nathanael from the outside but reorients the first letter, which we now realize we were reading over her shoulder rather than Lothar's. The passage that follows, in which the narrator personalizes himself as an acquaintance unsure how to begin, gives still a third turn to the revolving stage. The most difficult turn in the narrative is, I think, the necessity of detaching the reader's point of view from Nathanael's to a point sufficiently distant that we will not feel his madness and death as an act of aggression against us.

That turn, the most painful scene in the narrative, is the moment Freud identified as the counterpart of the alchemy scene: the episode of Olympia's dismemberment. There is a rough parallel here between the conclusion of *The Blind Owl*, where the narrator repeats the experience of the trial by cobra by sleeping with his wife and realizing after the murder that he is the old man, but Hedayat has a more conventional task because the lurid intensity of the murder, itself a dismemberment (especially if superimposed on the death of the ethereal woman in part one), works as a climax. In "The Sandman" it is too serious, too frightening for the point in the narrative at which it occurs. We have been following Nathanael's naive faith in Olympia's reality as a comic eccentricity; everything has suggested that we are meant to feel a gentle, satiric detachment in the manner of Jensen's *Gradiva*. But when Nathanael goes to Spalanzani's house with his mother's wedding ring to propose marriage and sees her dismantled, the shift in tone is shattering.

> The professor was grasping a female figure by the shoulders, the Italian Coppola had her by the feet, and they were twisting and tugging her this way and that, contending furiously for possession of her. Nathanael recoiled in horror upon recognizing the figure as Olympia's. Flaring up in a wild rage, he was about to tear his beloved from the grasp of these madmen when Coppola, wrenching the figure from the professor's hand with the strength of a giant, struck the professor such a fearful blow with it that he toppled backwards over the table on which vials, retorts, flasks, and glass test tubes were standing—everything shattered into a thousand fragments. Then Coppola [in a gesture reminiscent of the old man running out into the foggy street in the closing scene of *The Blind Owl*—MCB] threw the figure over his shoulder and with a horrible, shrill laugh, ran quickly down the stairs, the figure's grotesquely dangling feet bumping and rattling woodenly on every step. Nathanael stood transfixed; he had only too clearly seen that in the deathly pale waxen face of

Olympia there were no eyes, but merely black holes. She was a
lifeless doll.   (Kent and Knight trans., 119)

To the extent that we still identify with Nathanael we are seeing something that threatens to break the generic contract.
(This is why a passage of clowning, in which we are told the
comic reactions of other eligible bachelors, intervenes directly
afterward.) In romance there is a convention that the realm of
erotic feeling and the realm of social interaction are separate.
Madness, in the tradition of the Majnuns and Orlando Furi-
oso figures of literature, comes from beyond the former
sphere, from the deep well of emotion we like to feel drives
our erotic selves. "The Sandman" betrays those expectations
by placing madness closer to the shared world, in the processes of commerce between erotic feeling and social interaction. If Olympia is a being without interiority, a mirror, there
is no communication of souls in Nathanael's love: his only
intermediary with himself is society; his narcissism is acted out
in public. The power of "The Sandman" is in our fear that
Nathanael's madness is not an interior phenomenon at all, but
something out in the open that we could catch. It ceases to be
a story about an eccentric individual, or a psychoanalytic type,
and begins to be about the wars between the sexes, which we
all participate in. Nathanael's spying has finally penetrated to
the ultimate mystery that the overwhelming power of the ladies over the gentlemen is not a biological phenomenon but
another generic or social contract we willingly enter.

What we like to believe about madness, that it comes from
elsewhere (as we like to believe love comes from elsewhere),
we also like to believe about art. Nathanael not only believes
himself in love with Olympia but also convinces himself that
he is a poet. The narration makes it clear that he is a very bad
poet, and that this is not one of Hoffmann's apprenticeship
stories; but he is at least as much an artist as the hero of *The
Blind Owl*, who is a painter during the fantasy of part one.

Irving Massey, in a provoking and useful discussion of "The
Sandman" in *The Gaping Pig*, argues that Olympia is a kind
of test for Nathanael's imagination: "Klara would seem to be

the villain, the representative of the bourgeois world that sti-
fles art; Olympia, the image of the ideal that Nathanael should
have brought to life with his aesthetic vision to become a ful-
filled work of art. But he is unable to effect her metamorphosis."[28] It is easy to make fun of this notion (it is hard not to
think of the resurrection of Tinker Belle in *Peter Pan*), but it
has an outrageous thrust that seems to pierce the esthetic walls
of the story beyond which criticism ordinarily reaches. Clara
is indeed depicted with hardly less individuality than her mechanical counterpart, and Massey's intolerance for ambiguity
has a perverse appeal. He is right to imply that there is no
particular reason given within the narrative why Nathanael
should be a bad poet; homiletic criticism could argue that
"The Sandman" demonstrates that narcissistic personalities
make bad poets, but do we have any reason to believe that
poets should be well-adjusted people? Massey rightly wants
the answer to be in the open, like Nathanael's madness. As
evidence that the option is available to Nathanael to become
a real poet, he cites "The Golden Pot" (1814) as a Hoffmann
story in which the Nathanael figure succeeds. On the other
hand, there is also the epically bad poet Amandus in the "The
King's Betrothed" who defeats a supernatural army by reading them his poetry; there is not just one Hoffmann scenario,
just as there is no single use for victimization in the scenarios
of the Gothic.

Another way to argue that Nathanael can be an artist would
be to show him creating something. And Massey points out,
astutely, that Nathanael does indeed write a story remarkably
like "The Sandman" toward the middle of the narrative. (On
the other hand, that story is about Clara, not Olympia.) If we
want to see Olympia as an allegorical figure for an element of
the artistic process, she seems less a work who might come
alive like Pygmalion's statue or Hermione in *The Winter's
Tale*, or even a subject of Nathanael's writing, than a depiction of the audience. Her esthetic suction draws forth his creative power, and the scene in which we see him fishing out all
his previous writings, because he knows he can depend on her
to listen patiently to them, establishes her function in the ar-

tistic process most clearly. Art requires trust in an audience: to see that trust is the most efficient way to see into the artistic process.

> He lived only for Olympia, beside whom he sat every day, hour after hour, carrying on about his love, about mutual sympathy kindled into life, and about their psychic affinity—and Olympia listened to all of this with great reverence. From deep within his desk [*aus dem tiefsten Grunde des Schreibpults*], Nathanael dug up everything he had ever written—poems, fantasies, visions, romances, tales—and the number was increased daily by a plethora of hyperbolic sonnets, verses and canzonets; and all of this he read to Olympia tirelessly for hours at a time. Never before had he had such a splendid listener.
>
> (Kent and Knight trans., 118)

The anticlimax of the phrase *aus dem tiefsten Grunde des Schreibpults* (from deep within his desk) seems a purposeful parody of the notion of depth, both the depth he attributes to her responses and the depth in him from which the verses come. One might argue that Hoffmann isn't questioning the notion of depth, simply that Nathanael isn't an example of it, that for a better poet the depth might have come from deeper, from his depth of soul, but this again would refer us outside the narrative.

If we want to relate Nathanael to a more capable writer, there is another dimension of depth to pursue. There are three levels of narration identifiable in "The Sandman." First, there are the stories and poems Nathanael recites to Clara, later to Olympia, at least one of which is a miniature of "The Sandman," stories that seem to succeed best with an inert audience. Second, there is Nathanael's fuller story, similarly enclosed, embedded in a whimsical text by a narrator who is also concerned with the responses of an audience. On a third level, which we know by inference but do not see, there is the biographical Hoffmann, who may or may not have something in common with either narrator, but who is addressing a living audience (us, that is) through the framed artifact of the first two.

The second level, the parabasis where the narrator personalizes himself, is concentrated in that masterful transition where the epistolary introduction ends and the narrator introduces himself (masterful because it exploits the pretense of uncertainty with such authority). He begins by sketching a state of agitation like Nathanael's, projecting it first on the audience ("Have you, gentle reader, ever experienced anything that totally possessed your heart, your thoughts, and your senses to the exclusion of all else?"—Kent and Knight trans., 104), and then, in a passage that foreshadows the scene in which Nathanael will read to Olympia, projecting it on himself: "Sympathetic reader, no one, I must confess, asked me about the history of young Nathanael; you are, however, surely aware that I belong to that remarkable species of authors who, when they carry something within themselves as I have just described it, feels as if everyone who approaches—indeed, everyone in the whole world—is asking 'What is it? Do tell us, dear sir!' " (Kent and Knight trans., 105).

But it is not as if Nathanael's malaise passed outward inexorably from the fictional world to us. What distinguishes the narrator from Nathanael is irony: when he resembles Nathanael he alters the resemblance by acknowledging it. Whereas Nathanael thinks he is engaged in intersubjective relations when he is not, the narrator goes out of his way to acknowledge the possibility that his readers are ignoring him. This does not deny that Nathanael may be a frightfully intimate figure for Hoffmann: the story that Hoffmann became so scared writing it, late one night in November 1815, that he had to wake up his wife for human company is convincing.[29] But the immediacy of "The Sandman" as an artist's parable is in its representation of the dilemma of writing—the physical absence of the audience—as a psychological issue. Nathanael's crisis as a writer, which amounts to a confusion about what constitutes an audience, is structurally related to the crises that accumulate in the narrative in which he attempts to see and remain unseen.

The claim of the narrator in *The Blind Owl* that he is writing only for his shadow, which we have interpreted to mean, roughly, that we are witnessing a private act in which a writer is concerned only with his own therapy, is of course absurd applied to Hedayat: the effect of the statement is, like the exaggerated uncertainty of Hoffmann's narrator in "The Sandman," an ironic device, a piece of antirhetoric that invites the reader closer. There are indirect references to audiences, such as the clientele referred to in the opening pages who buy the pen cases in India. The speaker becomes a kind of audience when he digs up the vase with the portrait on it, but of course since the picture is identical to his deathbed portrait of the ethereal woman he is in a sense digging up something he painted himself: the mirroring effect puts into question the agency of the artist and the passivity of the observer. The motifs that lead outward to representations of community in "The Sandman" are regularly privatized in *The Blind Owl*: the ubiquitous emblems of representation, from the shadow on the wall to the painted curtain, are abstracted, frozen emblems in which community is not made an issue. In "The Sandman" the narrator compares effective communication to sketching a portrait; Spalanzani is even described through comparison with a portrait of Cagliostro in an eighteenth-century almanac that the nineteenth-century reader could, presumably, consult (like the Callot sketches that function as illustrations to "Princess Brambilla"). The motif of the portrait in *The Blind Owl*, however, leads inward. The communal art, as we have seen, is dance, and it is explicitly separated from the narrator's world.

The reticence or reserve that marks the shadow on the wall in *The Blind Owl* is also an index of its conventionality. Its enigmas are conventional enigmas; "The Sandman" is more enigmatic, but more open. The relation of Coppelius and Coppola is not quite that of the double as Otto Rank was to codify it. Hoffmann assembles the parts of the genre with rough edges showing. One feels reading him that the options of happy ending versus unhappy ending, supernatural versus explained supernatural, whether Nathanael will kill Clara or be killed himself, can go either way. Historically, Hoffmann occupies a moment when naive romance models are highly visible in the form of the Grimm brothers' collections and the narrative components of romance are seen as artificial, improvised.

In comparison, *The Blind Owl* is a more streamlined assembly of romance conventions. Instead of a Coppola and Coppelius who look suggestively alike, we have classical double figures whose reflections stretch to infinity, and the distinctions from one to the other become so problematic that we see the doubling process instead of the individual. *The Blind Owl* transforms horrific and painful thematic material by awareness of its conventionality. The narrative thrust is toward a sense of fate, of narrative inevitability. (The technique of "The Sandman" is to transform it by narrative speed.) "The Sandman" is finally the more disturbing work because of its exuberance and unpredictability; it is more subversive and vertiginous, less firmly embedded in Western narrative convention.

III

Seen next to each other, the parabolic dimensions of the Salome stories and "The Sandman" have channeled our attention repeatedly to their scenes of victimization. When I began examining instances of these motifs in an attempt to fit the events of *The Blind Owl* into a coherent pattern, it seemed clear to me that violence against women was the common element. Yeats's self-sufficient dancers, agents of violence against the poet, seemed eccentric, superfluous. "The Sandman," in which the violence bounces back and forth, now directed against Nathanael, now against Olympia or Clara, is in this respect an important document.

One way to visualize the violence that haunts the parable of the artist is spatial: if we see art as a separate world, an alternate creation, violence enters the system at the edges where they meet, where, for instance, imagination makes claims that the shared world will not support, where mortal voices wake us and we drown, and it may be more useful to speak of that zone of violence as the invariant in our narratives rather than particular acts of violence. At this point there remain a series

of relatively spare, straightforward parables of creation—
roughly isomorphic with the deathbed scene in part one of
The Blind Owl—Poe's "The Oval Portrait" and the conclusion of "The Sandman."

Of the many unpredictable transitions of "The Sandman"
the tower scene is one of the most peculiar shifts of direction.
Not only do we arrive at the outcome unprepared, but the
scene itself seems tacked on. The emphasis on setting is un-
characteristic, and it is the first unmotivated act or whim of
the narrative, the first action not set in motion from outside.
It seems about to turn into a tableau, a scene set in front of a
scrim.

It is not hard to come up with meanings for the setting.
Climbing stairs has one of the clearest cut interpretations in
the list of common motifs in Freud's *Interpretation of
Dreams*, and this in turn is consistent with a common romance ending in which a coda presents an indirect mimesis of
consummation. Towers and telescopes have at least two
things in common: their shape (roughly cylindrical) and that
they both represent modes of vision. The telescope brings
things closer in a confined circle, as with Olympia, whereas
the view from a tower accepts distance and enlarges the frame.
One insists on seeing things one at a time, the other on assembling them simultaneously. The family has recently inherited
land outside of town; the implication is that from the tower
they will see their patrimony in visible form. This is Clara's
mode of vision. (The Gothic theme of the hero's fear of having
children seems to enter here tangentially.) To find a telescope
in one's pocket on top of a tower is to be tempted to combine
two types of vision (an instance of excess that could serve as
an image of Hoffmann's narrative style). It is as if, to return
to our spatial metaphor, there is insufficient room for everyone at the place where the two worlds meet.

But who is dispensable does not seem predetermined. We
could imagine Nathanael succeeding in his attempt to kill
Clara or Lothar (an eventuality that threatened earlier when
the two began to duel), though coming to his senses does not
seem a narrative likelihood at this juncture. Irving Massey

makes of Nathanael's leap from the tower a communication to his author, a fall into silence that passes the responsibility of the narrative to Hoffmann: "In some way Nathanael's suicide, his inability or perhaps his refusal to produce the work of art, is the writing of the story, the breaking out of an impossible contradiction" (Massey, 119). It may seem a naive reading, a critic's attempt to scale prematurely the fiction's esthetic walls, like the device students develop of recounting the story in the past tense, but Massey's reading does suggest something the reader feels intuitively is there, in the story. The tower scene may be eccentric to the narrative seen from inside, but something in it is crucial, in a way central. We feel a release in Nathanael's fall; we detach ourselves from identification with his point of view and watch him descend, in a process like the esthetic closure effected by the jump from the bridge at the end of Kafka's "The Judgment."

"The Sandman," taken as a parable about the nature of art, conveys an idiosyncratic vision (consistent perhaps with its refusal to assimilate to the generic patterns of romance). If we take Nathanael's death as a sacrifice, the price of a beautiful work of art, the art is not anything that he has written. It seems tautological to say that he is sacrificed for Hoffmann's work of art (it seems to suggest that Hoffmann creates a bad artist in order to show what a good one he himself is), but the economy of the story does demand a reading in which Nathanael's death is intended to have significance. Massey's dictum that " 'The Sandman' is at least partly about the author's pretending that he is not in it and can do with his characters what he wants" (Massey, 122) does indeed succeed in reaching problematic aspects of the text.

What the flexible, comically self-deprecating narrator of "The Sandman" has that ensures his survival is irony,[30] irony being the ability to exist in two contexts simultaneously. The top and bottom of the tower are like the two contexts that irony binds; Nathanael's encounter with that distance is like his inability to bridge the two terminals of irony. This is not an esthetic of profundity, but of gaps. The comparable passage in Hedayat is the moment by the river (also the scene of an initiating fall), contemplating the clayey bank and listening to the sound of the water, "like the staccato, unintelligible syllables murmured by a man who is dreaming [*ke dar 'âlem-e khâb zamzame mikonad*]" (77/72). This is a more traditional image of writing, transcribing the flow of a medium with substantiality and depth. (The term *'âlem-e khâb*, "the world of sleep," suggests the same notion of parallel creations, or separate tracks, which we mentioned above as part of the vision of esthetic profundity.) Hoffmann, in comparison, is hardly a poet of water, but of things that clank together, of gaps crossed instantaneously, electrically. What is traditional is a vision of art as something that flows, curves, displays organic contours, such as a river that is figuratively a woman. ("I squeezed the warm, moist sand in my fists. It felt like the firm flesh of a girl who has fallen into the water and who has changed her clothes"—77/72.) Hoffmann represents a limit, a zero degree of organicism. Compare the dismemberment of Olympia and the ethereal woman in part one of *The Blind Owl*. The ethereal woman is dead; Olympia has never been alive.

More traditional still is the parable of the artist in Poe's "The Oval Portrait." There is little plot to speak of, and the framing tale is little more than a scene setting in which the narrator enters a deserted castle to recuperate from an unexplained wound. The ascension of this tower has no specific narrative to be appended to, but if we have read enough romances we know it already. In this turret above the familiar country of romance narrative instead of looking through a telescope he sees a portrait, or rather, reads a book that explains the portrait. That is the story. It develops its power not from internal mechanisms but from what we already know: it is the definitive expression of the screen of anxieties through which we like to look at the artistic process.

The portrait that catches his eye is suspended between two possible appeals: "it could have been neither the execution of the work, nor the immortal beauty of the countenance, which had so vehemently moved me" (*CWP* 2.664). An hour's thought finds the intermediate source of the effect: "I had found the spell of the picture in an absolute *lifelikeness* of expression, which, at first startling, finally confounded, subdued and appalled me" (*CWP* 2.664). But the solution is not complete until we know from the catalogue describing the painting what caused the expression portrayed in such a lifelike way, a quotation that accounts for the final third of the narrative. In it we have one of those equations we saw in "Berenice," in which the engaged couple have separate spheres of power, hers in life and his in art. They marry. He attempts to combine the two realms by painting her portrait: "And he *would* not see that the tints which he spread upon the canvass were drawn from the cheeks of her who sat beside him" (*CWP* 2.665). At the last stroke of the brush she dies, her vital juices depleted by the process of being painted. The sequence of events is clearer even than in the scene in which the narrator paints the deathbed portrait in part one of *The Blind Owl*. Patrick Quinn, in *The French Face of Edgar Allan Poe*, has connected this parable with Poe's characteristic running together of physical and spiritual categories:

> in the living economy of matter as Poe conceived it, the Whole— "vast, animate and sentient"—continues always to exist, although its parts die in feeding one another and in so bringing about new living structures. In "The Oval Portrait," the life of the woman was drained from her body, but instead of being dissipated this life was transferred to her portrait. The quantity of life remains constant. This principle is as basic to the story as it is to the cosmological treatise *Eureka*.[31]

We are at the element of the story with which Hedayat and Poe are most clearly in accord; but again it might be more accurate to say that their agreement is in the degree of explicitness with which they both say what is often expressed obliquely.

Poe's economy of forces acting in a universe of scarcity is unusually schematic. It articulates myths about art that are widely held but not ordinarily visible, and makes it possible to develop a germinal rationale for the floating violence we have been cataloging. But it would oversimplify things to say only that there is a limited amount of vitality available, and that art and life share that vitality between them. The polarity of art and life is projected on the two genders, the ladies on the side of life, the gentlemen on the side of art. The metaphor of art as an organic process becomes in Poe's hands something more specific, art as a kind of domestic quarrel, but still it is a recognizable extension of the original argument. The esthetic system in which women are the pattern of beauty, a model for the artist, thus ultimately expendable, is also not Poe's innovation. Misogyny is embedded in the system, perhaps even more clearly in *The Blind Owl*, where after creating his successful portrait he adds, "I had fixed on paper the spirit which had inhabited those eyes and I had no further need of the body. . . . Henceforth she was in my power and I had ceased to be her creature" (26/29). But this oversimplifies things too.

The aggression implicit in the system is often enough rechanneled in other directions too. A recurring motif of "The Oval Portrait" is that of frames that fail to contain. (An oval is both an image of organic enclosure, of hermetic sealing, and—since the egg shape connotes temporary dwellings—also a shape that breaks.) The portrait doesn't simply memorialize an act of aggression, but it passes one on to the viewer. The agency attributed to the portrait, its ability to confound, subdue, and appall its observer, is of a piece with the process undergone by its model (who is literally appalled, or turned pale by the process of being drawn). Even the framing story is incomplete: "The Oval Portrait" ends with the framed quotation, and the narrator never returns to sum things up. The implication is that the power of art is so great that it cannot be contained in its own realm. It redounds on the artist in the concluding passage of the story: "he grew tremulous and very pallid, and aghast, and crying with a loud voice, 'This is indeed *Life* itself!' turned suddenly to regard his beloved: —*She was dead!*" (*CWP* 2.666).

An earlier draft read "turned a round to his beloved—*who was dead*. The painter then added—'But is this indeed Death?' " (*CWP* 2.666). It is certainly a weaker version. The implication that the painter sees immediately the consequences of the process, that life remains a constant amount and therefore the wife is still "alive" in the portrait, makes him a figure outside the narration, someone who sees the whole picture in the manner of a detached reader. In the final version, where the artist's victimization makes him more clearly a participant in the proceedings, we can begin to see the victimization travel. The vision of the artist in front of a double vista, sharing his attention between the real woman and her picture, is also a picture of him confronting his own blindness, discovering another monomania like that of Egaeus in "Berenice." David Halliburton has described the concluding scene of "Ligeia" as a scene of victimization that reaches the narrator as well as Rowena: "If Ligeia's soul-mate shrieks when she returns, it is because that return in one sense confirms his inferiority—makes him, in a word, a victim. . . . He could never, if he wanted to, be rid of her. But does he want to be? For this defeat is also a kind of triumph. To experience the return of the other, to watch her emerge victorious, is to experience vicariously the reality of transcendence."[32] This process is perhaps clearer in "The Oval Portrait," where the big issue (Ligeia's will to live) is not part of the scenario and the process has been isolated further as a process.

In the world of "The Oval Portrait" art competes with natural beauty and wins, but art is also incomplete without the exhibition catalogue that describes it. The three interlocking realms of nature, painting, and writing combine to form a parable that reassures us of the power of art. The reassurance is bought at a high price—an act of aggression portrayed as inevitable—but it is perhaps not as high a price as that paid in "The Sandman," where the sense of reassurance is almost nonexistent. Nathanael could be said to be caught between his own art (that is, his poetry) and Professor Spalanzani's—a mastery of science or engineering so cunning that it creates a third, Olympia's gracefulness. The mechanism of Olympia imitates life so thoroughly that it threatens Nathanael's access to nature. The reassurance left us is in the narrator's irony—his ability to insulate himself from the illusion of the natural, to remind us that it is only a fiction.

If we rank the arts portrayed within the narrative world of *The Blind Owl*, dancing is clearly in the highest position. Although it is a pastiche of European allusions, dancing is our link with a native, innocent, prelapsarian world, an art in which eros has been absorbed, an art that is in turn absorbed into a unified society, integral and whole. The plastic arts that enter into the speaker's world directly—the pencil cases that provide his livelihood, and the portrait that is his link with an earlier Iran—are artifacts of furtive sexuality in a world otherwise walled off from the object of desire.

We have in *The Blind Owl* both parables, coexisting at arm's length from each other—the story of the poet's search for ethereal beauty in which the woman who is its model is done away with, and the story of the woman at the center of authority, through whom power flows to the detriment of the male observer. The dancer is in the privileged position, but as we acknowledge this, a counteresthetic is discernible behind that ranking. The unheard music of Bugam Dasi's dance is available to us only through words, and in spite of the esthetics of reserve that surfaces momentarily at the beginning of part two, where the narrator suggests the bittern as an emblem of exemplary silence (46/47), it is nonetheless the process of the narrator's confession that allows us, momentarily, to glimpse the crime that generated the telling of the story. In one sense writing in *The Blind Owl* is like the catalogue of "The Oval Portrait": it tells the story of the painting's violent effect. In another sense it undoes it, because its irony—like Hoffmann's—distances us to the degree we see the narrator's madness. We identify and distance ourselves simultaneously, as part of the same process. If we took the parables of the generation of art as the "message" of the book, a vista of uncontained victimization would open up in which the aggression of the artist against the model, or the subtler aggression of the dancer's beauty against the beholder, would open outward to the reader, in a kind of chain reaction of mirroring. It would, like the scenario of misogyny, render it intolerable, a kind of esthetic universal solvent. And what contains it is the final esthetic layer, the grain of the writing, the medium that allows us our distance.

Chapter Seven

PROLEGOMENON TO *THE BLIND OWL* AS AN EASTERN NOVEL

To say that the assorted phenomena and bric-a-brac of nationalism have a "material" basis and explanation is akin to saying that
individual neurosis has a sexual explanation. We all know the
generations of indignant evasion which have now gone into deny-
ing and disguising the latter theory (degrading, reductionist, un-
dervaluing consciousness, etc., etc.). These evasions were largely
ideological misunderstandings of Freud. His theory does not really "dismiss" the higher things of human consciousness at all:
it enables us to appreciate their genuine weight, their true function in the individual's history, by relating them to the unconscious and buried segments of that history—to the underlying,
forced dilemmas of personal development which have been willy-
nilly "solved" in neurosis. Following the metaphor in our own
terms, one might say: "nationalism" is the pathology of modern
developmental history, as inescapable as "neurosis" in the individual, with much the same essential ambiguity attaching to it,
a similar built-in capacity for descent into dementia, rooted in
the dilemmas of helplessness thrust upon most of the world.[1]

"By the Saints, by the Prophet, I'm losing my mind. You've buried me in here with three people. One of them, may he drop
stone-dead, is a damned foreigner—just looking at his face is a
sin, it makes you want to repent—standing there in the corner
like a scowling owl that'll swallow you with his evil eyes. The
other two don't understand a word people say."
                    (Mohammad Ali Jamalzade, "Persian Is Sugar")[2]

I

WE HAVE been focusing more or less insistently on the textual
particulars and the formal shapes that link it with neighboring

texts, but of course the impression persists that we should be able to pass beyond, to poke through the glass walls that surround the esthetic artifact and reestablish its connections in history. A standard critical move used to make that crossing is to identify satire, to locate the pointed commentaries that ground it in its social context. We have suggested that irony is the most frequent device—the strategy in which we pretend to praise, or when we enter an alien voice, leaving hints that the voice is not our own. The hints are the difficulty. When Voltaire praises the armies of the Abarians and the Bulgars in chapter three of *Candide* it is a straightforward task to reverse the flow of the surface intent and find it a powerful statement against the absurdities of war: "Nothing could be so beautiful, so smart, so brilliant, so well drilled as the two armies. Trumpets, fifes, oboes, drums, cannons formed a harmony such as was never heard even in hell. First the cannons felled about six thousand men on each side; then the musketry removed from the best of worlds some nine or ten thousand scoundrels who infected its surface."[3] If we haven't heard the mocking nature of the voice in the extravagance of its praise, we cannot help but hear it in the addition of a cannon to the musical instruments or the overt suggestion that the harmony is worthy of hell.

Hedayat's ironies are more complicated and (as we have been noticing) contradictory, more in the manner of Dostoevsky's *Notes from Underground*, where the narrator scores points with us in the attack on his society, but he leaves no route of escape for the reader because he criticizes himself as fiercely or more. Irony is even further suffused through the narrative fabric of *The Blind Owl*: the entire opening section, for instance, could be called ironic on the grounds that the narrating voice is telling a distorted form of his own story, which can be decoded largely by reversal (irony as a variant of Freud's *Verneinung*). If we had here a character like Seyyed Nasrollah Vali in Hedayat's "Mihan-parast" (The patriot, 1942),[4] who clearly represents positions to be rejected, we could use the tactic of reversal on the entire book. But applied to *The Blind Owl* this strategy would make it a satire on insanity—not a promising foundation for social criticism.

And then there are the occasions when the speaker satirizes Islam and sums up prayer as "bobbing up and down [*dowlâ va râst shodan*] in honour of a high and mighty Being, the omnipotent Lord of all things, with whom it was impossible to have a chat except in the Arabic language [*bâyad be-zabân-e 'arabi bâ u ekhtelât kard*]" (88/81). We recognize Hedayat's voice here in what seems a relatively undistorted form—perhaps licensed by the guise of an insane narrator to veer into equivocal, dangerous sentiments. (He would paraphrase that passage using nearly the same words in the speech of another eccentric speaker in *Tup-e morvâri* [The pearl cannon].)[5] More complicated still is the single reference to pre-Islamic culture, where in the course of a manifesto on straight speech (he is priding himself on having used the term *miân-e tan-am*, "the middle of my body," which Costello translates as "loins," source of his feeling for his wife) he says, "I have no taste for literary *huzvaresh*" (72/68). *Huzvaresh*, a form of circumlocution in Pahlavi writing in which an Aramaic word is substituted for a Persian one,[6] is a reasonable image for euphemism and indirection, but the obtrusive nature of the term outweighs its semantic meaning, and its effect is, consequently, equivocal: the text goes out of its way to introduce a term from pre-Islamic Iran in order to describe hypocrisy. There is probably a way of making some consistent cultural position out of this, but it would be like constructing epicycles in Ptolemaic astronomy.

And yet satire is so profoundly ingrained in the traditions of Persian literature (much more so than the tactics of novelistic narrative) that it is hard to think of Hedayat's writing apart from it.[7] It hovers intangibly about the book, not simply because there is a tradition of social commentary in Persian writing (or because an outsider persona such as the speaker of *The Blind Owl* suggests an insider's society to complement it), but because Hedayat has written a considerable body of satire himself. The stream of influence that runs through Dehkhoda's *Charand Parand* at the turn of the century and passes

through the absurd "cases" of *Vagh-vagh sâhâb* and its sequel, *Velengâri*, is still with us, and it has the weight of a sub-
stantial literary institution, parallel to the institutions of accepted fiction and poetry. In magazines such as *Towfiq*, the
comic journal of the Shah's day, satire took on the authority
of a countertradition, with its *Hezb-e khar* (the Ass Political
Party) and the exquisite graphics with which it created an esthetic vision of daily life in Tehran.

It would be reasonable to divide Hedayat's writing into two
parts—the measured, self-conscious, "Western" oeuvre of his
fiction, which suppresses explicit commentary, whose power
rests on a narrating voice that distances itself clinically from
the scene it describes; and the less controlled experiments of
his satires, the pieces of *Vagh-vagh sâhâb* or *Velengâri*, whose
style culminates in his last extended work, *Tup-e morvâri*. The
satires might be called self-indulgent writing, in which the
reader feels a strange force let loose, which seems almost out
of the writer's control. Hedayat's satiric voice is in a way the
other pole from the measured and careful voice of *The Blind
Owl*, but there is an ambivalence of affect that in a way they
do share. In *Tup-e morvâri* for instance, the language of gratuitous insult accumulates to an extent that the demand of
rhetorical intensity seems to have outweighed the demands of
precise targeting. (In the search for an increasingly powerful
figurative language, a cadence of escalating insults creates a
thematic demand for a particular kind of sexual insult—the
language of phallic disproportion and buggery. It is a landscape so charged with sexual aggression that it becomes point-
less to ask whether we are in the realm of machismo or ho-
mosexuality. The two turn out to be the same thing.)

Irony is an unstable medium. The ambiguity inherent in satire—that one risks a paradoxical magnification of the object
of ridicule (the cliché of the satirist who falls in love with the
satiric target)—is perhaps better known than the problem of
unpointed energy we observe in *Tup-e morvâri*. It can be studied in Butler, Swift, and Wyndham Lewis. It is by no means a
culture-bound problem. It is perhaps characteristic of Hedayat that he should take up satire with a ferocity that plunges

to its most problematic center, the area where its intensity compromises its aim; but I do not bring up satire so much to demonstrate where it shows Hedayat's lack of control as to show his available generic resources. *The Blind Owl* is not itself a satire, but the frameworks of satire loom behind it in the narrator's habits of looking. They haunt it, and sensing them links us to the primary element that identifies it as Iranian, or if we prefer, "deeply" Iranian.

There is a profitable line of research in Persian literature that would examine the institution of Persian satire as an alternative to the more austere traditions of novel and short story. There are works (such as Hedayat's *'Alviye Khânom*) about which we may speak of the two traditions as overlapping, but for the most part they draw from distinct esthetic systems. Fiction in the style of realism tends to focus on the individual scene with greater tenacity, more "realistically" we say, foregoing the convention of an explicit commentary, whereas satire foregoes the realistic convention of presenting representative or typical situations. It tends to move more rapidly and unpredictably, with a greater tolerance for extremes, for chaotic detail, and for the intensity of a charged language of insult or praise.[8] The research I visualize would demonstrate how satire penetrates farther into the cultural specificity of local issues and local styles, so that it is more difficult for the nonnative reader and it gives the native speaker the illusion of being more spontaneous, an unmediated and direct expression of national style. This may be one reason why the more detached, indirect restraints of proper fiction are often devoted to the project of defining national identity, of transcending specific targets and approaching the culture as a whole. We say of Hedayat's satires that they respond to regional and contemporary issues; we say of his short stories that they attempt to define Iranian national character.

There is one theme that has been represented with comparable frequency in both satire and narrative in the realist style, and this is the theme of cultural contact with the West. From Hasan Moqaddam's satirical play *Ja'far Khân az farang âmade* (Ja'far Khan is back from the west, 1922)[9] to the sketches of life in exile in the videos circulated among the Iranian community in California, there has been a recurring, uneasy acknowledgment of something probably incompatible between the two traditions. It is easy to see why the theme of the returned student, which we discussed in the introduction as a formative plot structure for Hedayat,[10] has persisted as a recurring, even an obsessive subject. The mysterious intimacy in which Iran and the West, specifically the United States, has lived since the Second World War goes well beyond our support of the Shah. Iran did not erupt into American awareness in our news and our popular culture until the hostage crisis, but long before its appearance as a conspicuous, reactionary Other, Iran was a secret, Westernized other: the number of Iranian students in the United States, the primacy of English as everyone's second language, the Shah's dependence on U.S. weapons and military advisers, the sense of Iran being closer to the United States culturally than to either Turkey, the USSR, Afghanistan, Pakistan, or Iraq—all were major facts of life. That intimacy has been perhaps the most significant constitutive element of Iranian experience.

Jalal Al-e Ahmad's famous critique of the Iranian fascination with the West, *Gharb-zadegi* (translated variously as "West-struckness," "Westoxication," and "Euromania"),[11] seems on the face of it an attack from within a firmly entrenched sense of Iranian identity, but in fact its authority is founded on a close familiarity with the Other. It is well known that it grows out of a reading of Heidegger's dialogue with Ernst Jünger on the shortcomings of European culture in *Über 'Die Linie'*;[12] it is less frequently mentioned that the epigraph is a translation of Tennessee Ernie Ford's version of "Sixteen Tons."

And here a problem intrudes that seems to me accessible only obliquely: once we begin to look at the treatment of the term "West" in Middle Eastern writing, a kind of Heisenberg uncertainty principle enters the system. Our perception of the issue becomes part of the subject. We might compare it to the problem faced by an editor preparing an annotated edition of Pope's "Dunciad": the object of his satire is the very process of glosses and critical apparatus that as readers we have come to rely on. The more specific cultural background we bring to our reading of Hedayat, however accurate or apt, the more I suspect we are courting a tone of expert detachment that falsifies our observations.

An appropriate cautionary text is a 1982 comic discussion of the *Encyclopedia Iranica* by the London-based Iranian satirist Hadi Khorsandi.[13] The *Encyclopedia Iranica* is an admirable, indeed monumental project. There is no reason to speak against it. Just by virtue of its generic form, however, it begins to look different in Khorsandi's treatment of it. It opens with a summary of the opening entry, *âb,* "water" (27–39). Khorsandi's account makes us notice that the categories under which the encyclopedia carves up its subject—first, water in pre-Islamic tradition, then the ritual uses of water in Shi'ite Islam, and finally a technical discussion of water resources and hydrological devices—divide the realm of something utterly familiar into diverse specialized categories that seem anything but familiar and recognizable. The specialist's complex account of ritual purity, as we see it through Khorsandi's summary of the *Encyclopedia,* produces an alien vision of the familiar world that ironically mirrors the excessive legalism it is Khorsandi's job to criticize in the writings of the new regime. The *Encyclopedia Iranica* is not Khorsandi's target: it is simply the occasion for a fanciful discussion of Khomeini's handbook, *Towzih al-masâ'el* (Clarification of questions), which also opens with a discussion of the ritual purity of water. Khorsandi quotes passages from the opening pages of *Towzih al-masâ'el* that do indeed sound ungainly and, to Western ears, comical. He appends fanciful commentaries and glosses (what about ice out of the freezer when it melts?) that sound like almost plausible clerical style.

Khorsandi didn't invent the tradition of clerical parody; there are, as Michael Fischer and Mehdi Abedi point out in their preface to the *Towzih al-masâ'el* in translation, a number of satires on the handbook genre within Shi'ite tradition.[14] What I point out here, however, is that there are at least three very distinct points of view visible in Khorsandi's essay, all of

which are relevant to our point of view as Western readers of
The Blind Owl: first we have the detached Western expert;
second, the traditional Iranian who is apart from the world of
modernization and Western thought; third is the position
Khorsandi has adopted, that of the Westernized Iranian who
attempts to combine the advantages of both traditions, the
middle figure, the mediator. An unintended irony, however,
acknowledged only in his slightly excessive praise for the *Encyclopedia Iranica* and in the parallels that invite the analogy,
emerges in the inevitable implication that the opposites reflect
each other, that conservative legalism is the mirror of scholarly research. There is an additional irony, not part of Khorsandi's design (as in *The Blind Owl* the triangle collapses into
a simple polarity: a narrative of failed mediation). The position that Khorsandi occupies is the one that interests me, however, because it is an ambiguous position: it implies something
very complex—that the legitimately "Iranian" perspective is
an eclectic one, neither of the East nor of the West, and that
furthermore the real Iran is in exile. It is this position that interests me, because it is related to Hedayat's position.

The middle position is historically ambiguous. When Jamalzade constructs his national allegory in "Persian Is Sugar"
around Iranians in a jail cell, the basic opposition is between
the speech of a Westernized Iranian and the dialect of an
âkhund (i.e., between a surplus of French and of Arabic loan
words). Jamalzade, however, doubles the middle position by
putting four characters in the cell: the uneducated Iranian
Ramazan and the narrator, recently returned from Europe,
thus leaving two possible claimants to the middle position. (It
is Ramazan who calls the narrator an owl in the second epigraph to this chapter.) Jamalzade's denouement allows for the
possibility of reconciliation between all parties. The prisoners
are released and the narrator hires a droshky to carry himself,
the Westernized friend, and the *âkhund* to the nearby town.
We might argue that all the themes of the middle position in
The Blind Owl are also present here, including the split middle
position: "I was about to get going, when I saw Ramazan running toward us. He handed me a handkerchief filled with dried

fruit and whispered, 'Forgive me, I talk too much, but God! it seems to me that their madness has also gotten to you, otherwise how could you have the nerve to ride with these two?' I said, 'Ramazan, I'm not a coward like you' " (*Once Upon a Time*, 42–43).

There is a logic of the middle position for the reader and analyst as well. The dilemma of a writer whose discourse is not contained by a single culture stems from the choice of dialects, the difficulty of visualizing how much the reader is likely to know. (We could describe that dilemma as a condition of freedom or one of vertiginous anxiety.) It is a dilemma for us as readers because of the disciplinary pressure to contain him within what Jonathan Culler has called the "pieties of nationalisms."[15] And so, when we call this chapter a prolegomenon to *The Blind Owl* as an Eastern novel the point is not to pass it on to a specialist's attention (as if having looked at it from the outside, we could now take it inside where it belongs).

The criticism that succeeds in standing outside of the pieties of national literature departments is a long-term project. Creating it is not a matter of accumulating more knowledge, of piling new bricks of information one on top of another to construct a permanent edifice of enlightenment. Glimpses of a future criticism that can deal with the cultural complexities of non-Western writing are not rare, but they are scattered. They suggest that it is a matter of reassessing what we already know, from processes of debate and negotiation such as the controversy between Fredric Jameson and Aijaz Ahmad over "Third World" literature in *Social Text* 15 and 17. Fredric Jameson's attempt to sketch a theoretical underpinning for a future study of non-Western literatures, "Third-World Literature in the Era of Multinational Capitalism,"[16] centers on the suggestion that "Third World" novels reflect a communal spirit (unlike that of the European intellectual community) that molds them as national allegories. His readings of *Xala* by the Senegalese writer Ousmane Sembène and "Diary of a Madman" by the Chinese writer Lu Xun certainly make them work as national allegories. (*The Blind Owl* could be read as a national allegory: in fact "Diary of a Madman" shows so many formal similarities to it that we could imagine a thoroughgoing comparison between their use of insane narrators.) The problem is not in the task of making the label stick; it is in distinguishing what is not a national allegory, since the same elements can be found in, for instance, mainstream American writing. As Aijaz Ahmad suggests in "Jameson's Rhetoric of Otherness and the 'National Allegory,' "[17] a

> wider application of "collectivity" establishes much less radical difference between the so-called first and third worlds, since the whole history of realism in the European novel, in its many variants, has been associated with ideas of "typicality" and "the social," while the majority of the written narratives produced in the first world even today locate the individual story in a fundamental relation to some larger experience. . . . what else are, let us say, Pynchon's *Gravity's Rainbow* or Ellison's *The Invisible Man* but allegorisations of individual—and not so individual—experience?   (Ahmad, 15)

It is in some ways a sad exchange (Ahmad's sense of betrayal by a theoretical system that oversimplifies his own experience is moving), but it is through the sum of such encounters that institutions humanize, or rehumanize, themselves.

Jameson's article concludes tellingly with reference to Hegel's master-slave relation (book four of *Phenomenology of the Spirit*). In that notorious paradigm we start with the image of a life-and-death struggle: once a potential adversary has backed off, and the roles of master and slave are established, there occurs a reversal. The master's dominance is made hollow and unsatisfactory because recognition by a nonmaster cannot confirm the master's status:

> a second reversal is in process as well: for the slave is called upon to labor for the master and to furnish him with all the material benefits befitting his supremacy. But this means that, in the end, only the slave knows what reality and the resistance of matter really are; only the slave can attain some true materialistic consciousness of his situation, since it is precisely to that that he is

condemned. The Master, however, is condemned to ideal-
ism. . . .

It strikes me that we Americans, we masters of the world, are
in something of that very same position. The view from the top
is epistemologically crippling, and reduces its subjects to the illusions of a host of fragmented subjectivities.   (Jameson, 85)

The implication that non-Western thinking for this reason has
a privileged access to reality overstates things, but the point is
devastatingly correct that "they" know us far better than we
know "them." And a criticism of the future that does not treat
texts such as *The Blind Owl* as Western novels (as I have been
attempting to do) will have to develop a way to stand provi-
sionally outside Western contexts. It would be a useless sentimental reaction to regret that the methods of comparative literature have evolved in a European setting, but it is
increasingly clear—as we have already argued—that there are
invisible constraints against taking non-Western culture seriously. The growing body of criticism dealing with colonial
and postcolonial writing, both in the mainstream publications
and in the smaller periodicals devoted exclusively to the subject, such as *Critical Exchange* or *Inscriptions*, is still
grounded in the West, and there is no easy way to will ourselves out of the invisible constraints of our assumptions.

One device is to differentiate between the histories of non-
Western cultures—between, say, the colonial experience of India and Algeria, or between those properly colonial experiences and those of Iran, whose domination from abroad was
always unnamed and ambiguous—so we are not stuck with a
single term to define disparate non-Western cultures. There
are, after all, elements that set Iranian culture radically apart
from its neighbors; for one thing there is the peculiar complication that we can identify two kinds of mediation or in-be-
tweenness—the middle position between Iranian and European culture, which *The Blind Owl* flirts with endlessly, is
one; but there is also the middle position between an indigenous, Indo-European language and Arabic (or between secular culture and religious culture), which already marks tradi-

tional Iran. Iran was, in other words, an international culture already, before Western influence. It was Western influence that made possible the chimerical vision of cultural purity with which we find Hedayat struggling.

To return to the question of reinserting *The Blind Owl* in a social context, it is clear that when the cultural complexity of Iranian life peeks into the fiction it does not necessarily do so on the story's own mimetic terms, but inverted, condensed, displaced, even allegorized. As we attempt to see the text both as an esthetic artifact and as an episode in the history of nationalism, an imaginative act that defines an Iranian voice and style, we may need to keep shifting the scale of the inquiry. (Both esthetics and nationalism are terms that broader contexts will redefine.) The middle position will, I think, continue to interest us because it brings the observer into the picture. The logic of Hedayat's writing, like that of Khorsandi in his satire on Khomeini, argues that an intermediate position between East and West is in fact more truly "Iranian" than cultural isolation. And Hedayat's concept of national identity must, however we read the book, come in contact with ours. Hedayat is accessible to me because of his Western education and his project of seeing his own society in defamiliarized terms. There is, in other words, an overlapping of values that draws me to him and puts me in a kind of complicity with him.

This complicity is not free from a kind of distant class identification (though the more we are aware of that identification the less we are determined by it). Hedayat was, it is often said, a representative of a family that came to power during the development of the Qajar bureaucracy in the late nineteenth century, a Westernizing class. As a Western reader I sense in Hedayat's outsider personas (and there are many of them in his writings) something I recognize, something I have myself felt as a visitor in Iran. Hedayat represents a Westernized style we understand; he speaks in "our" terms even when most dedicated to the task of defining Iranian identity. (The concept of defining a national identity is itself a Western project.) But there is a further complication. Hedayat's is a class often defined in modern times by its self-hatred, its anxiety about having sold out to corrupt powers during the Pahlavi years, a class whose fall from power Hedayat (in his writings and in his death) may, in his way, have prophesied.

It is not uncommon among Iranian intellectuals (a class I know mostly from Iranian students in the United States) to say that Hedayat's self-deprecating, aristocratic appeal no longer carries resonance. It was a phenomenon of the fifties. (The fifties in Iran do not represent the naive exuberance popularly associated with our fifties; it is a period rather more like our seventies—the aftermath of a time of experimentation and enthusiasm.) And yet there is a context in which we do find an ironic mirror reflection of Hedayat in a surprising place, at the heart of Iranian conservative culture. If we read the eulogy to death in Hedayat's juvenalia ("Marg" [Death], *NP* 237–39) next to one of the essays on the virtues of martyrdom (*sha-hâdat*) in the popular press of the eighties, the stylistic resemblance is uncanny.[18] Hedayat was horrified by Shi'ite martyrology, and the most obvious source for the style of his essay "Marg" is Western (my suspicion is the essays of Maurice Maeterlinck), and in any event Hedayat greets death as a kind of fuzzy, undefined nothingness that owes little to any religious notion. But the resemblance remains. There are numerous ways to account for it: we might speak of death as a powerful rhetoric that he needs for the intensity of his writing and readapts into western, Schopenhauerian terms. We might see it as a kind of return of the repressed, a native fatalism that haunts him even as he tries to introduce a Western esthetic of Cartesian certainty and materialistic optimism to his own culture. In the terms we have been using, it is a mark of the failure of the middle term, a place where the attempt to find middle cultural ground has led to an unsuspecting parody of the position he has abandoned.

If the thematics of death can in fact be traced to social anxieties as well as metaphysical ones, the linkage between social identity and the modes of character portrayal may be established even more easily. Of the many properties ascribed to Iranian national character, from Morier's caricatures in *Hajji Baba of Ispahan* (1824) to the hysterical portraits that we began to see in the aftermath of the hostage crisis,[19] one is un-questionable: a sense of themselves as a culture defined from outside, an entity not wholly itself. The history of contact with the West produces a crisis of authority after which there is in a sense nothing but middle ground. Hedayat's avowed project of defining the Iranian national character through pre-Islamic culture is a typically Western search for origins; even the fundamentalist claims of Persian cultural separateness in this generation are predicated on opposition to Western culture and would be meaningless if they did not see the West as a threatening Other watching them from afar. Now if we consider *The Blind Owl* as an attempt to write from within cultural middle ground, from the point of view of an outsider—part Western romantic hero, part pure Iranian plain speaker—the difficult, forbidding dimension of the project may seem to be reflected in the plot and setting. We could connect the deceptive settings marked by shadows and reflections with the difficulties of that cultural search and the figure of the old man who turns out to be his mirror image takes on greater and greater importance.

The figure of the old man is, as it turns out, not an uncommon image in the iconography of Persian culture, perhaps as important as the figure of Salome in the *fin de siècle* tradition behind the ethereal woman in the pen-case sketch. And putting it in the foreground, we have returned to the image that has been suspended in front of us all this time. In the Persian miniature tradition an old man with a young woman is traditionally a picture of the legendary Shaykh San'an, the Sufi leader who falls in love with a Christian girl in the parable from Farid al-Din 'Attar's *Mantiq al-Tayr* (The conference of the birds). The mystical readings of the story need not concern us here, but the theme of overlapping values located between seemingly contradictory worlds is not easy to miss, and in contemporary illustrations to poetry it is even more familiar as a picture of the poet (always portrayed as an old man apart from the world) confronting ethereal beauty.

In Reza Baraheni's essay "Masculine History"[20] he takes the figure of the old man victimizing a young one as the central theme of Persian literature, the Oedipus narrative in reverse.

English readers are likely to be familiar with the story of Ros-
tam and Sohrab, which provides the pattern: the young men,
Baraheni argues, "fall as the victims of a partiarchal [sic] pattern, dying so that men older than they, and less worthy, will
continue to live" (*Crowned Cannibals*, 66). In a brief summary of Persian literary history that follows, *The Blind Owl*
becomes the clearest concretion of that pattern:

> There is more than one old man in the novel: the protagonist's
> father, his uncle, the butcher, the driver of the hearse also ap-
> pear. The lonely young man could have been happy with his wife
> if only these old men had not existed. It seems that he could have
> resolved all his personal problems if only the old men had dis-
> appeared. The young man's failure entails the old men's tri-
> umph, and this in itself means the failure of a better and freer
> human world, with young and free men and women, a new na-
> tion of youths, a new nation, liberated from the bondage of pa-
> triarchs and kings.   (Baraheni, 77)

Baraheni is striking out for another kind of middle ground, in
a sentimental vision of a world without authority, and perhaps for this reason he does not see that the narrator's anxiety
in *The Blind Owl* is that he himself has become the old man—
an anxiety that argues that the middle position may not in fact
exist (still another way of collapsing the triangles into a simple
polarity). Baraheni argues to erase the old man's angle of the
triangle, but it would be equally easy to reverse those values
and see the old man as a representation of tradition, of the
redemptive value of the past, the old man as he enters the
Jungian system, as a benevolent sorcerer, the patriarch of
Yeats's "Sailing to Byzantium," the center of a country for old
men. And since we are talking about the posthistory of the
book, it becomes very hard not to remember that we are talking about a country in which people effected a revolution carrying portraits of an old man in the streets. The image of an
old man's face as it proliferated on posters, magazine pictures,
and embroidered wall hangings has been duplicated since the
end of the seventies in a manner no less uncanny than in the
narrative of *The Blind Owl*.[21]

But I oversimplify to suggest that this icon is a strictly Iranian possession. Khomeini was also a central figure in U.S. mythology, the concretion of all our fears of the Third World, and it would be naive to pretend that he didn't arrange this purposely, with a shrewd intuition for what a Western observer most shrinks from. In this respect we are repeating the narrative of *The Blind Owl* in this generation: the triangle collapses into two parts because the speaker and the old man turn out to be the same, and the process keeping those two figures apart is the Gothic vision, which portrays some mirrors as too frightening to look into. In his incarnation as an odds-and-ends man, that figure can exist only by virtue of his distance:

> On Thursday evenings he reads aloud from the Koran, revealing his yellow, gappy teeth as he does so. One might suppose that he earned his living by this Koran-reading for I have never seen anyone buy anything from him. It seems to me that this man's face has figured in most of my nightmares. What crass, obstinate ideas have grown up, weed-like, inside that shaven greenish [*mâzu'i*] skull under its embroidered turban, behind that low forehead?   (53–54/53)[22]

A similar passage in the account of the dying slave at Cap Juby in St.-Exupéry's *Terre des hommes* (1939) allows us to see the same trope (the barrier in communication between monads) aligned on an East/West grid:

> in a man's death, there dies an unknown universe, and I ask myself what images are foundering in him. What Senegalese plantations, what bleached villages of southern Morocco are crumbling into forgetfulness. I cannot know if inside that black form are fading only mundane concerns—the tea to prepare, animals to water—if it is the soul of a slave going to sleep or if, reviving in a shower of recollection, a man is dying in his grandeur. The hard cranium was for me like an ancient treasure chest.[23]

The difference is that Hedayat's other is also a doppelgänger. What is going on inside the old man's mind may be a mystery, but it is clear that he sees the narrator. It may be equally clear that the Iranian government, which seems so inscrutable, at least sees us and takes our distant reactions into account. Acknowledging the risk of creating ahistorical categories, archetypes that hide more than they reveal, we can nonetheless identify the figure of the old man with tradition. Hedayat's fiction shows us the patriarchal tradition as the source of horror, whereas the actors of the Iranian revolution used the same image to claim identification with it. The image is still in use by both sides. Not only is the old man the icon of so-called traditional power, but a recent satirical novella by Saʿidi Sirjani retells the story of Shaykh Sanʿan as a political allegory in which the old man suggests Khomeini and the name of the counterpart to the Christian swineherd is Qodrat Khânom, "Miss Power."[24]

If we were to extend our inquiry further into the question of *The Blind Owl* as an Iranian phenomenon, it is the polarity of public and private that will increasingly command our attention. The contrast between the individual, introspective, psychological perspective of *The Blind Owl* and the intuition of readers that it in some way addresses itself to public questions, the novelistic project of defining national identity, is not going to leave us, as indeed that polarity is always latent in the novel form. A novelist's solitude is always a public act. But even when we argue that its historical and political background is its ultimate horizon, locating a work of fiction in its social contexts will not necessarily tell us what side to take. *The Blind Owl* will not, I think, be what many opponents of the Islamic Republic want it to be, an effective tool against clerical power. Nor does it demonstrate the bankruptcy of westernized thinking. Two endings seem to me possible here. One takes a path of locating *The Blind Owl* in a history of forms, arguing simply that it belongs in a generic category with the narratives of students returned from the West, such as Jamalzade's "The Drainage Controversy," Yahya Haqqi's "Saint's Lamp," or Tayeb Saleh's *Season of Migration to the North*. Hedayat's pastiche of Western themes and styles is more concrete, detachable, clearly defined; such informing shapes as satire and the narrative of the returned student are more amorphous. Nonetheless the returned student theme is an important category, perhaps the source of a genre destined to be as resonant in the Middle East and as all-encompassing as the Western bildungsroman has been in the West, or as romance. But it is a genre that seems to require open-endedness, because it posits an impossible choice.

II

The other possible ending would be more demanding. It would pursue much further the textual relevance of expanding social contexts that surround the fictional text—biography, politics, mythology, folklore, culture. It would insist that those contexts are also constructed of texts and that they are open to the same forms of analysis. If we open the fiction out to its historical vistas (through the vehicle of national allegory), past the obvious opposition of public and private in the narrator's life to the same opposition in Iranian society—both in the lives of individual Iranians exposed to the pressures of global markets and mass culture and in the collective life of the country as a national entity—we begin to see that history has the properties of a novel too, not necessarily a realistic one. In both texts, fictional and social, the demanding distinction would be between those who are aware they occupy middle ground and those who are not.

There is certainly no one among the characters of *The Blind Owl* with whom we can identify if we are looking for that kind of middle ground (as we could in Jamalzade's "Persian Is Sugar"). A simplified expression of this model would begin by saying that *The Blind Owl* is a national allegory in which the old man represents a corrupt, traditional Iran, the woman some unmediated prelapserian state (perhaps India, perhaps the West), and the narrator thrashes about for a middle term. Our more complicated suggestion in Chapter Three was a model of reading in which the hero is in fact the reader, whose final obligation is to determine where the system describes a shared reality and where it does not; this amounts to an obligation to scrutinize our own sympathies, the identifications that make us forget we are reading fiction. (There is also a middle ground between fiction and history; it is inside us.)

My polemic against the esthetic of profundity is meant to include both the profundity of national identity and the profundity of literature. There are numerous ways criticism can praise the humanizing transformations of literature, but an imagery of depth, containment, and privacy is not in our case a productive one; it distracts us from the extent to which literature is a public phenomenon. Similarly with Iranian culture: to imagine it separate, unpenetrated by Arabic in its formative epoch, or by Western culture in this one, denies the resourcefulness and adaptability that Western readers can most learn from. The point of this twofold polemic is to make visible the double bind inherent in all treatment of national literatures, but particularly those of the Middle East, and perhaps, among those of the Middle East, particularly of Iran. Any discourse in a Western academic context finds itself responding to contradictory threats: there is nowhere to hide from them. To emphasize cultural difference is to risk the tone of exoticism; to treat the other culture as if it were ours is to risk an ethnocentric bias that judges everything according to our standards. It should be clear that the same double bind haunts the Middle Eastern writer, and that *The Blind Owl* is a comment on that dilemma.

The Blind Owl seems at first a critique of the dominant discourse, by a solitary voice who has woven his own authority out of his own being. That independence is the most fictional element of the fiction of *The Blind Owl*, though Hedayat may at moments have believed it. (One of the stories Hedayat burned before his suicide was, tellingly, about a spider that could not spin—*ASH* 376.) In an international context *The Blind Owl* becomes something else, something more public, perhaps equally intimate, and we can hear it as a mix of shifting voices speaking on mixed authority.

NOTES

CHAPTER ONE
NATIONALIST POETICS AND ITS SHADOWS

1. See, for instance, Iraj Bashiri, *Hedayat's Ivory Tower: Structural Analysis of the Blind Owl* (Minneapolis: Manor House, 1974); *The Fiction of Sadeq Hedayat* (Lexington, Ky.: Mazda, 1984).

2. The concept of national character seems to me a sensitive one, but not beyond the grasp of the social sciences. See M. C. Bateson, J. W. Clinton, J.B.M. Kassarjian, H. Safavi, and M. Soraya, "Safa-yi Batin: A Study of the Interrelations of a Set of Iranian Ideal Character Types," in *Psychological Dimensions of Near Eastern Studies*, ed. L. Carl Brown and Norman Itzkowitz (Princeton: Darwin Press, 1977), 257–73; William O. Beeman, "What Is (Iranian) National Character?" *Iranian Studies* 9.1 (Winter 1976): 22–48; and Mary Catherine Bateson, " 'This Figure of Tinsel': A Study of Themes of Hypocrisy and Pessimism in Iranian Culture," *Daedalus* 108.1 (Winter 1979): 125–34.

3. L. P. Elwell-Sutton, "The Influence of Folk-tale and Legend on Modern Persian Literature," in *Iran and Islam*, ed. C. E. Bosworth (Edinburgh: University Press, 1971), 247–54, 251.

4. William K. Archer, "The Terrible Awareness of Time," *Saturday Review*, 17 December, 1958: 24–25.

5. Christophe Balaÿ and Michel Kuypers, *Aux sources de la nouvelle persane* (Paris: Institut d'Iranologie de Téhéran, 1983).

6. Peter Avery, "Developments in Modern Persian Prose," *Muslim World* 45.4 (Oct. 1955): 313–23, 319.

7. Zaki Najib Mahmoud, *Qasâsât al-zujâj* (Cairo Dâr al-Shurûq, 1974). The word *qasâsât* is from the same stem as *qissa* (story); the pun is meaningful.

8. Ahmad Karimi-Hakkak, *Iranian Studies* 10.3 (Summer 1977): 217.

9. Edward Said, *Beginnings: Intention and Method* (Baltimore: Johns Hopkins University Press, 1975), 81.

10. Jalal Al-e Ahmad, "Hedâyat-e Buf-e kur" (The Hedayat of "The Blind Owl"), *'Elm va zendegi* 1(1951): 65–78, rpt. in *AA* 79–81. The quote is from the English translation by Ali Eftekhary in *FYA*

27–42, 30. The word *badi'tarin* (most novel) is from the stem *bid'a* alluded to above, used here without an implication of heresy.

11. Haideh Daraghi, in the introduction to her translation of Jamalzade's preface to *Yeki bud-o yeki na-bud*, compares his project to that of American local colorists in the late nineteenth century: "The Shaping of the Modern Persian Short Story: Jamalzadih's 'Preface' to *Yiki Bud, Yiki Nabud*," *Literary Review* 18.1 (Fall 1974): 18–37. The French translation of that preface in *Aux sources de la nouvelle persane* (131–37) includes a commentary (137–41) that updates Daraghi's translation and puts Jamalzade's manifesto in a larger theoretical context. There is an admirable, adventurous English translation by Heshmat Moayyad and Paul Sprachman, *Once Upon a Time (Yeki Bud Yeki Nabud)* (New York: Biblioteca Persica, 1985), which does not, however, contain Jamalzade's preface.

12. As an analogous situation compare George Steiner's discussion of Shakespeare in German translation in *After Babel* (New York: Oxford University Press, 1975), 380–82.

13. Hassan Kamshad, *Modern Persian Prose Literature* (Cambridge: Cambridge University Press, 1966).

14. This misinterpretation seems to trace back to Al-e Ahmad's allusions to Buddhism at the conclusion of his "Hedâyat-e Buf-e kur." Kamshad's expansion of these allusions is relatively innocent. In Iraj Bashiri's *Hedayat's Ivory Tower*, where it becomes the substance of an entire book, the connection seems to me to submit *The Blind Owl* to distortion.

15. G. M. Wickens, "Bozorg Alavi's Portmanteau," *University of Toronto Quarterly* (Jan. 1959): 116–33, 117.

16. Gianroberto Scarcia, " 'Hâǧi Aqâ' e 'Buf-e Kur', i cosidetti due aspetti dell'opera dello scrittore contemporaneo persiano Sâdeq Hedâyat," *Annali: Istituto Universitario di Napoli*, n.s., 8 (1958): 102–23, 120–21. See also his "Letteratura persiana," in *Storia delle letterature d'oriente*, ed. Oscar Botto, 4 vols. (Milan: F. Vallardi, 1960), 2:392–98. (Unless otherwise noted, translations are my own.)

17. I argue this position at more length in "Distance and Perception: Islamic Literary History and the Western Reader," *Alif: Journal of Comparative Poetics* 6 (Spring 1986): 47–61.

18. There are three extended biographical treatments of Hedayat's life in Western languages: Vincent Monteil, *Sâdeq Hedâyat* (Tehran: Editions de l'Institut Franco-Iranien, 1952); the section on Hedayat in Kamshad, *Modern Persian Prose Literature*; and D. S. Komissarov's *Sâdek Khedâyat: Zhizn' i tvorchestvo* (Sadeq Hedayat: Life and

works) (Moscow: Nauka, 1967), to which we can add a forthcoming full-length biography in English by Homa Katouzian. In Persian, Abulqasem Djannati-Atai's popular biography, *Zendegâni va âsâr-e Sâdeq-e Hedâyat* (Life and works of Sadeq Hedayat) (Tehran: Majid, 1978), is by far the most detailed account. The other standard references include Bozorg Alavi, *Geschichte und Entwicklung der modernen persischen Literatur* (History and development of modern Persian literature) (Berlin: Akademie-Verlag, 1964), 159–68; Vera Kubickova, "Persian Literature of the Twentieth Century," in *History of Iranian Literature*, ed. Jan Rypka, trans. P. van Popta-Hope et al. (Dordrecht: D. Reidel, 1968), 410–12; and Mohammad Ebrahim Shari'atmedari, *Sâdeq-e Hedâyat va ravânkâvi-ye âsâr-ash* (Sadeq Hedayat and the psychoanalysis of his works) ([Tehran]: Piruz, n.d. [1964]). With Mohammad Golbon's bibliography of works by and about Hedayat in Persian, an exemplary work of scholarship that sifts through countless ephemeral periodicals and includes a year-by-year chronology of Hedayat's life, Hedayat scholarship enters a wholly new level of precision: *Ketâbshenâsi-ye Sâdeq-e Hedâyat* (Bibliography of Sadeq Hedayat) (Tehran: Tus, 1976). Except for Golbon's chronology, with its unsymmetrical catalogue of fortuitous details, all of these treatments convey a sense of belatedness, of a personality explained by his own career, reduced to the myth of himself as artist. In this respect, the memoires and anecdotes collected in Siavosh Danesh's introduction to his English translation of Hedayat short stories, *Sadeq's Omnibus* (Tehran: Mehre Danesh, n.d.), and the testimonials collected in Esmail Jamshidi's *Khod-koshi-ye Sâdeq-e Hedâyat* (Sadeq Hedayat's suicide) (Tehran: 'Atâ'i, 1971), as well as Bozorg Alavi's passing recollections in Donné Raffat's *Prison Papers of Bozorg Alavi: A Literary Odyssey* (Syracuse: Syracuse University Press, 1985), 35–37, 48–49, 61–65, 91–93, and 216, are invaluable supplements to the biographical notices because they provide so much contingent detail that resists the myth-making process. The 420 pages of recollections in M. F. Farzaneh's *ASH*, a meticulous and often moving account of their friendship during Hedayat's last years, offers useful, abundant examples of both contingent detail and the myth-making process. I would add to this list the historical background provided by Maurizio Pistoso to the Italian translation of *Buf-e kur* by Lisetta Cerato, in *Esotismo di riflesso e autodenigrazione: Due voci dell'Islam di ieri* (Rome: Istituto per l'Oriente C. A. Nallino, 1983), supplement no. 2 to *Oriente moderno*, 105–16.

19. Edward G. Browne, *A Literary History of Persia*, vol. 4 (1924; reprint, Cambridge: Cambridge University Press, 1969), plate 12, facing p. 344.

20. See ibid., 224–26, for a commentary on Reza-Qoli Khan's politeness.

21. Trans., with admirable attention to its citations of classical poetry, by Jerome Clinton as "The Man Who Killed His Passions," *Literary Review* 18.1 (Fall 1974): 38–52.

22. Rahmat Mostafavi, in *Bahs-e kutâhi darbâre-ye Sâdeq-e Hedâyat va âsâr-ash* (A short inquiry into Sadeq Hedayat and his works) (Tehran: Amir Kabir, 1971), argues that Hedayat's familiarity with French interfered with his Persian and accounts for a series of stylistic defects in his early writings (162). In this Hedayat resembles Mohammad Ali Jamalzade, who taught himself to write Persian while living abroad; see Kamshad, *Modern Persian Prose Literature*, 93–94.

23. Bozorg Alavi's account of the group, in his interview with Donné Raffat, suggests that the group was less tightly knit than the standard histories imply, and even the name was a kind of joke (Raffat, *Prison Papers of Bozorg Alavi*, 34–35).

24. Jan Rypka, "Mes souvenirs de Sâdegh Hedâyat," *Mélanges d'Orientalisme offerts à Henri Massé* (Tehran: Imprimerie de l'Université, 1963), 355–56.

25. Eugène Flandin, *Voyage en Perse* (Paris: Gide et J. Baudry, 1854), 2:355–56.

26. Hedayat, "Seeking Absolution," trans. Minoo S. Southgate, *Iranian Studies* 9.1 (Winter 1976): 49–51, 52 (cited here); trans. Brian Spooner as "The Search for Mercy," *ANTH* 53–62.

27. Hedayat, "The Mongol's Shadow," trans. D. A. Shojai, *Chicago Review* 20.4/21.1 (combined issue, May 1969): 95–104. The initial publication was in a collection of three short stories, *Anirân* (Non-Iranian, 1931). The Persian text is collected in *NP* 69–81. Hedayat's illustration is printed in Hasan Qa'emyan, *Darbâre-ye zohur va 'alâ'em-e zohur* (About the last days and signs of their coming) (Tehran: Amir Kabir, 1965), 73.

28. Hedayat, "Abji Khânom," trans. Siavosh Danesh as "The Spinster," *ANTH* 137–44.

29. Hedayat, "Hâjji Morâd," trans. Iraj Bashiri, in *The Blind Owl and Other Hedayat Stories* (Minneapolis: Sorayya Publishers, 1984), 3–7.

30. Hedayat, "Buried Alive," trans. Carter Bryant, *FYA* 43–59; trans. Brian Spooner, *ANTH* 145–62.

31. See, for instance, Theodore Ziolkowski's chapter, "The Metaphysics of Death," in his *Dimensions of the Modern Novel* (Princeton: Princeton University Press, 1969), for a discussion of this theme in modern German literature.

32. Manoutchehr Mohandessi, "Hedayat and Rilke," *Comparative Literature* 23.3 (1971): 209–16.

33. Hedayat, "Three Drops of Blood," trans. Guity Nashat and Marilyn Robinson Waldman, *FYA* 60–67; trans. Brian Spooner, *ANTH* 93–101.

34. Alavi, *Geschichte*, 166.

35. Hedayat, "Madame Alviye," trans. Gisèle Kapucinsku and Mahin Hambly as "The Pilgrimage," *ANTH* 3–39.

36. "Qaziye-ye român-e 'elmi" (The case of the scientific novel), *Vagh vagh sâhâb*, 3d ed. (Tehran: Amir Kabir, 1962), 175–79.

37. Letter of 29 January 1937, quoted in Rypka, "Mes souvenirs," 358.

38. Al-e Ahmad speaks eloquently about this aspect of Hedayat's career, *AA* 86–87; *FYA* 35–36.

39. See Carter Bryant, "Hedayat's Psychoanalysis of a Nation," in *FYA* 153–67, 159, and *Sadeq's Omnibus*, 19–23. The question of Hedayat's sexual orientation is a source of some controversy, which I consider to be outside the scope of this study. I discuss this problem in my review of *FYA* in *Edebiyât* 3.2 (1978): 229–36, 233–34. Today one would want to include the evidence of Farzaneh's interviews with Hedayat, *ASH* 76–82.

40. Hedayat, *Hâjji Agâ*, trans., with extensive annotations, G. M. Wickens as *Haji Agha: Portrait of an Iranian Confidence Man* (Austin: Center for Middle Eastern Studies, 1979), Middle East Monographs, no. 6.

41. Hedayat, "Fardâ," trans. Lucien Ray in *New Left Review* 24 (March–April 1964): 91–99, and by Iraj Bashiri in *The Blind Owl and Other Hedayat Stories*, 165–75; trans. into French by Vincent Monteil in *Deux nouvelles (L'impasse—Demain)* (Tehran: Institut Franco-Iranien, 1952), 24–40.

42. Vincent Monteil, *Sâdeq-e Hedâyat: Neveshte-hâ va andishe-hâ-ye u*, trans. Hasan Qa'emyan (Sadeq Hedayat: His writings and thoughts), 2d ed. (Tehran: n.p., 1952–53), 100–127.

43. Hedayat, *Tup-e morvâri* (Tehran: Sâzmân-e Janbash-e Nâsyunalisti-ye Dâneshgâhiân va Dânesh-pezhuhân va Rushan-binân-e

Irân, 1980). There is an edition available abroad: Hedayat, *Tup-e morvâri*, ed. Iraj Bashiri (Lexington, Ky.: Mazda Publishers, 1986).

44. There is a briefer account in Jamshidi, *Khodkoshi-ye Sâdeq-e Hedâyat*, 52–57.

45. Hasan Qa'emyan, ed. and trans., *Nazariyyât-e nevisandegân-e khâreji darbâre-ye Sâdeq-e Hedâyat va âsâr-e u* (Observations of foreign writers concerning Sadeq Hedayat and his works) (Tehran: Parastu, 1964–65), 102–3.

46. "Chakâvak," trans. Khodabande Farsandegi, in *Yâdbudnâme-e Sâdeq-e Hedâyat be monâsebat-e sheshomin sâl-e dar-gozashte-ye u* (Memorial to Sadeq Hedayat on the occasion of the sixth anniversary of his passing), ed. Hasan Qa'emyan (Tehran: Amir Kabir, 1958), 274–77.

47. Ibid., 40–44. A. J. Arberry's translation of that poem into English can be found in *Life and Letters* 63.148 (Dec. 1949), Persian Writers Issue.

48. Althea Hayter, *Opium and the Romantic Imagination* (Berkeley: University of California Press, 1970), and M. H. Abrams, *The Milk of Paradise* (1934; reprint, New York: Harper and Row, 1970).

CHAPTER TWO
THE BOOK OF LOVE

1. M. Y. Qotbi, *In-ast Buf-e kur* (This is "The blind owl") (Tehran: Daftar-e Tahqiq-e Ra'in, 1973), 5.

2. Even *ezhâr kardan*, the colorless newspaper word in the second sentence of *The Blind Owl*, recalls a characteristic Hedayatian verb, *tazâhor kardan*, "to demonstrate, appear, materialize, become manifest." (Both are from the Arabic stem *z-h-r*, "to appear, become visible," whose variations, again, suggest the Hedayatian theme of materialization, the abstract made tangible.)

3. Ibrahim Desouqi Shitta, trans., *Al-bûma al-'amyâ'* (Cairo: Al-Hai'a al-Misriyya al-'amiyya li'l-kitâb, 1976), 44.

4. E.g., Bahram Meghdadi and Leo Hamalian, "Oedipus and the Owl," *FYA* 142–52.

5. My Italian text is Dante's *Vita nuova*, ed. Ludovico Magugliani (Milan: Rizzoli, 1952). Citations include chapter and sentence number as marked in that edition.

6. *NP* 608, p. 9 in European pagination.

7. See Leonard Forster, *The Icy Fire: Five Studies in European Petrarchism* (Cambridge: Cambridge University Press, 1969), 79, 175.

8. Erich Auerbach, *Dante: Poet of the Secular World*, trans. Ralph Manheim (Chicago: University of Chicago Press, 1961), 45.

9. See, for instance, Gayatri Spivak, "Finding Feminist Readings: Dante-Yeats," *Social Text* 3 (Fall 1980): 73–87.

10. Costello and Lescot both guess "turban," but the word is not Persian and to my knowledge has not been identified. Iraj Bashiri's solution in his translation (*The Blind Owl and Other Hedayat Stories* [Minneapolis: Sorayya Publishers, 1984], 38–99) may be the most logical: he simply transcribes the word.

11. Not to my knowledge an Iranian custom.

12. Etienne Gilson, *Dante the Philosopher*, trans. David Moore (London: Sheed and Ward, 1948), 69.

13. I use Dante Gabriel Rossetti's English translation of the *Vita nuova*, anthologized in *The Portable Dante*, ed. Paolo Milano (New York: Viking, 1947), 547–618.

14. Giovanni Pascoli, *La Mirabile visione: abbozzo d'una storia della Divina comedia* (The admirable vision: Sketch of a history of the Divine Comedy) (Bologna: Nicola Zanichello, n.d. [1923?]), 8.

15. Trans. by Rossetti in *Dante and His Circle* (Boston: Roberts Bros., 1887), 127.

16. Spivak, in "Finding Feminist Readings," makes a more specific use of the dream imagery, linking it with the lover's awkwardness and inability to function in the world of affairs: "If I decide to describe the events of this dream-vision through psychoanalytic structures, I can treat it as telling the story of a fantasy where the woman allows the man to acquire a 'passivity' that would prohibit 'activity.' By devouring Dante's phallus—the bleeding heart is a thin disguise—Beatrice 'incorporates' him, 'identifies' with him, acts for him" (87).

17. The words of Homer are from the *Iliad* 24.258.

18. Mark Musa, *Dante's Vita nuova: A Translation and Essay* (Bloomington: Indiana University Press, 1973), 170.

19. This relation has been examined, famously, by Northrop Frye: see, especially, *The Anatomy of Criticism* (New York: Atheneum, 1966), 189–92, and *The Secular Scripture* (Cambridge: Harvard University Press, 1977).

20. Dante's control is not always unacknowledged; he is not, as is often implied, always on the receiving end of the mockery in the *Vita nuova*. If the women in chapter 22 to whom he addresses the poem "Voi che portate la sembianza umile" are the same who teased him in chapter 18 about the contradictory nature of his love (about whom Musa has commented, "One cannot fail to notice the untranscenden-

tal nature of his Muse"—148), it would explain the backhanded compliment in that poem, where he says he knows they have been in the presence of Beatrice "perch'io vi veggio andar sanz'atto vile." It is no difficult task to read the line as translated by Rossetti, who has Dante's heart "marking your grave and sorrowful advance," but the literal meaning remains that the women addressed must have come from Beatrice because they are without their (evidently customary?) *viltà*, "baseness, cheapness."

21. Philippe Sollers, "Dante et la traversée de l'écriture," in *L'écriture et l'expérience des limites* (Paris: Seuil, 1968), 13–47, 30. The English translation is *Writing and the Experience of Limits*, trans. Philip Barnard and David Hayman (New York: Columbia University Press, 1983), 11–43, 25.

CHAPTER THREE
CHAPTER ONE SAYS YOU LOVE HER

1. This is not to my knowledge a common term (though the *Oxford English Dictionary* lists occurrences of it as "the science of light, optics"). Jacques Derrida has resurrected it in order to amplify its far-reaching historical resonance: the photological metaphor is "the metaphor of darkness and light (of self-revelation and self-concealment), the founding metaphor of Western philosophy as metaphysics." See "Force and Signification," *Writing and Difference*, trans. Alan Bass (Chicago: University of Chicago Press, 1978), 27.

2. M. Y. Qotbi, *In-ast Buf-e Kur* (Tehran: Daftar-e Tahqiq-e Ra'in, 1973). I pass over Qotbi's historical allegory, that the recurring interval of two months and four days stands for the two thousand and four hundred years since the ancient wisdom of Iran and India was imported to Greece and made the foundation of European philosophy. (Qotbi attributes this idea to an article by Parviz Daryush, "Edâye dayn be Sâdeq-e Hedâyat" [A debt paid to Sadeq Hedayat] in *Kayhân* 1.2 [Shahrivar 1341/1962]: 3–32.) Though it does not establish the validity of the historical allegory, it is worth observing that the equation of years with amounts of money (such as the 2 dirhems and 4 peshiz he offers to the odds-and-ends man—108/98) enters into a dream interpretation of Freud's (in *The Interpretation of Dreams*) where 3 florins and 65 kreuzers stand for a year. See *The Standard Edition of the Complete Psychological Works of Sigmund Freud* (London: Hogarth Press and the Institute of Psychoanalysis, 1953), 5.414–15.

3. Qotbi touches on this connection (*In-ast Buf-e Kur*, 25n).

4. The painting is reproduced in Hasan Qa'emyan, *Darbâre-ye zohur va 'alâ'em-e zohur* (Tehran: Amir Kabir, 1965), 144.

5. An English translation can be found in John D. Yohannan, ed., *Joseph and Potiphar's Wife in World Literature* (New York: New Directions, 1968), 174–79.

6. My source is Hedayat's *Tarâne-hâ-ye Khayyâm* (Songs of Khayyam), 4th ed. (Tehran: Amir Kabir, 1963), stanza 95.

7. Stanza 8, 1868 and subsequent editions. My text for Fitz-Gerald's translations is *Rubàiyàt of Omar Khayyàm*, ed. Dick Davis (New York: Penguin, 1989).

8. *Tarâne-hâ-ye Khayyâm*, stanza 105.

9. A. J. Arberry, *The Romance of the Rubàiyàt: Edward Fitz-Gerald's First Edition Reprinted with Introduction and Notes* (London: George Allen & Unwin, 1959), 220. I am thankful to Ahmad Karimi-Hakkak for pointing out to me a mistranslation in Arberry's version, which I have corrected. (Arberry misreads *dân* in line 3 as a suffix, and the result is a lamp stand rather than a lamp.)

10. A peculiar biographical anecdote that one sometimes hears about Hedayat would pass unnoted except that it has such striking appropriateness to the line of imagery that makes receptacles into erotic objects: "Asked once whether he ever intended to have children, Hedayat took a glass full of semen from its hidden place in his room and announced that its contents were his children" (cited by Carter Bryant, *FYA* 159). That glass has its place in the Hedayat museum, alongside the Rey vase and Khayyam's clay pots.

11. I am not familiar with the expressions, but do not doubt their authenticity. If authentic, they suggest the degraded and antifeminist form of a much less violent language. Compare another form of the same analogy in this sixteenth-century Arabic passage: "It is called the vulva. God has furnished the object with a mouth, a tongue, two lips; it is like the impression of the hoof of a gazelle in the sands of the desert." *The Perfumed Garden of Shaykh Nefzawi*, trans. Sir Richard F. Burton (Secaucus, N.J.: Castle Books, 1964), 7.

12. Sorush Abadi, *Bar-rasi-ye Sâdeq-e Hedâyat az nazar-e ravân-shenâsi* (An examination of Sadeq Hedayat from the point of view of psychology) (Tehran: Ibn Sina, 1959); Hushang Paymani, *Râje' be Sâdeq-e Hedâyat sahih va dâneste qazâvat konim* (Let's judge Sadeq Hedayat accurately and learnedly) (Tehran: Aban, 1963).

13. Mohammad Ibrahim Shari'atmadari, *Sâdeq-e Hedâyat va ra-*

vânkâvi-ye âsâr-ash (Sadeq Hedayat and the psychoanalysis of his works) (n.p. [Tehran]: Piruz, n.d. [1969?]).

14. André Breton, "Des Capucines violettes," *Médium* 8 (June 1953). The irregularly published periodical *Médium* was in the early fifties little more than a polycopied page. I am grateful to Mahshid Amir-Shahy for this reference; she located a researcher to copy the article in the Bibliothèque Nationale.

15. Janette S. Johnson's judgment (in *FYA* 130) that Nerval comes to mind for a French reader of Hedayat, as Poe comes to mind for the anglophone reader, has symmetry and justice. If we dwell on Poe (in Chapter Five, below) and ignore Nerval, it is in part because Poe is a verifiable influence, also because Poe's generic patterning allows us to discuss tradition in a way that we can't with Nerval. The evidence seems good that Hedayat did not read Nerval until after *The Blind Owl*, though the relevant references are not entirely without contradictions. Henri Massé, in a speech commemorating the third anniversary of Hedayat's death, says: "Mr. Roger Lescot has related to me that one day in Tehran he asked Hedayat if he knew the writings of Gérard de Nerval, and Hedayat answered, 'Yes, but unfortunately I became familiar with them rather late' " (trans. in Hasan Qa'emyan, *Nazariyyât-e nevisandegân-e bozorg-e khâreji*, 146). Lescot's account, eleven years earlier, differs only in his own role in things: "It would not properly speaking be a question of imitation, since S. Hedayat wasn't familiar with Nerval, except by name, until the author of these lines suggested that he read him" (Roger Lescot, "Le roman et la nouvelle dans la littérature iranienne contemporaine," *Bulletin d'études orientales* 9 [Beirut, 1943]: 95).

16. The French translation appeared shortly after Hedayat's return to Iran: *Délire et rêves dans la "Gradiva" de Jensen*, trans. Marie Bonaparte (Paris: Gallimard, 1931), prefaced by Jensen's *Gradiva*, trans. E. Zak and G. Sadoul. The English *Gradiva*, trans. Helen M. Downey, is appended to Freud, *Delusion and Dream and Other Essays*, trans. Harry Zohn et al. (Boston: Beacon Press, 1956).

17. See the anti-Oedipal reading of Freud's appreciation of Jensen in Sylvère Lotringer, "The Fiction of Analysis," *Semiotext[e]* 2.3 (1977): 173–89. Lotringer documents Freud's overreliance on Jensen's narrative, an overreliance that makes the fiction of *Gradiva* seem a case history, even a theoretical manifesto, rather than a novel. The result is not just a critique of Freud's mode of argument, but an attack on analysis as a social system that (like romance) functions to normalize and domesticate.

18. Reza Baraheni has referred to this aspect of *The Blind Owl* in his *Safar-e Mesr va hâlât-e man dar tul-e safar* (Journey to Egypt and my experiences there) (Tehran: Iranmehr, 1973), 83–84.

19. Hedayat, *Hâji Aghâ: Portrait of an Iranian Confidence Man*, trans. G. M. Wickens (Austin: Center for Middle Eastern Studies, 1979), Middle East Monographs, no. 6.

20. Cited in Adaline Glasheen, *A Census of Finnegans Wake* (London: Faber and Faber, 1956), xi.

21. The chronology of the second part of *The Blind Owl* can be worked out with somewhat more precision than is immediately apparent. The five nights described may not be consecutive, but they are nearly so. The first night (68/65) is the occasion of her nocturnal visit. The second (79–83/74–77) is the night after his walk to the Suran River. The third (90–95/83–87) is the night after his upsetting the soup and smoking the opium prescribed by the family doctor. The fourth (115–19/104–7) is the night following the wife's visit to him, the occasion of his first aborted attempt to kill her. The fifth and last night (124–28/111–14) is the scene of the murder and the conclusion of the narrative.

22. In the 1978 Massey Lectures, now rewritten as a chapter of *The View from Afar*, Lévi-Strauss draws a connection in folkloric science between the motifs of the harelip and of twins, a harelip being perceived as a kind of incipient or incomplete twinning: see "An Anatomical Foreshadowing of Twinship," *The View from Afar*, trans. Joachim Neugroschel and Phoebe Hoss (New York: Basic Books, 1985), 201–9. The detail that the old-man figure in his role as odds-and-ends man has a harelip is a gratuitous arabesque beyond the already exuberant plenitude of doubling that characterizes *The Blind Owl*.

23. There seems to be a vague parallelism between the list of goods the odds-and-ends man sells and the items the speaker describes his father and uncle selling in India. Both lists (53/52, 55/54) have eight items. The old man's list ends with a spade and a jar; the merchants' inventory concludes with fuller's earth (*gel-e sar-shur*, approximately, "shampoo") and pen cases, presumably like the pen cases of part one.

24. Otto Rank, *The Double*, trans. and ed. Harry Tucker, Jr. (Chapel Hill: University of North Carolina Press, 1971), 76.

25. See Otto Rank, *The Myth of the Birth of the Hero*, trans. F. Robbins and Smith Ely Jelliffe (New York: Robert Brunner, 1952),

esp. 61–94. Freud summarizes the theory at the beginning of *Moses and Monotheism*.

26. He would have consulted the French version: *Don Juan: Une étude sur la double*, trans. S. Lautman (Paris: Denoël and Steele, 1932). See Rank, *The Double*, vii–viii, for further bibliographical details.

27. "Character and Psychology in Hedayat's *Buf-e kur*," *Edebiyât* 1.2 (1976): 207–18.

28. The last two paragraphs are expanded from my review of *FYA* in *Edebiyât* 3.2 (1978): 245–49.

29. Iraj Bashiri, *Hedayat's Ivory Tower: Structural Analysis of the Blind Owl* (Minneapolis: Manor House, 1974), 17.

30. The letter is quoted in Abulqasem Djannati-Atai, *Zendegâni va âsâr-e Sâdeq-e Hedâyat* (Tehran: Majid, 1978), 143–44.

31. D. S. Komissarov, *Sâdek Khedâyat: Zhizn' i tvorchestvo* (Sadeq Hedayat: Life and works) (Moscow: Nauka, 1967), 43–44.

32. José Ortega y Gasset, *The Dehumanization of Art and Other Writings on Art and Culture*, trans. Willard R. Trask (Garden City, N.Y.: Doubleday, Anchor, 1956), 92–95.

33. Contradictory because the preceding narrative has built up such a powerful portrait of a sexual anxiety based on the fear of entering the role of the father. The desire to kill her is founded on her pregnancy, not its termination. We have, I think, a case here for a biographical analysis: a moment when Hedayat represses the painful clarity of his own insight.

34. The fortress itself does not have an intrinsic importance in the unfolding of the narrative, but it is a matter of some interest that the dismembered body in part one is buried in a spot that resembles the site of the fortress in part two. In Jacques Lacan's essay on the mirror stage (written by coincidence the same year as *The Blind Owl*) the fragmented body is described as an image that occurs "when the movement of analysis encounters a certain level of aggressive disintegration in the individual." Images of fortresses, on the other hand, symbolize for Lacan the formation of the I (*Ecrits I* [Paris: Seuil, 1966], 89–97, 94; trans. Alan Sheridan, *Ecrits: A Selection* [New York: W. W. Norton, 1977], 1–7, 5). See also note 20 of Chapter Four, below. Is it significant in this regard that the proverbial description he cites to describe sleeping with his wife is "taking the fortress by storm" (62/60)?

35. Ebrahim Golestan, *Esrâr-e ganj-e Darre-ye Jenni*, 2d ed. (Tehran: Rowzan, 1978), 118, paraphrased by Paul Sprachman in "Ebra-

him Golestan's *The Treasure*: A Parable of Cliché and Consumption," *Iranian Studies* 15.1–4 (1982): 155–80, 160.

36. See the lucid association of those two scenes in John T. Irwin's *Doubling and Incest/Repetition and Revenge: A Speculative Reading of Faulkner* (Baltimore: Johns Hopkins University Press, 1976), 44–47. In the personal, long unpublished introduction that Faulkner wrote for *The Sound and the Fury*, the generating image of Caddy as a young girl is transformed into an inanimate object familiar to readers of Hedayat: "One day I seemed to shut a door between me and all publishers' addresses and book lists. I said to myself, Now I can write. Now I can make myself a vase like that which the old Roman kept at his bedside and wore the rim slowly away with kissing it" (cited in Irwin, *Doubling and Incest*, 171).

37. Jacques Derrida, *La dissémination* (Paris: Seuil, 1972), 195–96; *Dissemination*, trans. Barbara Johnson (Chicago: University of Chicago Press, 1981), 169–71.

38. In "Imaginary and Symbolic in *La rabouilleuse*," *Social Science Information* 16.1 (1977): 59–81, 59.

CHAPTER FOUR
GOTHIC I

1. Gianroberto Scarcia, in " 'Hâgi Aqâ e *Buf-e kur*', i cosiddetti due aspetti dell'opera dello scrittore contemporaneo persiano Sadeq Hedayat," *Annali* 8 (1958): 112–13, comments at some length on the similarities between Iranian society in Hedayat's day and tsarist Russia. See also Wickens, "Bozorg Alavi's *Portmanteau*" *University of Toronto Quarterly* (Jan. 1959): 132, and Roy Mottahedeh, *The Mantle of the Prophet: Religion and Politics in Iran* (New York: Simon and Schuster, 1985), 306–7.

2. Rainer Maria Rilke, *The Notebooks of Malte Laurids Brigge*, trans. M. D. Herder Norton (New York: W. W. Norton, 1949), 47–48. The German text consulted is *Die Aufzeichnungen des Malte Laurids Brigge* (Frankfurt: Insel Verlag, 1963). My source for the French translation that Hedayat would have read is by Maurice Betz, *Les cahiers de Malte Laurids Brigge* (1923; reprint, Paris: Emile Paul Frères, 1945).

3. Sartre, *Nausea*, trans. Lloyd Alexander (New York: New Directions, 1959), 212–13.

4. See, for instance, Peter Ruppert, "The Aesthetic Solution in *Nausea* and *Malte Laurids Brigge*," *Comparative Literature* 29.1

(Winter 1977): 17–34, and Laurence Gill Lyon, "Related Images in *Malte Laurids Brigge* and *La Nausée*," *Comparative Literature* 30.1 (Winter 1978): 53–71. It is not rare to see *Nausea* and the *Notebooks* compared, though it is not to my knowledge considered certain that Sartre had read Rilke at that time. He had certainly read him by 1943, since he cites him approvingly and familiarly in *Being and Nothingness*.

5. Sartre, *Being and Nothingness*, trans. Hazel E. Barnes (New York: Washington Square Press, 1966), 651.

6. Vincent Monteil, *Sâdeq Hedâyat* (Tehran: Editions de l'Institut Franco-Iranien, 1952), 20.

7. See Joseph Frank, *The Widening Gyre: Crisis and Mastery in Modern Literature* (Bloomington: Indiana University Press, 1968), 3–62.

8. Monteil, *Sâdeq Hedâyat*, 17. One of these marginal comments is reproduced in Hassan Tahbaz, *Yâdbud-nâme-ye Sâdeq-e Hedâyat be monâsebat-e hashtâdomin sâl-e tavallod-e u/Gedenkschrift für Sadeq Hedayat zu seinem 80. Geburtstag* (Memorial to Sadeq Hedayat on the occasion of his eightieth birthday) (Cologne: Bidar, 1983), 137.

9. Émile Zola, *Thérèse Raquin* (Paris: Livre de Poche, 1975), 12.

10. Geoffrey Hartman, *The Unmediated Vision: An Interpretation of Wordsworth, Hopkins, Rilke and Valéry* (1954; reprint, New York: Harcourt, Brace & World, 1966), 134–35.

11. Our text is Charles Baudelaire, *Oeuvres complètes*, ed. Y.-G. Le Dantec (Paris: Gallimard, 1961), 29–31. Translation by Richard Howard, *Les Fleurs du mal: The Complete Text of the Flowers of Evil in a New Translation by Richard Howard* (Boston: David R. Godine, 1983), 35–36.

12. Baudelaire, *Correspondences*, ed. Claude Pichois (Paris: Gallimard, 1966), 676, trans. in Marie Bonaparte, *The Life and Works of Edgar Allan Poe: A Psychoanalytic Interpretation*, trans. John Rodker (1949; reprint, New York: Humanities Press, 1971), 669.

13. Hedayat, "Payâm-e Kâfkâ" (Kafka's message) preface to *Goruh-e mahkumin* (Hasan Qa'emyan's translation of Kafka's *In der Strafkolonie*/"In the Penal Colony"), (Tehran: Amir Kabir, 1958), 71. It is a particularly gratuitous reference: " 'In the Penal Colony' is one of Kafka's moving stories, which is not without resemblance to Edgar Allan Poe."

14. Killis Campbell, ed., *The Poems of Edgar Allan Poe* (1917; reprint, New York: Russell and Russell, 1962), 1917, 34–38.

15. A persistent researcher could put together in a few pages a little encyclopedia of faint noises in literature. A starting point would be Gaston Bachelard's chapter, "Miniature," in *The Poetics of Place*, trans. Marie Jolas (Boston: Beacon Press, 1969), 173–80, where he cites imagined sounds of plants in obscure poems by René-Guy Cadou and Claude Vigée. M. H. Abrams, in *The Milk of Paradise* (New York: Harper and Row, 1970), quotes a passage from Roger Dupouy's *Les Opiomanes* (1912), which suggests that such images may be characteristic of opium experience: "The hearing develops an exquisite delicacy; the least sounds are perceived . . . an insect walking across the ground . . . the sounds of growing grass" (*Milk of Paradise*, 25). As for the sleeping bird, Killis Campbell (*Poems of Edgar Allan Poe*, 187) mentions Moore's *Lalla Rookh* and Shelley's "Lines Written in the Bay of Lerici" as possible sources for Poe. It may have been an image of some personal significance for Hedayat. Among his extant paintings is a portrayal of a European goose in flight. The wings are extended wide as if motionless, floating. The visible eye is open but expressionless, as if in a trance. The light comes from below as if buoying it up in flight (Hasan Qa'emyan, *Darbâre-ye zohur va 'alâ'em-e zohur* [Tehran: Amir Kabir, 1965], 144).

16. Thomas Moore, *Lalla Rookh*, 18th ed. (London: Longman, Rees, Orme, Green and Longman, 1836), 194.

17. To say that footnotes are strictly for the reader's assistance oversimplifies things slightly. There is a complex set of unwritten rules at work in the selection of footnotes in long poems of the Romantic period, particularly in the Oriental tale, such as *Lalla Rookh*, where the dazzling array of footnotes seems part of the sublimity of the genre. The footnotes to the English version of Beckford's *Vathek*, over half the length of the narrative itself, are so extensive and often so obtrusive and meandering that they could not possibly be thought to elucidate the text. In some strange way they seem to validate the story, like magically solidified crystals of inspiration, a peep behind the curtain of the creation of the work.

18. "I slept through my existence like the Simorgh in the Eastern fable." Charles Robert Maturin, *Melmoth the Wanderer*, ed. William F. Axton (Lincoln: University of Nebraska Press, 1961), 76.

19. See Allen Burdett Thomas, *Moore en France* (Paris: Honoré Champion, 1911), 156ff.

20. In fact there is a ruined Sassanid tower in Rey. (See Karl Baedeker, *Russia: A Handbook for Travelers* [1914; reprint, New York: Arno Press/Random House, 1971], 505.) Presumably this will be the castle (Persian *qal'e*, "fortress") where the narrator sees the young

woman by the river Suran (75/71). Baedaker does not record its height. (See Chapter Three, note 34, above.)

21. Freud, *Complete Psychological Works* (London: Hogarth, 1953), 4.138.

22. F. Gaffary, "La chouette aveugle et le cinéma," *Bizarre* 1 (1954): 64, cites specifically *Dr. Caligari* and Murnau's *Nosferatu* as influences on *The Blind Owl*.

23. The list of critical works that have made this possible includes Robert Kiely's *Romantic Novel in English* (Cambridge: Harvard University Press, 1972), Dan J. McNutt's thorough bibliography, *The Eighteenth Century Gothic* (New York: Garland Publishing, 1975), and the initial, tentative feminist readings of Ellen Moers's *Literary Women* (New York: Doubleday, 1976), as well as the witty, sensible correction (and reversal) of standard Gothic wisdom in Eve Kosofky Sedgewick's *Coherence of Gothic Conventions* (New York: Arno Press, 1980). The regrounding of a single, problematic Gothic work in its historical particularity in the essays of George Levine and U. C. Knoepflmacher's *Endurance of Frankenstein* (Berkeley: University of California Press, 1979) succeeds so admirably that for many readers it may seem a step backward for us to reintroduce the generalizing grid of genre at all.

24. Michel Foucault, "What Is an Author?" in *Language, Counter-Memory, Practice: Selected Essays and Interviews*, trans. Donald F. Bouchard and Sherry Simon (Ithaca: Cornell University Press, 1977), 113–38, 131–32.

25. René Wellek and Austin Warren, *Theory of Literature* (New York: Harvest, 1956), 222–23.

26. George Steiner, *Tolstoi or Dostoevsky* (New York: Dutton, 1971), 192–214.

27. See, particularly, Lee Sterrenburg, "Mary Shelley's Monster: Politics and Psyche in *Frankenstein*," in *The Endurance of Frankenstein*, 143–71.

28. Geoffrey Hartman, ed., *Psychoanalysis and the Question of the Text* (Baltimore: Johns Hopkins University Press, 1978), Selected Papers from the English Institute, 1976–77, n.s. 2, vii.

29. Tzvetan Todorov, *The Fantastic: A Structural Approach to a Literary Genre*, trans. Richard Howard (Ithaca: Cornell University Press, 1975), 17.

30. Gérard Genette, *Figures* I (Paris: Seuil, 1966), 94; Todorov, *The Fantastic*, 96.

31. Christine Brooke-Rose, "Historical Genres/Theoretical Genres: A Discussion of Todorov on the Fantastic," *New Literary His-*

tory 8.1 (Autumn 1976): 145–57; Theodore Ziolkowski, *Disenchanted Images: A Literary Iconology* (Princeton: Princeton University Press, 1977), 230–35.

32. Gérard Genette, "Genres, 'types', modes," *Poétique* 32 (Nov. 1977): 389–421, 408. See also Jacques Derrida's commentary on that essay in *Glyph* 7 (1980): 202–32.

33. Fredric Jameson takes an initial step toward the task of historicizing our understanding of romance in *The Political Unconscious: Narrative as a Socially Symbolic Act* (Ithaca: Cornell University Press, 1981), 103–50.

34. Angus Fletcher, *Allegory: The Theory of a Symbolic Mode* (Ithaca: Cornell University Press, 1964), 261–68. See also Jean Starobinski, *The Invention of Liberty: 1700–1789*, trans. Bernard C. Swift (Geneva: Skira, 1964), 171–81.

35. Julien Gracq, *Au chateau d'Argol* (Paris: José Corti, 1945), 10; trans. Louise Varèse, *The Castle of Argol* (New York: New Directions, n.d. [1951?]), 145.

36. See Robin Magowan, *Narcissus and Orpheus: Pastoral in Sand, Fromentin, Jewett, Alain-Fournier and Dinesen* (New York: Garland Publishing, 1988), 26.

37. See, for instance, Leo Spitzer's demonstration, in "A Reinterpretation of 'The Fall of the House of Usher,' " in *Essays on English and American Literature* (Princeton: Princeton University Press, 1962), 51–66, 62, of the common ground between Poe's use of atmosphere in that story and a novelistic use of it in Balzac's *Père Goriot*.

38. Robert Kellogg and Robert Scholes, *The Nature of Narrative* (New York: Oxford University Press, 1966), 87–88.

39. Francis Russell Hart, "The Experience of Character in the English Gothic Novel," in *Experience in the Novel*, ed. Roy Harvey Pearce (New York: Columbia University Press, 1968), 83–105.

40. Ermanno Krumm, "Sadègh Hedayàt par Antonin Artaud," *Il piccolo Hans* 34 (April–June 1982): 169–81.

41. Matthew G. Lewis, *The Monk* (New York: Grove, 1978), 237–38.

CHAPTER FIVE

GOTHIC II

1. David Halliburton, *Edgar Allan Poe: A Phenomenological View* (Princeton: Princeton University Press, 1973), 199.

2. This passage contains a mistranslation that can be cited to refute

the common misperception that Costello's translation is derived from Lescot's French. Costello continues: "the glory and splendour of the star," rendering "va be 'azamat va shokuh-e ân pay bordam." The problem is the antecedent of *ân* (that), which Costello takes to be the heavenly apparition (logically enough), but which in fact must refer grammatically to the speaker's life. The error is not in Lescot's version: "me permit d'entrevoir . . . toute la misère de mon existence, d'en comprendre aussi la grandeur et la beauté" (26). Komissarov's Russian translation repeats the word "life" in order to make that antecedent clearer still (Sadeq Hedayat, *Izbrannye proizvedeniya*, trans. D. S. Komissarov and A. Z. Rozenfeld [Moscow: Nauka, 1969], 287). Qotbi, in *In-ast Buf-e kur* (Tehran: Daftar-e Tahqiq-e Ra'in, 1973), explicitly confirms this interpretation (22). It is an error that could not have been made through the Western intermediaries.

3. "Heaven knows how long ago" is in Persian the proverbial expression *dar 'ahd-e Doqyânus* (in the age of Decius). Decius is traditionally taken to have reigned at the time the seven sleepers of Ephesus took to their cave (a story known in the Islamic world from the Sura of the Cave in the Koran). The use of a cliché to amplify the theme of reclusion is typically indirect and complex.

4. Roland Barthes, *S/Z*, trans. Richard Miller (New York: Hill and Wang, 1974), 26–28.

5. The contemporary popular romance that has grown out of that tradition is about nearly nothing else, a kind of rationalization of women's powerlessness. See, for instance, Ann Barr Snitow, "Mass Market Romance: Pornography for Women Is Different," *Radical History Review* 20 (Spring/Summer 1979): 141–61.

6. Marie Bonaparte, *The Life and Works of Edgar Allan Poe: A Psychoanalytic Interpretation*, trans. John Rodker (1949; reprint, New York: Humanities Press, 1971), 224–36; Daniel Hoffman, *Poe Poe Poe Poe Poe Poe Poe* (New York: Doubleday, Anchor, 1973), 229–58.

7. Hoffman refers to the theory held by Bonaparte and Joseph Wood Krutch that Poe was impotent; there does not seem to be any way to investigate it as a biographical problem, but since Al-e Ahmad says the same of Hedayat in his famous essay, it does seem necessary to acknowledge it. The problem is that fear of impotence and regret over actual impotence might generate much the same imagery. Impotence as a biological phenomenon is less interesting in this context than impotence as an essential part of the sexual system we inherit and recognize in the writings of both sexes. I discuss this further in my review of *FYA* in *Edebiyât* 3.2 (1978): 229–36, 233–34.

8. Eve Kosofsky Sedgewick, "Imagery of the Surface in the Gothic Novel," *PMLA* 96.2 (March 1981): 255–70, 261.

9. Ellen Moers, *Literary Women* (New York: Doubleday, 1976).

10. Leslie Fiedler, *Love and Death in the American Novel* (New York: Dell, 1960), 113.

11. Fredric Jameson, *The Political Unconscious: Narrative as a Socially Symbolic Act* (Ithaca: Cornell University Press, 1981), 107–8.

12. Iraj Bashiri, *Hedayat's Ivory Tower: Structural Analysis of the Blind Owl* (Minneapolis: Manor House, 1974), 152.

13. The contradictions of describing castration anxiety do not end with the ambiguities of the fetish object. Images of violation through dismemberment are already images of impotence, simply because they are accompanied by a protective veneer that the pain is somehow not real. That muffling of intensity, lessening of nerve input, which allows the dispassionate (hardheaded) observation of unpleasant realities is conceived as a preliminary step in the acquisition of knowledge; it is also an image of impotence, for which fantasies of intensified transgression are compensation.

14. Georges Bataille, *Oeuvres complètes* (Paris: Gallimard, 1970), 1:69. I have translated from the 1928 version, which Bataille rewrote extensively in 1940. It is within the realm of possibility that Hedayat read the first edition—though there were only 134 copies printed, so it is only barely within the realm of possibility. There is a translation of the 1940 version by Joachim Neugroschel, *Story of the Eye by Lord Auch* (New York: Urizen Books, 1977).

15. In the murder scene of *The Blind Owl* the knife lands "somewhere" in her body (*be-yek jâ-ye tan-e u*); we are, I think, to assume that the cutting out of the eye follows in an undescribed scene, the ambiguity of the initial wound ("somewhere") working to avoid distracting us from the equation of eye and vagina, intercourse and murder.

16. Claude Lévi-Strauss, "The Structural Study of Myth," in *Structural Anthropology*, trans. Claire Jacobson and Brooke Grundfest Schoepf (Garden City, N.Y.: Doubleday, Anchor, 1967), 202–28.

CHAPTER SIX

SALOME

1. *NP* 578–98 (1–21 in Western pagination); trans. Mary K. St. John in *The Blind Owl and Other Hedayat Stories* (Minneapolis: Sorayya Publishers, 1984), 100–108.

2. Iraj Bashiri, *Hedayat's Ivory Tower: Structural Analysis of* The Blind Owl (Minneapolis: Manor House Press, 1974), xii.

3. Hedayat may have used *vav* to render the *é* as it is sometimes used to render the *e muet* in transcribing French words (though the *e* in *bégum* is obviously not an *e muet*), or to avoid orthographic confusion (*begam* and *begâm* both being possible units of meaning in Persian). The transformation of the second vowel is more easily accounted for. The 1875 edition of Littré's *Dictionnaire de la langue française* notes: "We ought to write *begam*, which is the true spelling, *begum* being the English transcription of the native word in which the mute pronunciation [*son muet*] of the *a* is rendered by the English *u*." Hedayat may have learned the Urdu pronunciation in India, or he may have read it in Littré.

4. It would be wrong to make Indian music an ideal against which the other arts are measured: *khorâfât*, the word translated "legends," connotes ignorance and superstition, but the emphasis of the passage is clearly on the process by which the music successfully expresses or represents the concerns of its society. The music depicted here resembles the narrator's project at least in this; it is both a process of foreshortening or concentration (*mokhtasar*) and inclusion, totality (*jam'*).

5. See Pierre Grimal, ed., *Larousse World Mythology*, trans. Patricia Beardsworth (London: Hamlyn, 1973), 233. Jung refers to the anima in much the same terms as an Indian goddess: "The East calls it the 'Spinning Woman'—Maya, who creates illusion by her dancing" ("Aion: Phenomenology of the Self," in *The Portable Jung*, ed. Joseph Campbell [New York: Viking, 1971], 139–62, 148).

6. Paul de Man, in an essay on Kleist, singles out a germinal instance of this image much earlier, in a 1793 letter of Schiller, where an English dance becomes the image of a well-ordered society. In de Man's analysis Kleist's essay on the puppet theater becomes part of a dialogue on this image: "Aesthetic Formalization: Kleist's *Über das Marionettentheater*," in *The Rhetoric of Romanticism* (New York: Columbia University Press, 1984), 263–90.

7. Frank Kermode, *The Romantic Image* (New York: Vintage, 1964), 53.

8. Joris Karl Huysmans, *Against Nature*, trans. Robert Baldick (London: Penguin, 1959).

9. The translators are perhaps less in agreement here than anywhere else in the text. Costello's "morning glory" would, strictly speaking, have been *nilufar-e pich* in Persian, but "morning glory"

like *capucine* (English nasturtium) could describe the flowers in the border in Hedayat's sketch of the vase in the headpiece of the Bombay edition. Iraj Bashiri translates "black lily"; D. S. Komissarov's Russian translation gives the word for lotus. *Nilufar* comes from Sanskrit *nil utpala* (blue lotus), and is a cognate of the French word *nenuphar* (water lily). *Nilufar-e âbi* (blue *nilufar*) is the usual word for lotus, *nilufar* alone being the term for "water lily." Another English solution might have been the word *nenuphar*.

10. Mario Praz, *The Romantic Agony*, trans. Angus Davidson, 2d ed. (Oxford: Oxford University Press, 1970), 305–20.

11. Gustave Flaubert, *Trois contes* (Paris: Garnier, 1967), 197.

12. Jane Marcus, "Salome: The Jewish Princess Was a New Woman," *Bulletin of the New York Public Library* 78.1 (Autumn 1974): 95–113, 98.

13. "Some critics have objected to Wilde's freehanded use of history. He has purposefully telescoped three Herods into one. He wished to juxtapose the rise of Christianity with the fall of the Roman Empire in order to write in *Salomé* a kind of Christian *Gotterdämmerung*" (Marcus, "The Jewish Princess Was a New Woman," 100).

14. Richard Ellmann's notorious biographical reading offers a rough parallel, in which Wilde's esthetic Paterism and ascetic Ruskinism face each other through the figures of Salome and Iokanaan. "Overtures to Wilde's *Salomé*," in *Golden Codgers: Biographical Speculations* (New York: Oxford University Press, 1973), 60–80.

15. Michel Foucault, *The Order of Things*, trans. anon. (New York: Vintage, 1973), 300.

16. Jacques Derrida, *Dissemination*, trans. Barbara Johnson (Chicago: Chicago University Press, 1981), 175–85.

17. Hoffmann's comparable statement is in the opening of "Kreisleriana": "Not so much in dream, as in the condition of delirium at the onset of sleep, especially if I have been listening to a lot of music, I feel a blending of colors, tones and fragrances." *E.T.A. Hoffmanns Sämtliche Werke*, ed. Eduard Grisebach, 15 vols. (Leipzig: Max Hesse Verlag, 1900), 1:46.

18. The classical essay is of course Freud's "The Uncanny" (1919), trans. Alix Strachey, in *On Creativity and the Unconscious* (New York: Harper, 1958), 122–61, or *Complete Psychological Works* (London: Hogarth, 1953), 17.219–56. There is also a classic commentary on "The Uncanny," Hélène Cixous's "Fiction and Its Phantoms: A Reading of Freud's *Das Unheimliche* (The 'uncanny'),"

trans. Robert Dennome, *New Literary History* 7 (Spring 1976): 525–48, now a chapter in her *Prénoms de personne* (Paris: Seuil, 1974), 13–38, followed by a reading of "The Sandman," 39–99. See also Samuel Weber, "The Sideshow, or: Remarks on a Canny Moment," *Modern Language Notes* 88.6 (Dec. 1973): 1102–33, and Neil Hertz, "Freud and the Sandman," *Textual Strategies: Perspectives in Post-Structuralist Criticism*, ed. Josué Harari (Ithaca: Cornell University Press, 1979), 296–321.

19. See Fredric Jameson's discussion in *Marxism and Form: Twentieth-century Dialectical Theories of Literature* (Princeton: Princeton University Press, 1971), 404–5.

20. Trans. as "The Doll Behind the Curtain" by Ya'kov Mashiah and Aubrey Hodes in *New Outlook* 4.4 (Feb. 1961): 40–48; and by Ahmad Karimi-Hakkak in *ANTH* 127–36.

21. My text is the Dover edition, *The Best Tales of Hoffmann*, ed. E. F. Bleiler (New York: Dover, 1967), 130–82.

22. This is, as Cixous demonstrates, the issue on which Freud's intolerance for the uncertainties of fiction is most visible, his insistence that Coppola and Coppelius are "identical."

23. Even more than owls, snakes are creatures of bad omen in Persian culture. The mild oath *zahr-e mâr* (snake poison) is widespread (it is a particularly common expression of anger among schoolchildren), a phenomenon worth noting in a country where snakes are so rare.

24. This coinage is a central element in Iraj Bashiri's reading of *The Blind Owl*.

25. Gaston Bachelard, *The Psychoanalysis of Fire*, trans. Alan C. M. Ross (Boston: Beacon Press, 1964), 85–86, 90–92.

26. *Tales of E.T.A. Hoffmann*, trans. Leonard J. Kent and Elizabeth C. Knight (Chicago: Chicago University Press), 97–98.

27. E.T.A. Hoffmann, *The Devil's Elixirs*, trans. Ronald Taylor (London: John Calder, 1963), 160.

28. Irving Massey, *The Gaping Pig: Literature and Metamorphosis* (Berkeley: University of California Press, 1976), 118.

29. See Charles Passage, trans., *Three Märchen of E.T.A. Hoffmann* (Columbia: University of South Carolina Press, 1971), xv.

30. Paul de Man assesses Hoffmann's irony and its refusal to hide behind claims of transcendence in "The Rhetoric of Temporality," in *Interpretation: Theory and Practice* (Baltimore: Johns Hopkins University Press, 1969), 173–209, 198–200.

31. Patrick Quinn, *The French Face of Edgar Allan Poe* (Carbondale: Southern Illinois University Press, 1957), 266.

32. David Halliburton, *Edgar Allan Poe: A Phenomenological View* (Princeton: Princeton University Press, 1973), 218.

CHAPTER SEVEN
PROLEGOMENON TO *THE BLIND OWL*

1. Tom Nairn, *The Break-Up of Britain: Crisis and Neo-Nationalism* (London: NLB, 1977), 379.

2. Mohammad Ali Jamalzada, "Persian Is Sugar," from *Once Upon a Time*, trans. Heshmat Moayyad and Paul Sprachman (New York: Bibliotheca Persica, 1985), Modern Persian Literature Series, no. 6, 40–41.

3. Voltaire, *Candide, Zadig and Selected Stories*, trans. Donald Frame (New York: New American Library, 1961), 20.

4. Hedayat, *Sag-e velgard*, 9th ed. (Tehran: Amir Kabir, 1968), 215–63. Trans. Iraj Bashiri in *The Blind Owl and Other Hedayat Stories* (Minneapolis: Sorayya Publishers, 1984), 132–48.

5. Hedayat, *Tup-e morvâri* (The pearl cannon), 33; in the American edition, ed. Iraj Bashiri, 29.

6. See E. G. Browne, *Literary History of Persia* (Cambridge: Cambridge University Press, 1969), 1:72–75.

7. See the extensive treatment of this side of Persian culture in Hasan Javadi, *Satire in Persian Literature* (Rutherford, N.J.: Fairleigh Dickinson University Press, 1988).

8. See George Steiner's discussion of the culture-specific nature of satire in "Black Danube," *New Yorker* (21 July 1986): 90–93.

9. There is a recent edition that includes the author's French translation, *Djaafar Khan est revenu d'occident: Comédie en un acte*, ed. Hasan Javadi (Oakland, Calif.: Jahan Book Co., 1984).

10. See also my review of Nahid Rachlin's *Foreigner* in *World Literature Today* 53.2 (Spring 1979): 341–42.

11. Jalal Al-e Ahmad, *Gharb-zadegi* (unauthorized edition, [Tehran]: n.p., n.d. [the 1964 version]); for background on Al-e Ahmad, see the introduction to the English translation by John Green and Ahmad Alizadeh in *Gharbzadegi* (Westruckness) (Lexington, Ky.: Mazda, 1982). See also the discussion of Al-e Ahmad in Roy Mottahedeh, *The Mantle of the Prophet* (New York: Simon and Schuster, 1985), 287–323.

12. Jünger's essay is *Über die Linie* (Frankfurt: Vittorio Kloster-

mann, 1950); Heidegger's contribution, "Über 'Die Linie,' " is translated by William Kluback and Jean T. Wilde as *The Question of Being* (New Haven: College and University Press, 1958).

13. *Asghar Agâ* 129 (16 Oct. 1982): 5; *Encyclopedia Iranica*, ed. Ehsan Yarshater (London: Routledge and Kegan Paul, 1982).

14. The introduction to J. Borujerdi's translation of the *Towzih almasâ'el*, titled *A Clarification of Questions* (Boulder: Westview Press, 1984), ix–xxxii, seems to me a good example of scholarly tact. Acknowledging the objections to its emphasis on "frivolous anecdotal material" in a review by Hamid Algar in the *International Journal of Middle East Studies* 19.2 (May 1987): 245–46, I would argue that it is one of the rare summaries of the subject that does not get lost in apologetics or legalisms. It addresses the subject straightforwardly from the point of view of an outsider; but as an outsider willing to construct a believable sensibility for his subject, it may represent the third position I look for in the pages that follow. For the tradition of parodies see page xxviii. For a sociological treatment of *The Blind Owl* that I think occupies that middle perspective, see Fischer's "Towards a Third World Poetics: Seeing Through Short Stories and Films in the Iranian Cultural Area," *Knowledge and Society: Studies in the Sociology of Culture Past and Present* 5 (1981): 171–241, 197–213.

15. "Literature as the repository of national genius and monument to national pride," in "Comparative Literature and the Pieties," *Profession* 86 (1986): 30–32.

16. Frederic Jameson, "Third-World Literature in the Era of Multinational Capitalism," *Social Text* 15 (Fall 1986): 65–88.

17. Aijaz Ahmad, "Jameson's Rhetoric of Otherness and the 'National Allegory,' " *Social Text* 17 (Fall 1987): 3–25.

18. A good example is the back inside cover of the Iranian government periodical *Peyâm-e Emâm* (The Imam's message) 17 (Tir 1360/ 1981): a handwritten essay entitled "Martyrdom and the Martyr," which begins "Martyrdom is the last step in the road that leads to God. Martyrdom is growth and liberation, liberation from the prison of the body, this prison of earth. Martyrdom is a flight, the flight of a bird from the cage to its own nest."

19. See Edward Said's discussion of those portraits in the preface to *Covering Islam: How the Media and the Experts Determine How We See the Rest of the World* (New York: Pantheon, 1981), xxvi–xxx.

20. Reza Baraheni, "Masculine History," in *The Crowned Cannibals* (New York: Vintage, 1977), 19–84.

21. At an earlier period in the history of Iranian oppositional politics, Iranian students in the United States developed the tactic of wearing masks at demonstrations in order to draw attention to the danger of being identified. Its effect was uncanny (and, if I may use the term, characteristically Iranian), another example of thematics from *The Blind Owl* taking form in a public context.

22. There is a typographical error in the Amir Kabir edition: *kaleme*, "word," for *kalle*, "head" or "skull."

23. Antoine de St.-Exupéry, *Terre des hommes* (Paris: Gallimard, 1939), 118.

24. Saʿidi Sirjani, *Shaykh-e Sanʿân* (n.p. [San Francisco?]: Sâzmân-e Farhangi-ye Mashreq, n.d.). It was partially serialized in Iran in *Negin*, and later in the exile publication *Shânzdahom-e Azar*.

INDEX